BY THE
SWORD
DIVIDED

BY THE SWORD DIVIDED

EYEWITNESS ACCOUNTS OF
THE ENGLISH CIVIL WAR

John Adair

SUTTON PUBLISHING

First published in 1983 by Century Publishing Co Ltd

This edition first published in 1998 by Sutton Publishing Limited

Text copyright © John Adair, 1983, 1998
Design copyright © Shuckburgh Reynolds Limited, 1983, 1998

British Library Cataloguing in Publication Data
A catalogue record for this book is available from the British Library

ISBN 0 7509 1858 6

Cover illustration: detail from The Wounded Cavalier, *by W.S. Burton (The Guildhall, London/photograph Bridgeman Art Library, London)*

Printed in Great Britain by
WBC Limited, Bridgend, Mid-Glamorgan.

Picture Sources

Illustrations on the following pages are reproduced by gracious permission of Her Majesty the Queen: 8, 20–21, 135*b*; the following painting is from the Royal Collection, reproduced by courtesy of Her Majesty Queen Elizabeth the Queen Mother: 216. Grateful acknowledgement is made to the following: Ashmolean Museum 33, 34, 75, 81, 96, 207; John Bethell 52; British Library 13, 16*l*, 16*r*, 17, 25*l*, 25*r*, 27, 40, 101, 106, 137, 149; Trustees of the Chatsworth Settlement 72*l*; The Broadlands Collection 129; The Buccleuch Collection, Bowhill, Selkirk 193; Department of the Environment/The Armouries, HM Tower of London 56–7; Department of the Environment/House of Lords 105, 204; Fotomas Index 36, 42, 90, 93, 111, 113, 167, 173, 179, 186, 194, 225*l*, 232, 234; Behram Kapadia 69; Mansell Collection 135*t*, 164*l*, 199; Musées Nationaux/Musée du Louvre 49; National Gallery of Scotland/courtesy the Duke of Hamilton 225*r*; National Gallery of Scotland/by permission of the Earl of Rosebery 212–13; National Portrait Gallery 87, 115, 124–5, 164*r*; Museum of Oxford/courtesy Lord Dartmouth 200–201; Pennington-Mellor-Munthe Inheritance 72*r*; Pitkin Pictorials 140, 141; Private collections 29, 204*r*; Sotheby Park Bernet 72*b*; The Earl Spencer 132; Sir Ralph Verney 60, 65, 66, 68, 71; Walker Art Gallery, Liverpool 196–7; York City Art Gallery 139.

Contents

Preface	page	*7*
1	FOR KING OR PARLIAMENT?	*9*
2	A NATION DIVIDED	*23*
3	EDGEHILL	*39*
4	THE VERNEYS OF CLAYDON HOUSE	*58*
5	CAVALIERS IN OXFORD	*74*
6	WESTERN WONDERS	*85*
7	LONDON'S BRAVE BOYS	*100*
8	HOPTON AND WALLER	*114*
9	THE NORTHERN STRUGGLE	*130*
10	CIVIL STRIFE IN THE MIDLANDS	*144*
11	IN CROMWELL COUNTRY	*153*
12	THE IMPACT OF WAR	*163*
13	THE DEFEAT OF THE CAVALIERS	*185*
14	THE SECOND CIVIL WAR	*209*
15	ROUGH JUSTICE	*230*
Bibliography		*238*
Index		*239*

Preface

'You would think it strange if I should tell you there was a time in England when brothers killed brothers, cousins cousins, and friends their friends.' So wrote Sir John Oglander, a Royalist in the Isle of Wight. He captures in a sentence the agony of civil war as the sword divided families, friends and neighbourhoods.

This book contains passages from the chief eyewitness accounts of this great tragedy in English history. These personal experiences are set within the broader story of the war. But space does not allow me to explore the politics or strategic aspects of the conflict; still less can I describe in detail all the campaigns, battles and sieges. My concern is rather to give an impression of the nature and course of the whole war, and its influences upon the lives of ordinary Englishmen and women.

Houckgeest's painting of the King and Queen dining at Whitehall conveys the characteristic combination of grandeur and informality in palace life, the spectators in the gallery, and dogs chasing each other round the room.

I

For King or Parliament?

In July 1642 the English nation sensed that it stood 'at the pit's brink, ready to plunge ourselves into an ocean of troubles and miseries'. Those words, spoken to the House of Commons by Bulstrode Whitelocke, led him to reflect: 'It is strange to note how we have insensibly slid into this beginning of a civil war by one unexpected accident after another, as waves of the sea which have brought us thus far and we scarce know how, but from paper combats, by declarations, remonstrances, protestations, votes, messages, answers and replies we are now come to the question of raising forces and naming a general and officers of an army. . . . What the issue of it will be no man alive can tell. Probably few of us now here may live to see the end of it.'

The quarrel between the King and the nation's representatives was a long-standing one; it predated both Charles I and the Long Parliament. The issues were both deep-rooted and densely interwoven, making it difficult for us to disentangle them in a few sentences. At the core of them, however, lay a fundamental division in the country over religion. The vast majority of the English were strongly Protestant, but the King's policies at home and abroad seemed to herald the return of popery to these islands. An absolute monarch supporting the Church of Rome or its Anglican satellite would spell the end of English liberties as personified by the freedom and integrity of Parliament.

Deeply attached though they were to the Protestant religion and their national liberties, the English were noted for their peculiar reverence for their monarch: one foreign visitor to Queen Elizabeth's court had called it the second religion of England. That same religion still survives today. Therefore it seems extraordinary to us that in forty years King James I and King Charles I could have so depleted the gold reserves of confidence and loyalty built up by their glorious predecessor as to bring the nation to the brink of civil war. Yet Queen Elizabeth did not commit blunders on their scale. She may have frustrated the more extreme Puritans by her resolute maintenance of episcopacy as the national form of church government, but her archbishops were men of impeccable Calvinist theology. She never lost the trust of her people; towards the close of her long reign she basked in the warmth of their affection.

The story of the gradually deteriorating relations between King and Parliament after 1603, the year of James I's accession, is a long and oft-told one. The first real crisis came in 1629, when Charles I dissolved Parliament, imprisoned its popular leaders in the Tower (where Sir John Eliot died three years later) and ruled himself for eleven years through strong ministers in Church and State, Archbishop William Laud and the Earl of Strafford. The King's attempt to impose the Church of England on the presbyterian Scots precipitated the second great crisis. Charles unwillingly succumbed to pressure and summoned the Short and Long Parliaments in 1640 to vote him some much-needed money to pay the bills of his disastrous northern adventure. Having secured its own existence, the Long Parliament promptly launched into a preconceived programme of reforms designed to remove forever the possibility of arbitrary rule in England. The third crisis overtook them in the autumn of 1641 when the Irish Catholics arose in rebellion. The King delayed in condemning this dangerous and bloody rising. Could he be trusted with the army that would have to be raised in order to suppress it? Might the King or his evil counsellors not seize this opportunity and use these forces to crush all opposition in England?

In this atmosphere of mutual distrust and growing suspicion King Charles resolved upon a singularly inept action. Having accused John Pym, John Hampden and three other members of the Lower House, together with Lord Mandeville (later the Earl of Manchester), of treason, he demanded the wanted men. Parliament refused to hand them over. On 4 January 1642 the King walked down to Westminster from his palace at Whitehall in order to arrest them in person. Word of the attempt arrived from the court that morning and the 'five members' withdrew to a safe refuge in the City of London. Sir Ralph Verney sat on the crowded bench in the House of Commons as the King made his entrance:

A little after, the King came with all his guard, and all his pensioners, and two or three hundred soldiers and gentlemen. The King commanded the soldiers to stay in the hall and sent us word that he was at the door. The Speaker was commanded to sit still, with the mace lying before him, and then the King came to the door, and took the Palsgrave [his nephew, the Elector Charles of the Palatinate] in with him, and commanded all that came with him – upon their lives – not to come in. So the doors were kept open, and the Earl of Roxburgh stood within the door, leaning upon it.

Then the King came upwards, towards the chair, with his hat off, and the Speaker stepped out to meet him. Then the King stepped up to his place and stood upon the step, but sat not down in the chair. And, after he had looked a great while, he told us he would not break our privileges but treason had no privilege. He came for those five gentlemen, for he expected obedience yesterday and not an answer. Then he called Mr Pym and Mr Holles by name, and no answer was made. Then he asked the Speaker if they were here, or where they were.

Upon that the Speaker fell on his knees and desired his excuse, for he was a servant of the House and neither eyes nor tongue to see or say anything but what they commanded. Then the King told him he thought his eyes were as good as his, and then said his birds were flown but he did expect the House would send them to him. And if they did not he would seek them himself, for their treason was foul and such a one as they would thank him to discover. Then he assured us they should have a fair trial, and so went out, putting off his hat till he came to the door.

The next day the King rode into the City to call upon his loyal subjects to deliver up the accused men. All the previous night the citizens stood to arms, with men running from gate to gate crying out, 'The Cavaliers are coming to fire the City!' The Lord Mayor called together the Common Council to receive him. The King promised to secure the Protestant religion and to put down the Irish Catholics. But when he demanded the five members, the newly-elected majority of Puritan members on the Council in Guildhall cried out, 'Privilege!' Others, but not many, countered with 'God Save the King!' The King drove back to Whitehall empty-handed through crowds roaring 'Privilege of Parliament! Privilege of Parliament'. Among those who followed the coach ran a fellow calling out in a loud voice the rebellious words, 'To your tents, O Israel!'

On 10 January a great crowd began to gather in Westminster. That evening Charles suddenly left London by coach. Arriving late that night at a cold and unprepared Hampton Court the King, Queen and three children went straight to bed, all in one four-poster for mutual comfort and warmth. Next morning Westminster rang with cheers as a procession of gaily-decorated boats brought back Pym and Hampden, together with Denzil Holles, Arthur Heselrige and William Strode, in triumphant mood. Meanwhile London's trained bands, marching with colours flying and drums beating, escorted Mandeville to the doors of the House of Lords. As the citizen soldiers passed the gates of Whitehall they shouted, 'Where is the King and his Cavaliers?'

At Hampton Court the King and Queen put on brave faces. Queen Henrietta Maria assured a foreign envoy that her husband was beloved everywhere in his dominions – except in London. But their error of judgement had confirmed many fears in the nation and played into the hands of Pym and his fellow leaders. They could now paint Charles as a tyrant in the making, who must be kept in bounds at whatever cost. Clarendon observed that Hampden 'was much altered, his nature and carriage seeming much fiercer than it did before'. Sir William Waller, who entered the House later that year, called the event such a 'horrid violation of privilege that although his Majesty was pleased to withdraw the prosecuting of it and to promise a more tender respect for the time to come, yet nevertheless this spark (as his Majesty terms it) kindled such flames of discontent as gave occasion first to the raising of guards and afterwards to the levying of an army'.

The first hint of these flames soon appeared. Parliament asked the City to provide a guard of militia for it, while the King also countenanced plans to raise more bodyguards for himself. Soon London seethed with rumours of military preparations, armed risings and invasions. At Kingston-on-Thames Lord Digby and Colonel Sir Thomas Lunsford mustered local Royalists into three troops of horse, but Sir Richard Onslow marched up at the head of the Surrey trained bands and scattered them. Onslow secured the Kingston magazine of arms and gunpowder for Parliament and he also took the precaution of occupying Farnham Castle in order to dominate the main road to Portsmouth.

In mid-February King Charles accompanied the Queen to Dover, where she took ship for the continent – ostensibly to attend the wedding of her daughter Mary to William, Prince of Orange but in reality to obtain money, munitions and men by pawning her personal jewels. Parting in tears from the King, she made her husband promise he would never give in to the chief demands of his political enemies. The King, who wept at their farewell, galloped along the cliffs of Dover to keep her ship in sight for as long as possible.

Outwardly the King seemed composed as he made a royal progress north-wards that spring. At Cambridge he visited two colleges, and the eleven-year-old Prince of Wales was entertained with a play. The royal party spent some time at Nicholas Ferrar's religious community in Little Gidding. In mild sunshine the King shot a March hare in the neighbouring fields while Prince Charles lunched on the cheese-cake and apple pie provided for him in the pantry. The King gave the Ferrars as a parting gift for charity the five gold pounds he had won from the Elector Palatine at the card-table the previous evening. 'Pray, pray for my speedy and safe return,' he added.

At York the King and his court carried on their normal round of pastimes in the halls and gardens of the great houses within the white city walls. Meanwhile, in the kingdom as a whole, anxiety fed upon uncertainty and bred the most violent fears. In the North news spread that the wild Irish Catholics would shortly invade and put English Protestants to the sword as they had done to their unfortunate co-religionists in Ireland. Puritan families knew what to expect from the graphic woodcuts of martyrdom in Foxe's *Book of Martyrs*, by far the most popular book in England after the Bible. They were frightened out of their wits. Joseph Lister of Bradford remembered those panic-filled days in Puritan homes: 'O what fears and tears, cries and prayers, night and day, was there in many places, and in my dear mother's house in particular. I was then about 12 or 13 years of age, and though I was afraid to be killed, yet was I weary of so much fasting and praying.' On one occasion a messenger announced to a packed church that the Irish papists had landed and marched through Lancashire towards Bradford, which caused the congregation to leave their pews and run off into hiding.

On 11 June the King answered the nineteen propositions, Parliament's ultimatum on the eve of war. It demanded from him control of all high offices in government and the armed forces, the prosecution of the laws against the Roman Catholics, the reform of the Church, the control of all fortresses, and support for the Protestant cause in war-torn Europe. In plain terms, Parliament asserted for itself the right to shape England's policies. Charles rejected this outright challenge to his sovereignty out of hand. It was framed, he declared, by 'raisers of sedition and enemies of my sovereign power'. Shortly afterwards he

Opposite A Puritan satirical picture of the call to arms in 1642: the scholar on the left, the bishop in the centre, and the Cavalier on the right each urge the reader to fight for his own and the Kingdom's defence.

despatched Commissions of Array to all his Lords Lieutenant throughout the kingdom, empowering them to secure the militia and all county magazines of weapons, ammunition and gunpowder. It amounted to a declaration of war.

When it came to choosing sides in this domestic quarrel between King and Parliament some Englishmen were at a loss to know what to do. Everyone agreed that England was governed by a mixed constitution. 'Better laws and a happier constitution of government no nation ever enjoyed,' wrote Lucy Hutchinson, 'it being a mixture of monarchy, aristocracy and democracy, with sufficient fences against the past of every one of these forms – tyranny, faction and confusion.'

Both sides asserted, each with some truth, that they were taking up arms to maintain that time-honoured constitution. In order to gain the moderate ground and present themselves as upholders of King and Parliament both sides relied upon fictions. Parliament claimed it made no war against the person of the King, but merely sought to rescue him from the clutches of evil counsellors and restore him to their bosom at Westminster. The King saw the rebellion as inspired and led by a handful of dangerous fanatics out to destroy his Church and kingdom. Most people, however, had the wit to see that these respectful nods to that constitutional convention disguised the underlying political and religious power struggle.

The outcome of this tussle depended upon the support which each side could enlist in its service. At the time there was a wide spectrum of religious and political views, but the two were much more closely linked with each other then than they are now. The Cavaliers and the Roundheads, to use the popular nicknames that came into currency in 1642, soon formed the two poles at either end of that spectrum. They can be clearly contrasted with each other. In the

middle of the spectrum, however, the differences between the supporters of each side could be almost imperceptible. Here is a profile of each.

The Royalists were essentially conservatives in Church and State. Apart from the small minority of Roman Catholics, who supported the King to a man, their ranks included all Church of England men who adhered to rule by bishops and cherished the Book of Common Prayer. The more High Church members of the Church of England, led by those Laudians among the clergy and laity, accepted wholeheartedly the divine origins of kingship, which inclined them to submit themselves to his authority. Richard Bulstrode, who served in the King's Lifeguard, said it was 'some kind of sacrilege' to take up arms against him. For the true Cavalier, wrote Sir Francis Wortley, 'conceives the King to be the Head of the Church' and 'dares call his Sovereign the Anointed of God. . . . He conceives passive obedience always due to the power of the King'.

Sir Edmund Verney, the Knight-Marshal, who had been a courtier for thirty years, may have seen too much of Charles to be swayed by such considerations. As a Protestant he had no liking for the Laudian bishops; but to fight against the King's person was so unthinkable that he was shocked when his eldest son, Sir Ralph, sided with Parliament. From Ireland, where he was serving with the army sent to suppress the Irish rebellion, Sir Edmund's son Edmund wrote to remonstrate with Ralph: 'Brother, if what I feared is proved too true, which is your being against the King, give me leave to tell you in my opinion 'tis most unhandsomely done, and it grieves my heart to think that my father already and I, who so dearly love and esteem you, should be bound in consequence (because in duty to our King) to be your enemy. I hear it is a great grief to your father. I beseech you to consider that Majesty is sacred. . . . I believe you will all say you intend not to hurt the King, but can any of you warrant any one shot to say it shall not endanger his very person? I am so much troubled to think of your being of the side you are, that I can write no more, only I shall pray for peace . . .'

Most Royalists felt the same holy if inarticulate reverence for kingship as personified in King Charles I. They were moved by class loyalties to the Crown which had its roots in feudal England. For England in 1642 was far closer to the medieval than to the modern world. Honour, the code of chivalry which swayed every English gentleman, consisted of a proper sense of what was due to people, together with a strict adherence to these social obligations. No English gentleman would deny that the monarch could lawfully command his services when he took the field either to oppose a foreign foe or else to suppress a rebellion at home. Honour pressed him to be the first in the field. Loyalty, family tradition and the desire for an honourable reputation among his peers spoke with one voice on the matter. Sir Bevil Grenville responded with such a spirit when summoned to serve King Charles in the Scots war. In a letter to a fellow Cornishman he writes: 'I cannot contain myself within my doors when the King of England's standard waves in the field upon so just occasion, the cause being such as must make all those that die in it little inferior to martyrs. And for mine own part, I desire to acquire an honest name or an honourable grave. I never loved my life or ease so much as to shun such an occasion, which if I should I were unworthy of the profession I have held as to succeed those ancestors of mine who have so many of them sacrificed their life for their country.'

Invading an old enemy north of the Border was quite a different matter from fighting against fellow Englishmen. Yet Grenville, a friend of Sir John Eliot and other leading Puritans, a man of deep Protestant piety himself, did not hesitate to support the King when called upon to do so again in the summer of 1642. The King's greatest strength lay in this instinctive loyalty which pervaded the nobility and the gentry.

For those who held positions of trust at court, class obligations were complemented by delicate ties of loyalty and affection, and some individuals felt themselves to be trapped. Their religious and moral sympathies drew them towards the popular cause, but honour and loyalty anchored them firmly at the King's side. Sir Edmund Verney obeyed the King's summons to arms in 1642, but he spoke to Clarendon plainly about his misgivings: 'I do not like the quarrel and do heartily wish that the King would yield and consent to what they desire; so that my conscience is only concerned in honour and in gratitude to follow my master. I have eaten his bread and served him near thirty years, and will not do so base a thing as to forsake him; and choose rather to lose my life (which I am sure I shall do) to preserve and defend those things that are against my conscience to preserve and defend. For I will deal freely with you, I have no reverence for the bishops for whom this quarrel subsists.'

At the other end of the spectrum stood the 'more godly and honest part of the Kingdom'. It is as difficult to write a profile of a typical Puritan as it is of a Cavalier, but one central characteristic that Puritans shared in common was a burning zeal for the Protestant religion. According to Richard Baxter 'the religious serious people of these countries' were characterized by a suspicion 'of all that is ceremonious in God's service, and of all which they find not warrant for in scripture and a greater inclination to a rational convincing earnest way of preaching and prayers than to the written forms of words which are to be read in churches. And they are greatly taken with a preacher that speaks to them in a familiar natural language, and exhorteth them as if it were for their lives; when another that readeth or says a few composed words in a reading tone, they hear almost as a boy that is saying his lesson. And they are much persuaded that a just parochial discipline would greatly reform the Church, and that diocesans by excluding it cherish vice. . . .

'The name Puritan was put upon them, and by that they were commonly known. When they had been called by that name awhile, the vicious multitude of the ungodly called all Puritans that were strict and serious in a holy life, were they ever so conformable! So that the same name in a bishop's mouth signified a nonconformist, and in an ignorant drunkard's or swearer's mouth, a godly obedient Christian. But the people being the greater number, became among

THE

World turn'd upside down:

OR,

A briefe defcription of the ridiculous Fafhions
of thefe diftracted Times.

By T. J. a well-willer to King, Parliament and Kingdom.

London : Printed for *John Smith*. 1644.

Anti-Cavalier (and anti-smoking) propaganda (*left*): a portrait of the 'roaring boys . . . children of spiritual fornication, such as go a-whoring from God after the idols of their own brains'. *Right* The title page of a well-known tract published at the end of the war.

themselves the masters of the sense.'

For the true Puritan loyalty to God took precedence over loyalty to the King; God's will could be plainly known through reading Scripture and by prayer. The services and buildings of the Church of England must be cleansed from the 'dregs of popery'; the swelling number of Puritan preachers should be helped to bring the nation under the sway of the Word of God. True religion and England's liberty were bound up together: to forward one and preserve the other was the work that God called his servants to perform. 'When I put my hand to the Lord's work in 1642,' wrote a Yorkshireman called John Hodgson who became a Roundhead captain, 'I did not do it rashly, but had many an hour and night to seek God to know my way.'

The events of that year, wrote Hodgson, caused serious thought in many, and amongst the views he read and heard expressed were the following: 'That the safety of the people is the supreme law both of nature and nations; and that there was a people before there were rulers and governors chosen and set over them . . . the fountain has been the agreement of the people; and that rulers and governors are accountable to the people for their misgovernment, when they transgress the laws and rules by which the people did agree they would be governed (that is, the people assembled in parliaments or chief councils). Now, I have found that England was never a pure monarchy (for that is tyranny), but a political monarchy governed by laws.'

16

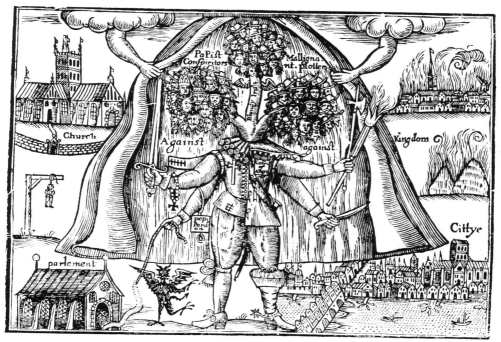

A vivid portrayal of the Protestant image of their foes as a composite monster, made up of 'Popish conspirators, Malignant plotters and cruel Irish', united by their single aim to destroy the Kingdom and its institutions.

For the politically sophisticated, it was this defence of English freedoms against an incipient tyranny which formed the chief plank of 'the Good Old Cause'. The religious issues were real, but they lay in the background. Mr John Hutchinson, son of the MP for Nottinghamshire, went home in 1642 to his native county and carefully read all the published papers exchanged between King and Parliament, as well as many private treatises, 'whereby he became abundantly informed in conscience of the righteousness of the Parliament's cause in point of civil right; and though he was satisfied of the endeavours to bring back Popery and subvert the true Protestant religion, which was apparent to everyone that impartially considered it, yet he did not think that so clear a ground of the war as the defence of the just English liberties'. As Richard Baxter makes clear, however, it was religion which provided the chief motive force for Parliament's epic struggle:

But though it must be confessed, that the public safety and liberty wrought very much with most, especially with the nobility and gentry, who adhered to the Parliament, yet was it principally the differences about religious matters that filled up the Parliament's armies, and put the resolution and valour into their soldiers, which carried them on in another manner than mercenary soldiers are carried on. Not that the matter of 'Bishops or no Bishops' was the main thing (for thousands that wished for good bishops were on the Parliament's side), though many called it *Bellum Episcopale* (and with the Scots that was a greater part of the controversy). But the generality of the people through the land (I say not *all* or every *one*) who were then called Puritans, Precisians, religious persons that used to talk of God and heaven and scripture and holiness, and to follow sermons and read books of devotion, and pray in their families and spend the Lord's day in religious exercises, and plead for mortification and serious devotion, and strict obedience to God, and speak against swearing, cursing, drunkenness, prophaneness, etc., I say, the main body of this sort of men, both preachers and people, adhered to the Parliament. And on the other side, the gentry that were not so precise and strict against an oath, or gaming, or plays, or drinking, nor troubled themselves so much about the matters of God and the world to come, and the ministers and people that were for the King's Book, for dancing and recreations on the Lord's days; and those that made not so great a matter of every sin, but went to church and heard Common Prayer, and were glad to hear a sermon which lashed the Puritans, and which ordinarily spoke against this strictness and preciseness in religion, and this strict observation of the Lord's day, and following sermons and praying extempore, and talking so much of scripture and the matters of salvation, and those that hated and derided them that take these courses, the main body of these were against the Parliament. Not but that some such for money, or a landlord's pleasure, served them; as some few of the stricter sort were against them, or not for them (being neuters): but I speak of the notable division through the land. . . .

But as to the generality, they went so unanimously the other way, that upon my knowledge many that were not wise enough to understand the truth about the cause of the King and Parliament, did yet run into the Parliament's armies, or take their part (as sheep go together for company) moved by this argument, 'Sure God will not suffer almost all his most religious servants to err in so great a matter'. And 'if all these should perish what will become of religion'. But these were insufficient grounds to go upon. And abundance of the ignorant sort of the country, who were civil, did flock in to the Parliament, and filled up their armies afterward, merely because they heard men swear for the Common Prayer [Book] and bishops, and heard others pray that were against them; and because they heard the King's soldiers with horrid oaths abuse the name of God, and saw them live in debauchery, and the Parliament's soldiers flock to sermons, and talking of religion, and praying and singing psalms together on their guards. And all the sober men that I was acquainted with, who were against the Parliament, were wont to say, 'The King has the better cause, but the Parliament has the better men'.

Thus Puritans at home or in the colonies solidly supported Parliament. In Puritan New England, it is true, Captain Jenyson of the Watertown militia did express some doubts. He accepted that Parliament stood for the godly people in the Kingdom, but he did not think he would take sides with them against their prince. If the King attacked New England, he hastily added, he would defend it with his life. His shocked neighbours reported him to Governor John Winthrop but friendly pressures soon made him recant fully and declare himself wholly for Parliament. Soon a steady stream of New Englanders reached these shores to fight or preach for the common cause.

Parliament evoked an enthusiasm amounting to fervour among those who cared deeply for the Reformation and for England. Sir William Waller of Devon wrote that 'my passion for Parliament embolden'd me to offer my service as far as to the raising of first a troop and after of a regiment of horse'. In neighbouring Cornwall, where only a handful of gentlemen, headed by Lord Robartes, sided with Parliament, a contemporary could describe them as 'a passionate company'.

The King's party called their opponents most commonly 'Rebels', while the Parliamentarians usually referred to the Royalists as 'Malignants'. But the committed on both sides were also given nicknames with religious overtones: Cavaliers and Roundheads. 'Cavalier', adopted from the Spanish *Cavaliero*, identified the Royalists with the Papist horse-soldiers of Spain who plundered and despoiled the countryside of Europe during the Thirty Years War; while 'Roundhead' lumped all adherents of the Parliamentary party with those Puritans who wore their hair short as a badge of zeal, along with other affectations. As Lucy Hutchinson explains, it was not a very appropriate name: 'From this custom of wearing their hairs, that name of Roundhead became the scornful term given to the whole Parliamentary party, whose army indeed marched out so, but as if they had only been sent out till their hair was grown. Two or three years after, any stranger that had seen them would have inquir'd the reason of that name, which was very ill applied to Mr Hutchinson, who having a very fine thickset head of hair naturally kept it clean and handsome without any affectation, so that it was a great ornament to him, although the godly of those days, when he embrac'd their party, would not allow him to be religious because his hair was not in their cut, nor his words in their phrase, nor such little formalities altogether fitted to their humour, who were, many of them, so weak as to esteem rather for such insignificant circumstances than for solid wisdom, piety and courage, which brought real aid and humour to their party . . .'

Many Englishmen in the middle band of the spectrum of political and religious beliefs preferred to remain neutral. But there was constant social pressure from family and friends upon those who hesitated. Both sides tended to apply the principle that those who are not for us are against us. They suspected neutrals as being tacit supporters of the enemy. In 1643, when a Royalist advance into Hampshire seemed imminent, Colonel Herbert Morley told the Speaker: 'This approaching cloud, I fear, may raise a storm in Sussex, which county is full of neuters and Malignants; and I have ever observed neuters to turn Malignants upon such occasions.'

Even more suspect was the supporter who seemed to be moving into neutrality. In 1643 Sir Ralph Verney withdrew from the House of Commons because he would not take the Covenant and commit England to a presbyterian form of Church government. His cousin Henry Parker remonstrates with him: 'In my opinion you steer a course wherein there is almost no hope of indemnity

Overleaf Daniel Mytens' portrait of the King and Queen about to go hunting. The dwarf was the Queen's favourite, Jeffrey Hudson.

on either side, but certainty of great loss and blame from both. If you shall say there is much to be disliked in either party, methinks that should not seem strange or alienate you totally from either. For in these public divisions, where religion and liberty are endangered, all men ought to adhere to that cause which is dictated to them to be the better and more harmless by the light of nature and the most forcible indication of reason.

'No man can say that God has left him no part to act, nor no station to make good. And if some poor mechanick might plead himself to be wholly unuseful and inconsiderable in these grand cases, yet you are apparently bereft of such excuse. You have an account to make to God, your Country, to your friends, to yourself, and the charge of that account will be high and valuable. And to think that you can exonerate all by saying you were dubious and not satisfied in some particulars is most strange. 'Tis impossible that you should be equilibrious in the main or the generality of the controversy, and if either scale have but one odd grain in it to sway you, you are as much bound to obey that sway as he that has the greatest propension of judgement.'

Henry Verney, one of Ralph's Royalist brothers, added his voice. He was a passionate horse-racing and sporting man, without much grasp of politics, and he fell back on cock-fighting language. He urged his brother 'to take the pit one way or another' – to stand his ground or fly out of the cock-pit like a craven bird. 'For these times are likely to hold very long, and believe it, none will be in so sad a condition as those that stand neuters.'

Arguments such as these must have persuaded many reluctant Englishmen to plump for one side or other. Therefore the parties at either end of the spectrum were really coalitions of moderates and extremists of various kinds, sitting uneasily together. Sometimes the mutual suspicions and animosities which arose within these moving, shifting coalitions overshadowed the enmity they cherished for their opponents in the field. Genuine neutrals were probably few for it was not an age of reason, but it made good sense to pass yourself off as such if you happened to live in country dominated by the other side. Such a view does not contradict Clarendon's judgement that 'the number of them who desired to sit still was greater than those who desired to engage in either party'.

For families and individuals, for communities in towns, cities and villages, the summer of 1642 was a time for decision. Never had the whole nation been so involved in this manner. Pamphlets daily appeared from the presses, preachers expounded the moral interpretations of events from pulpits, husbands and wives talked politics over dinner, friends sent each other persuasive letters while neighbours reasoned or argued with each other in taverns. Even strangers would challenge each other. As John Corbet wrote, 'fears and jealousies had so possessed the Kingdom that a man could hardly travel through any market town but he should be asked whether he were for the King or Parliament'.

2

A Nation Divided

'Before the flame of the war broke out in the top of the chimneys, the smoke ascended in every country,' recalled Lucy Hutchinson. Like her contemporaries she frequently referred to counties as 'countries'. Similar to independent states, virtually ruled by the aristocracy and gentry who held lands within them, counties were close-knit societies deeply conscious of their distinct identities. In June 1642 the call to arms sundered these local unities of interest. The King's Commissioners of Array and the members of Parliament sent home to execute the Militia Ordinance clashed in a series of fierce contests and disputes up and down the country, some almost ending in bloodshed, so that 'every county had more or less the civil war within itself'.

In some areas the struggle soon resolved itself in favour of one side or other. London, and the home counties which supplied its markets with corn, meat, vegetables and logs, and the eastern counties, generally supported Parliament. With the exception of the royal Duchy of Cornwall, rural Wales and parts of the North, which were fairly solidly Royalist, the rest of the country was divided with each county experiencing its own conflict between the rural partisans.

The forces at work to produce this quiltwork pattern of civil war can be illustrated by looking at the North, a region which is often described as wholly loyal to the King. There, Royalist land-owners such as the Earl of Derby and the Earl of Newcastle used their great influence to call out their tenants and neighbours for the King. To stiffen their resistance to Lord Derby the more Puritan-minded tenants in Lancashire and Cheshire coined a proverb, 'God is greater than the Earl of Derby'.

The gentry of Yorkshire and Lancashire were divided in the King's favour in their allegiance. In Yorkshire, it has been estimated, some 138 out of a total of 679 gentry families were Puritan. In Lancashire the gentry families supplied 178 officers for the King and 84 for Parliament; most of them on both sides served their causes in their native county. In terms of the known allegiance of Lancashire gentlemen, 272 supported the King against 138 for Parliament, while nine changed sides.

In the country districts where the Royalists did most of their recruiting, social conservatism was matched by adherence to the old religion. The large size of parishes and the widespread practice of pluralism produced too few capable clergymen as shepherds to too many people. Moreover, as Puritan preachers discovered, working people such as farm labourers and their families were peculiarly resistant to the inward soul-searching which they enjoined. Northern countrymen in particular clung to the past. In 1628 Sir Benjamin Rudyard wrote that 'there were places in England which were scarce in Christendom, where God was little better known than amongst the Indians. I exampled it in the utmost skirts of the North where the prayers of the common people are more like spells and charms than devotions'.

Throughout the nation the situation in the towns was quite different. In general Puritanism was especially strong among the class of middling merchants, shopkeepers and tradesmen and their families, who carried the most votes in municipal matters. Writing about Gloucester, Corbet could say that 'the King's cause and party were favoured by two extremes in that city, the one of wealthy and powerful men, the other of the basest and lowest sort, but disgusted by the middle rank, the true and best citizens'. About a quarter of the population of England and Wales, some five and a half millions in 1642, lived in cities and towns, and so Parliament enjoyed here a considerable advantage.

The clothing industry was England's chief one at the time of the Civil War, and the clothiers in the towns of Yorkshire and Lancashire were noted for their staunch Puritan faith, the fruit of much labour by the preaching ministry. Puritan schools complemented the pulpit by training men for leadership. Halifax Grammar School, founded in 1591 by a Puritan wool-merchant family, existed to help some of its pupils 'to become in time ambassadors of reconciliation from God to his Church'. The schoolmaster in charge must be 'an enemy to popish superstition' – the fires of 'Bloody Mary' were still warm in England's imagination. But Halifax school produced lay Puritan leaders as well, such as the merchant Sir Richard Saltonstall who sailed with Winthrop in 1630 to found the colony of Massachusetts Bay in America.

By 1642 the monopoly of the Gospel enjoyed by the established Puritan ministry in the Church of England, educated at such schools as Halifax and at certain favoured colleges in the universities, was being challenged by preachers from the lower middle-classes, men who lacked degrees but had graduated by religious experience. Without the ballast of book-learning these Puritan preachers rode lightly over the rocks of theology, blown by impulses from the Spirit. A hostile writer in *The Schismatick Stigmatized* (1641) described how these men 'do affect an odd kind of gesture in their pulpits, vapouring and throwing heads and shoulders this way and that way, grinning and gerning, showing their teeth and snuffling through their noses . . .' Henry Oxinden, a Kentish gentleman who visited Leeds in November 1641, conveys in a letter home something of the religious ferment they helped to create.

For these parts, they are divided into so many sects and schisms that certainly it denotes the latter day to be very near at hand. Some whereof deny St Paul and upbraid him with bragging, fantastical and inconstant; others say that there is no national church, and so separate from us and the Puritans as being no true church, of which kind

Two more satirical portraits of the Royalist: *left* as a wolf with eagle's claws, and *right* as an 'English antick . . . with ridiculous habits and apish gestures'. The spots on his face are intentional, as is the hat shaped like a 'closet-pan'.

here are a great number. There is another which preach against the keeping of holidays and Christmas day, and exhort the people to follow their vocation thereon, and in their pulpits vilify and blaspheme our Saviour's name, affirming that it ought to be of no more account than Jack or Tom, and begin to deny the sacrament to noted sinners or drunkards, etc, and these are Puritans; there is another and they are conformalists, and they resort most to this place; priests which must needs have a specious, pompous religion, all glorious without; bishops must continue their dignities and authorities least despised and brought into contempt. . . .

Before the Civil War towns were mostly happy communities, united in civic pride despite their religious differences. Even during the war minorities were generally respected and tolerated, not least because the town expected them to share fully in the financial burdens of the war. The same unity persisted in the country as a whole. The marriage-ties between manor-house and manor-house were drawn so close and bound together over so many generations, that to live in an English shire was to be in the midst of a large and usually harmonious family party. Most people acknowledged cousinship as well as neighbourhood; strong friendships grew up between the members of these families; there was always a new baby to be 'made a Christian' amidst a gathering of god-parents and friends, or a valued friend now leaving their pleasant company to be escorted to his last rest. A note of passing annoyance may be detected in their correspondence when a low-born intruder outside the magic circle set a determined foot over the borderline, or even in the second generation sought a grant of arms. Apart from such incidents there was a proper good feeling between yeoman and squire, squire and his tenants and labourers. Only in the background there was still much ignorance, prejudice and savagery against such social deviants as poor witches.

The months before the outbreak of war saw a sharp decline in those harmonious relationships. Religion proved to be the most divisive factor. Richard Baxter recalls the effects in Kidderminster as Puritan zeal, sanctioned by Parliament, manifested itself:

About that time the Parliament sent down an order for the demolishing of all statues and images of any of the three persons in the blessed Trinity, or of the Virgin Mary, which should be found in churches, or on the crosses in churchyards. My judgment was for the obeying of this order, thinking it came from just authority; but I meddled not in it, but left the churchwarden to do what he thought good. The Churchwarden (an honest, sober, quiet man) seeing a crucifix upon the cross in the churchyard, set up a ladder to have reached it, but it proved too short. Whilst he was gone to seek another, a crew of the drunken riotous party of the town (poor journey-men and servants) took the alarm, and ran altogether with weapons to defend the crucifix, and the church images (of which there were divers left since the time of popery). The report was among them that I was the actor and it was me they sought; but I was walking almost a mile out of town, or else I suppose I had there ended my days. When they missed me and the churchwarden both, they went raving about the streets to seek us. Two neighbours that dwelt in other parishes, hearing that they sought my life, ran in among them to see whether I were there, and they knocked them both down in the streets, and both of them are since dead, and I think never perfectly recovered that hurt. When they had roamed about half an hour, and met with none of us, and were newly housed, I came in from my walk, and hearing the people cursing at me in their doors, I wondered what the matter was, but quickly found how fairly I had escaped. The next Lord's Day I dealt plainly with them, and laid open to them the quality of that action, and told them, seeing they so requited me as to seek my blood, I was willing to leave them, and save them from that guilt. But the poor sots were so amazed and ashamed, that they took on sorrily and were loth to part with me.

About this time the King's Declarations were read in our market-place, and the reader (a violent country gentleman) seeing me pass the streets, stopped and said, 'There goes a traitor', without ever giving a syllable of reason for it.

And the Commission of Array was set afoot (for the Parliament meddled not with the militia of that county, the Lord Howard their Lieutenant not appearing). Then the rage of the rioters grew greater than before! And in preparation to the war they had got the

Heraclitus' dream, published in 1642, is an elaborate allegory: in the centre the shepherd (the Church) is being shorn by his own sheep – the 'rude people, without authority, law or reason'.

word among them 'Down with the Roundheads!' Insomuch that if a stranger passed in many places that had short hair and a civil habit, the rabble presently cried 'Down with the Roundheads!'and some they knocked down in the open streets.

In this fury of the rabble I was advised to withdraw a while from home; whereupon I went to Gloucester. As I passed through a corner of the suburbs of Worcester, they that knew me not, cried, 'Down with the Roundheads!' and I was glad to spur on and be gone. But when I came to Gloucester, among strangers also that had never known me, I found a civil, courteous, and religious people, as different from Worcester, as if they had lived under another government. There I stayed a month. . . .

When I came home I found the beggarly drunken rout in a very tumultuating disposition, and the superiors that were for the King did animate them, and the people of the place who were accounted religious were called Roundheads and openly reviled and threatened as the King's enemies (who had never meddled in any cause against the King). Every drunken sot that met any of them in the streets would tell them, 'we shall take an order with the Puritans ere long'. And just as at their shows and wakes and stage-plays, when the drink and the spirit of riot did work together in their heads, and the crowd encouraged one another, so was it with them now. They were like tied mastiffs newly loosed, and fled in the face of all that was religious, yea, or civil, which came in their way. It was the undoing of the King and bishops that this party was encouraged by the leaders in the country against the civil religious party. Yet, after the Lord's day when they had heard the sermon they would awhile be calmed, till they came to the alehouse again, or heard any of their leaders hiss them on, or heard a rabble cry, 'Down with the Roundheads!' And when the wars began, almost all these drunkards went into the King's Army, and were quickly killed, so that scarce a man of them came home again and survived the war.

Baxter alludes to the militia which each county possessed, survivals from feudal days refurbished when Spain threatened to invade England at the time of the Armada. The King appointed a Lord Lieutenant and a commission of Deputy-Lieutenants to command these forces. Many gentlemen served on this commission and held commands in the trained bands, which gave those without previous military experience, such as John Hampden and Sir Edmund Verney in Buckinghamshire, some knowledge of how to muster, equip and drill soldiers. In numbers they were strong. The Hampshire trained bands in 1633, for instance, numbered 5,486 officers and men, divided into eight foot regiments, a Winchester company and three troops of horse. In Yorkshire in 1642 Sir Hugh Cholmley tells us that the trained bands could muster thirteen thousand men, even more than the regiments that London could put in the field. But the militia lacked more than basic training; they saw their role as local defence; and the divided loyalties of officers and men meant that neither side could really count upon them except in the heartlands. For these three reasons the real prizes in the summer of 1642 were the arms, ammunition and gunpowder stored in local arsenals for the use of each county's militia.

The King, in particular, needed to secure these stands of pikes and muskets, helmets, back-and-breast plates, swords and pistols, barrels of powder and bags of shot. He had lost the Tower of London and he failed to secure the second largest magazine in the land at Hull, which was denied him by Sir John Hotham and some trained bands of the East Riding. Portsmouth, third in order of size, seemed to be safely in Parliament's hands until its trusted governor, Colonel George Goring, betrayed his charge by declaring for the King in the last week in July. Although it contained 100 guns and 1,400 barrels of powder Goring could send nothing to the King at York. The Hampshire Parliamentarians invested him on land, while the ships of the Royal Navy, which had come out for Parliament under the Earl of Warwick, mounted a blockade of the port. Except for two or three small ships, which had deserted to the King, the fleet stood poised to intercept any vessels carrying the arms and munitions which Henrietta Maria was buying on the continent. In this unpromising situation every grain of gunpowder and every set of arms seemed precious to the King's commanders.

In Nottingham these prizes were denied to the Royalists at first by a young

Lucy Hutchinson, author of *Memoirs of the Life of Colonel Hutchinson*, portrayed after the war with her son for whom she wrote this fine biography of his father.

Parliamentarian gentleman. John Hutchinson was twenty-seven years and had recently returned from London to live at Owthorpe Hall, about seven miles south-east of Nottingham, together with his wife Lucy, who was twenty-two. She shared his Puritan ardour, and left an incomparable memoir of her husband for their surviving children. John Hutchinson was well-connected in the county, his father being Sir Thomas Hutchinson, member of Parliament for Nottinghamshire. But their Byron cousins sided with the King. Sir John would soon become a trusted Royalist cavalry general, while Sir Richard, Sir Robert and Sir Thomas all served the King as colonels.

The most important family resident in the county was also divided in its allegiance. The Earl of Kingston was 'a man of vast estate and not less covetousness', wrote Lucy Hutchinson, 'who divided his sons between both parties and conceal'd himself, till at length his fate drew him to declare absolutely on the King's side, wherein he behav'd himself honourably and died remarkably'. When asked to cast his lot with Parliament, Kingston had replied, 'When I take up arms with the King against the Parliament, or with the Parliament against the King, let a cannon bullet divide me between them.' Later, as a prisoner of war sailing down river towards Hull, these words came home to roost. The Parliamentarian boat carrying him came under fire from a Royalist battery on the bank and a cannon ball literally cut the Earl in two.

Two of Kingston's sons served Parliament: William Pierrepont as one of the better orators in the House of Commons and Francis with much less ardour as a colonel of a town regiment in Nottingham. His eldest son, Viscount Newark, who was Lord Lieutenant of the county, for his part did not hesitate before declaring for the King; he received for his generous loans and loyal services during the war the title of Marquess of Dorchester. On 13 July 1642 he could be found exhorting the Nottinghamshire trained bands at Newark to obey the King. Lord Newark was a little man in stature with a very fiery temper. In describing the conflict of wills between her husband and the Lord Lieutenant over possession of the county's magazine, Hutchinson's good manners or social deference were evidently combined with a desire not to trigger off one of Lord Newark's rages. But that did not prevent him from speaking his mind plainly, as Lucy Hutchinson recounts.

At that time most of the gentry of the country were disaffected to the Parliament. Most of the middle sort, the able substantial free-holders and the other commons who had not their dependence upon the malignant nobility made a petition to him to return to the Parliament, which, upon their earnest entreaty, Mr Hutchinson went with some others and presented at York, where, meeting his cousins the Byrons, they were extremely troubled to see him there upon that account. After his return, Sir John Byron being also come to his house at Newstead, Mr Hutchinson went to visit him there and not finding him return'd to Nottingham, five miles short of his own house.

There, going to the Mayor to hear some news, he met with such as he expected not; for, as soon as he came in, the Mayor's wife told him that the sheriff of the county was come to fetch away the magazine that belonged to the trained bands of the county, which was left in her husband's trust, and that her husband had sent for the country to acquaint them, but she fear'd it would be gone before they could come in. Whereupon Mr Hutchinson presently went, and taking his brother from his lodging along with him presently came to the town's hall, and going up to my Lord Newark, Lord Lieutenant, told him that hearing some dispute concerning the country's powder he was come to wait on his Lordship, to know his desires and intents concerning it. My Lord answer'd him that the King having great necessities desir'd to borrow it of the country. Mr Hutchinson asked my Lord what commission he had from his Majesty. My Lord told him he had one, but had left it behind him. Mr Hutchinson replied that my Lord's affirmation was satisfactory to him, but the country would not be willing to part with their powder in so dangerous a time without an absolute command. My Lord urged that he would restore it in ten days. Mr Hutchinson replied, they might have use of it sooner, and he hoped my Lord would not disarm his country in such a time of danger. My Lord condemn'd the mention of danger, and ask'd what they could fear while he was their Lord Lieutenant and ready to serve them with his life. Mr Hutchinson told him of some grounds to apprehend danger by reason of the daily passing of armed men through the country, whereof there was now one troop in the town, and that before they could repair to my Lord they might be destroy'd in his absence, and withal urg'd to him examples of their insolence. But my Lord replied to all the urgency of the King's occasions of it, where were such that he could not dispense with it. It was in vain to argue with him the propriety the country had in it, being bought with their money and therefore not to be taken without their consent: my Lord declar'd himself positively resolv'd to take it. Whereupon Mr Hutchinson left him. There were in the room with him Sir John Digby, the high Sheriff of the County, who was setting down the weight of the powder and match, and two or three captains and others that were busy weighing the powder.

By that time Mr Hutchinson came down, a good company of the country were gather'd together, whom Mr Hutchinson acquainted what had pass'd between him and my Lord; and they desir'd him that he would but please to stand to them and they would part with all their blood before he should have a grain of it, and said moreover they would go up and tumble my Lord and the Sheriff out of the windows. Mr Hutchinson, seeing them so resolv'd, desir'd them to stay below while he went yet once again up to my Lord, which they did; and he told my Lord some of the country were come in, at whose request he was again come to beseech his Lordship to desist from his design of taking their powder, which pursued might be of dangerous consequence. My Lord replied, it could not be, for the King was very well assured of the cheerful compliance of the greatest part of the country with his service. Mr Hutchinson told him, whatever assurance his Majesty might have, if his Lordship pleas'd to look out he might see no inconsiderable number below that would not willingly part with it. My Lord replied they were but a few factious men; whereupon Mr Hutchinson told him, since it was yet the happiness of these unhappy times that no blood had been spilt, he should be sorry the first should be shed upon my Lord's occasion in his own country. My Lord scornfully replied, 'Fear it not, it cannot come to that; the King's occasions are urgent and must be serv'd'. Whereupon Mr Hutchinson looking out at the countrymen, they came very fast up the stairs; and Mr Hutchinson told him, however he slighted it, not one there but would part with every drop of their blood before they would part with it, except he could show a command or request for it under the King's hand, or would stay till the country were call'd in to give their consents; for it was their property and they all had interest in it as bought with their money for the particular defence of the county.

Then my Lord fell to entreaties to borrow part of it, but that being also denied, he took the Sheriff aside, and after a little conference they put up their tools and left the powder; when my Lord, turning to the people, said to them: 'Gentlemen, His Majesty was by some assur'd of the cheerfulness of this country's affections to him, whereof I am sorry to see so much failing, and that the county should fall so much short of the town, which have cheerfully lent his Majesty one barrel of powder, but it seems he can have none from you. I pray God you do not repent this carriage of yours towards his Majesty, which he must be acquainted withal.' A bold countryman then stepping forth, by way of reply asked my Lord whether, if he were to take a journey with a charge into a place where probably he should be set upon by thieves, if any friend should ask to borrow his sword he would part with it. 'My Lord,' said he, 'the case is ours: our lives,

31

wives, children and estates all depend upon this country's safety, and how can it be safe in these dangerous times, when so many rude arm'd people pass daily through it, if we be altogether disarm'd?' My Lord made no reply, but bade the men who were weighing the powder desist, and went down. Mr Hutchinson follow'd him down the stairs; when an ancient gentleman that was with my Lord came and (whispering him) commended his and the country's courage and bade them stand to it and they would not be foil'd.

As they passed through a long room below, my Lord told Mr Hutchinson he was sorry to find him in the head of a faction. Mr Hutchinson replied, he could not tell how his Lordship could call that a faction which was so accidental as his being at that time in the town, where, hearing what was in hand, out of respect to his Lordship he only came to prevent mischief and danger which he saw likely to ensue. My Lord replied, he must inform the King, and told him his name was already up. To which Mr Hutchinson answer'd that he was glad, if the King must receive an information of him, it must be from so honourable a person; and for his name, as it rise, so in the name of God let it fall; and so took his leave and went home. The rest of the country that were there determin'd to give my Lord thanks for sparing their ammunition, and locked it up with two locks, whereof the keys of the one was entrusted with the Mayor of Nottingham, the other with the Sheriff of the County; which accordingly was done.

Meanwhile King Charles was raising his army at York. He issued commissions for eight regiments of horse and one of dragoons, fifteen regiments of foot and a train of artillery. Landed Royalists brought some of their own tenants but most commissioned officers raised volunteers by the beat of the drum. In the towns they met some opposition. Lieutenant John Roane, Yeoman Pricker to the King, tried to recruit men for his company in Walsall, but the mayor 'refused to let him beat up his drum and apprehended him'. What recruits came forward lacked arms. When the King marched southwards from York in mid-August so few officers had completed their regiments that no more commissions were issued for the time being. 'My Lord Crawford had spoken to the King for me to have a commission for a regiment of foot,' wrote Sir Henry Slingsby, 'but the King had so many that wanted for employment that unless I could find arms for them when they were raised, it would not be granted.'

In mid-August the Royalist army reached Nottingham. While the Sheriff broke open the lock of the county magazine the Royalist soldiers searched the houses of the citizens for their weapons. One of them had taken a musket and, as Hutchinson passed, was heard to say that he wished it was loaded for his sake, adding he hoped the day would shortly come when all such Roundheads would be targets for them. Hutchinson ignored the threat and hurried to his father's town house, where he found a quarter-master requisitioning it for the Earl of Lindsey, the King's General. Having tried without success to persuade Lindsey that the house was too inferior for him they parted on civil terms. Hearing a rumour that he would shortly be arrested, Hutchinson then made his way to the Parliamentarian army at Northampton.

On 22 August, about six o'clock, in the presence of Charles I and a small train

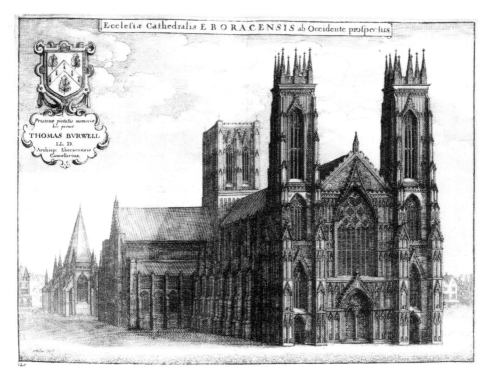

York Minster, one of the finest cathedrals in the country, is an example of the many great churches which, contrary to the common myth, survived the Civil War with relatively little damage at the hands of Parliament's Puritan soldiers.

of courtiers, the royal standard was raised to the sound of drums and trumpets on the top of Castle Hill in Nottingham. From time immemorial this formal act had made all who took the field against their king into self-declared traitors. It was a very blustery evening with grey rain clouds scudding across the sky, and that night the standard blew down – an ill-omen carefully noted by 'melancholic' men in the King's entourage. Even the King appeared more melancholic than usual at this joyless ceremony. The standard bore the royal arms with a quarter showing a hand pointing to the crown with a motto: GIVE CAESAR 'HIS DUE. By this time the High Sheriff had broken open the lock of the county's magazine and the Royalist soldiers had seized the weapons of the citizens.

The arrival of the King's dashing young nephew, Prince Rupert, lifted Royalist hearts at Nottingham. His mother, despite being the King's sister, wavered indecisively between the two sides; she did her best to keep him from the struggle. His eldest brother, the Elector Palatine, had already withdrawn from the King's camp, but the family loyalty to the Calvinist religion does not seem to have influenced Prince Rupert. Committed, fiery and impetuous, he was a natural cavalry leader. A superb horseman, a skilled swordsman and an excellent shot with his pistols, Prince Rupert was also 'very sparkish in his dress'. With feminine good looks inherited from his mother, Elizabeth of Bohemia, Prince Rupert had charisma or star quality. Unlike such archetypal

A true and exact Relation of the manner of his Maiesties setting up of His Standard at *Nottingham*, on Munday the 22. of August 1642.

First, The forme of the Standard, as it is here figured, and who were present at the advancing of it

Secondly, The danger of setting up of former Standards, and the damage which ensued thereon.

Thirdly, A relation of all the Standards that ever were set up by any King.

Fourthly, the names of those Knights who are appointed to be the Kings Standard-bearers. With the forces that are appoynted to guard it.

Fifthly, The manner of the Kings comming first to *Coventry*.

Sixtly, The *Cavalieres* resolution and dangerous threats which they have uttered, if the King concludes a peace without them, or hearkens unto his great Councell the Parliament : Moreover how they have shared and divided *London* amongst themselves already.

The raising of the King's standard at Nottingham in August 1642.

cavaliers as George Goring, Thomas Wentworth and George Porter, he did not frequently drink himself under the table. After spending nearly three years as a prisoner in Austria Rupert thirsted more for action than for wine. With his formidable energy and military flair, he was a potential war-winner.

King Charles appointed Prince Rupert to command his Cavaliers, the horse of his army. Rupert's second-in-command, a man he did not care for personally, was Henry, Lord Wilmot. Adept at court intrigue, Wilmot nonetheless possessed courage and some useful professional experience as a soldier. His motives for engaging in the war were far from disinterested; he once told a friend in a jocular letter that he expected fat pickings from confiscated estates of Parliament men when the war was won. Such covetous men on both sides already glimpsed the bonanza of lands which awaited the victors.

Despite his weakness in numbers one of the King's greatest strengths was the quality of those officers flocking back from foreign parts to serve him. Foremost among them was Patrick Ruthven, later Earl of Forth, who was to become Lindsey's successor after the battle of Edgehill. Ruthven had become a veteran in the Swedish army under the great Gustavus Adolphus, and married a Swedish wife. In 1640 he had held Berwick Castle with resolution against his fellow Scots. More than seventy years old, over fond of the bottle and plagued by gout, he was still an invaluable military adviser to the King's younger commander. Sir Jacob Astley, a little silver-haired veteran from the Dutch service, whom Elizabeth of Bohemia had once playfully called her 'monkey', received command of the Royalist foot regiments, while the dragoons were entrusted to Sir Arthur Aston, a peppery unpopular Roman Catholic who had fought for Russians, Poles and Swedes during a long and distinguished career.

Still too weak to face Parliament's army in battle, the King marched west in mid-September, recruiting as he went among the Derbyshire miners and labourers. Expecting 5,000 foot and 400 horse from Wales he moved to Shrewsbury, a crossing point on the River Severn. In his three weeks there the army began to take shape. Three regiments from Cheshire joined him as well as a Somersetshire regiment under Sir Thomas Lunsford, some Welshmen under Sir Edward Stradling, many of them armed with pitchforks and stout cudgels, and Sir John Beaumont's better-equipped Staffordshire foot. Clarendon declared it 'the wonderful providence of God' that within twenty days of coming to Shrewsbury 'the King could resolve to march, in despite of the enemy, even towards London with 6,000 foot, 2,000 horse and a train of artillery in very good order'.

The Royalists thought this army sufficient to resist the rebels, although it was inferior to the enemy in numbers. But not all of the King's officers were fire-eaters. If a way of avoiding a fight without dishonour could have been found many would have welcomed it with joy. Lord Henry Spencer, who was then twenty-two, was clearly among this number. Parliament had appointed him its own Lord Lieutenant of Northamptonshire, a sign of some hope for him, but

Few lived through the war without strong partisanships; but this cartoonist at least shows both sides in equal terms.

Spencer could not take up arms against the Crown. Like all Protestant English-men, however, he was vehemently anti-Catholic, and it was galling for him to be in the same political bed as such papists as Aston. At nineteen he had married Lady Dorothy Sidney. In some letters written in September in cypher from quarters in Shrewsbury, he shared his news and unburdened his feelings to his young wife.

My dearest Heart,

The King's condition is much improved of late; his force increases daily, which increases the insolency of the papists. How much I am unsatisfied with the proceedings here, I have at large expressed in several letters. Neither is there wanting, daily, handsome occasion to retire, were it not for grinning honour. For let occasion be never so handsome, unless a man were resolved to fight on the Parliament side, which, for my part, I had rather be hanged, it will be said without doubt, that a man is afraid to fight. If

there could be an expedient found, to salve the punctilio of honour, I would not continue here an hour. The discontent that I, and many other honest men, receive daily, is beyond expression. People are much divided; the King is of late very much averse to peace . . . it is likewise conceived that the King has taken a resolution not to do anything in that way before the Queen comes . . . nevertheless honest men will take all occasions to procure an accommodation. I fear the papists' threats have a much greater influence upon the King. . . . What the King's intentions are, to those that I converse with, are altogether unknown; some say he will hazard a battle very quickly; others say he thinks of wintering; which as it is suspected, so if it were generally believed, Sunderland and many others would make no scruple to retire; for I think it as far from gallant, either to starve with the King, or to do worse, as to avoid fighting. It is said the

King goes on Friday towards Chester, for a day or two, leaving his forces here; which are 6000 foot, 1500 dragoons, and above 2000 horse. There are 4000 foot more raised, they say 2000 by my Lord Strange, 1000 by Sir Thomas Salusbury, and 1200 by Sir Edward Stradling; all which will be here within a very few days. This a Lightning before Death.

I am yours, etc.

Shrewsbury, the 21 Sept. 1642.   Spencer

My dearest Heart,

I have received your letter of the 10 of this instant, but have had none else a good while, though you mentioned two others in this. Since we have been upon our march, I have had neither time nor opportunity to write, but I sent Alibone yesterday, to Althorpe, with a short letter to you, and a long one to my Lady; for which trouble I beseech you to make my excuse. Above one more than this, I believe I shall not have time to write, and opportunity to send, before we come to London; which by the grace of God, will be as soon as so great an army can march so many miles. For not only the papists but most men believe, that the King's army will make its way, though Lord Essex's army is five times as many as we are. If the King, or rather the papists prevail, we are in sad condition, for they will be insupportable to all, but most to us who have opposed them, so that if the King prevails by force, I must not live at home, which is grievous to me, but more to you. I cannot fancy any way to avoid both; for the King is so awed by the papists, that he dares not propose peace, or accept. I fear though by his last message, he is engaged. But if that be offered by the Parliament, I and others will speak their opinion, though by that, we were threatened by the papists.

My Lord Southampton, who presents to you his service, has lain in the bedchamber. I had above an hour's discourse with the King about the treaty, which I would be glad you knew, but it is too long with cyphers and unfit without, else we have had no commerce since we came from Nottingham. I thank you for your care to supply me with money. I should be sorry not to see you till I wanted it, for yesterday I gave six score pounds for a horse of my cousin Clumsey's, who kisses your hands. This may appear an argument that I shall want the sooner, but if I had been in danger of that, I would have ventured my body upon a worse horse. If I durst write thus freely of all things, you should have volumes, but by this constraint, I fear I have written too much nonsense; for I can truly say of my writing in characters, as a great man of this kingdom said of his speaking; that he never knew what he meant to speak, before he spoke, nor what he had said, after he had spoken.

The Parliament's confidence which you spoke of in your letter is put on, for really they are in ill condition, and it is impossible but they must know it. I never saw the King look better; he is very cheerful, and by the bawdy discourse, I thought I had been in the drawing room. Money comes in beyond expectation, the foot are reasonably well paid;

the horse have not been paid but live upon the country. The King is very good of himself, and would be so still, were it not for evil counsellors. For he gives very strict order, that as little spoil be made as is possible. Tomorrow we march to Birmingham, and so on the road to London, from whence by the Grace of God I will come to Penshurst, where I hope to see you past all your pains. I wrote to you last, to desire you to invite all my sisters to you, for I doubt London will be shortly a very ill place. I am yours, and my Lady Carlisle's humble servant. . . .

Not twelve months after writing these letters Henry Spencer, the first Earl of Sunderland, for so he had become, lay dead and stripped naked on the battlefield of Newbury.

3
Edgehill

In July 1642 Parliament entrusted its army to Robert Devereux, Earl of Essex, who was fifty-one years old. He had rebellion in the blood, as the Royalists said, for his mercurial father, the great favourite of Queen Elizabeth's declining years, had paid for that crime with his head. King James directed that Robert should be brought up as a companion to his eldest son Prince Henry, whose premature death in 1612 had paved the way to the accession of Charles. In the Prince's godly household Essex may have acquired his Puritan leanings. He had served in an expedition to support Prince Henry's sister Elizabeth of Bohemia, and then as vice-admiral in an unsuccessful naval assault on Cadiz. In 1628 he had voted for the Petition of Right, Parliament's call for a redress of outstanding grievances. King Charles gave him command of the army to invade Scotland, but it saw no glorious action and the King dismissed him 'without ordinary ceremony' which doubtless annoyed him. For Essex possessed a proud nature which made him exceptionally touchy, and a vanity which led him to enjoy his new title of 'His Excellency' and all the pomp of being Lord General. He puffed away at a white clay tobacco pipe and his soldiers called him 'old Robin'.

By late summer the Lord General's army had come into being. The cavalry was originally raised in troops, each numbering about sixty men, but commissions had been issued to six colonels to organise them into regiments of horse, besides two for dragoon regiments. Nineteen well-equipped regiments of foot, mainly from London, the home counties and the south Midlands, and a train of artillery completed the forces. Puritan members of both Houses supplied most of the colonels, although Essex had upon his staff some experienced professional officers, notably Scots Presbyterians such as Sir John Meldrum and Sir James Ramsey. As few of his new colonels of horse or foot had served more than a brief military apprenticeship they also commissioned some of these English and Scots professionals to manage their regiments for them. Colonel John Hampden, for example, appointed Joseph Wagstaffe to be lieutenant-colonel of his regiment of Buckinghamshire greencoats. Wagstaffe had soldiered for many years in France. Major William Barriffe, the next most senior officer, was also a professional who had written one of the more popular drill manuals of the day.

These seasoned veterans with their loud, authoritative orders laced with swear words were generally not so popular with the Puritan recruits. They

objected in particular to their use of oaths, which were religious (or blasphe-
mous to Puritan ears) rather than sexual as today. It should not be supposed,
however, that soldiers on either side confined themselves to blasphemies when
they came within shouting distance of each other. Henry Townshend recorded

*Robert Earle of Essex his Excellence, Generall of ý Army
Raised for the Preservation of Religion defence of King Parliment & Kingdom*

Robert Devereux, Earl of Essex, Lord General of the main Parliamentary army, of whom the
Royalists said that 'he had rebellion in the blood'. In the background the artist gives us an
impression of troops of horse and regiments of foot at Edgehill, the pikemen at the centre, with
files of musketeers on their flanks.

a typical exchange of 'ill-railing language' one night during the siege of Worcester in 1646: 'the enemy calling ours "Papist dogs", "Washington's Bastards", "Russell's Apes", "Where is the King of you rogues?", "Where is your tottered King?" (pardon the expression); ours replying and calling them "Traitors", "Villains", "Rogues to your King and Country", "The sons of a Puritan Bitch", "Bid you go preach in a crab tree", "Come and fetch their Colours which they lost", "Where are the Scots, you rogues, whom you hired to fight against your King?".'

Many feared that the professional soldiers, serving only for pay and plunder, would do all they could to prolong the fighting for their own ends, turning England into another province of the Thirty Years War. As Lord Brooke said at a commissioning ceremony for his officers: 'In Germany they fought only for spoil, rapine and destruction; merely for money it was and hope of gain that excited the soldier to that sense. It is not here so required as the cause stands with us. We must employ men who will fight merely for the cause's sake, and bear their own charges rather than those who expect rewards and salaries.' To hire such 'foreign and mercenary auxiliaries' would mean 'we shall never have a conclusion of these wars. For it is obviously in their self-interest to spin out our war to a prodigious length, as they have done in other countries, rather than see them quickly brought to a happy end. . . . I shall speak freely my conscience, I had rather have a thousand or two thousand honest citizens that can only handle their arms, whose hearts go with their hands, than two thousand of mercenary soldiers that boast of their foreign experience'.

The conduct of some professional soldiers bore out Lord Brooke's fears, as most of the English mercenaries had sided with the King; the allegiance of those who joined Essex's army was always suspect. Joseph Wagstaffe, for example, changed sides in 1643 and received a knighthood from the King. The Scots and Dutch officers proved to be more loyal as a body, but even some of them became turncoats as the war progressed.

In August 1643 the Lord General ordered his army to rendezvous at North-ampton before seeking to engage the Royalist forces in a decisive battle before Christmas. The letters of Nehemiah Wharton, a London apprentice turned sergeant in the redcoats of Colonel Denzil Holles, gives us a vivid picture of the mood in Essex's army as these regiments of raw, shaven-headed apprentices and other young men made their disorderly way through the quiet English countryside. His letters are addressed to his master, one Willingham, at home in the City.

Worthy Sir,   Aylesbury, August the 16th, 1642

On Monday, August the 8th, we marched to Acton; but being the Sixth Company, we were belated, and many of our soldiers were constrained to lodge in beds whose feathers were above a yard long. Tuesday, early in the morning, several of our soldiers

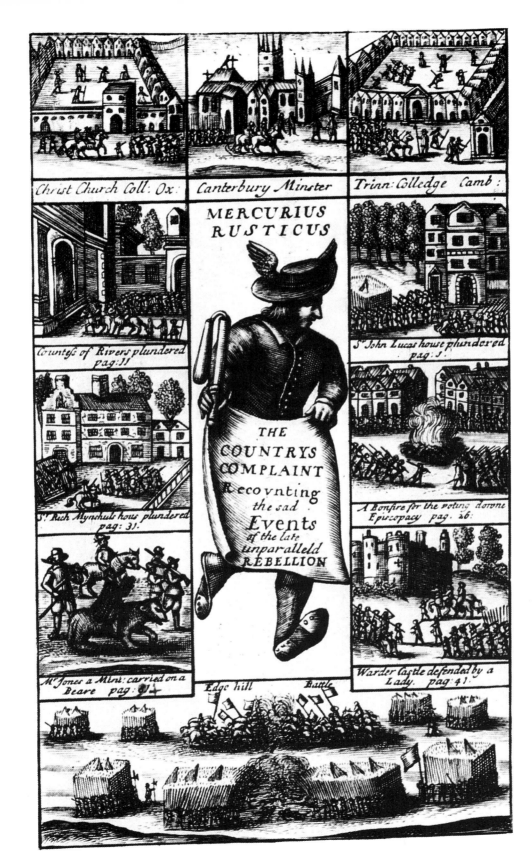

Christ Church Coll: Ox: Canterbury Minster   Trinn: Colledge Camb:

MERCURIUS
RUSTICUS

Countess of Rivers plundered
pag:11

S.t John Lucas house plundered
pag:5

S.r Rich Minshuls hous plundered
pag:31

A Bonfire for the voting dovne
Episcopacy pag: 26:

THE
COUNTRYS
COMPLAINT
Recounting
the sad
Events
of the late
unparalleld
REBELLION

M.r Jones a Mini: carried on a
Beare pag:41

Warder Castle defended by a
Lady. pag: 43.

Edge hill   Battle

inhabiting the out parts of the town sallied out unto the house of one Penruddock, a papist, and being basely affronted by him and his dog, entered his house, and pillaged him to the purpose. This day, also, the soldiers got into the church, defaced the ancient and sacred glassed picture and burned the holy rails. Wednesday: Mr Love gave us a famous sermon this day; also, the soldiers brought the holy rails from Chiswick and burned them in our town. At Chiswick they also intended to pillage the Lord of Portland's house, and also Dr Duck's, but by our commanders they were prevented. This day our soldiers generally manifested their dislike of our Lieutenant-Colonel, who is a Godamme blade, and doubtless hatch in hell, and we all desire that either the Parliament would depose him or God convert him, or the Devil fetch him away quick. This day, towards even, our regiment marched to Uxbridge, but I was left behind, to bring up thirty men with ammunition the next morning. Thursday I marched toward Uxbridge; and at Hillingdon, one mile from Uxbridge, the rails being gone, we got the surplice, to make us handercherchers, and one of our soldiers wore it to Uxbridge. This day the rails of Uxbridge, formerly removed, was, with the service book, burned. This even Mr Harding gave us a worthy sermon. Friday, I, with three other commanders, were sent with one hundred musketeers to bring the ammunition to Amersham in Buckinghamshire, which is the sweetest country that ever I saw, and as is country so also is the people. . . . Every day our soldiers by stealth do visit papists' houses, and constrain from them both meat and money. They give them whole great loaves and cheeses, which they triumphantly carry away upon the points of their swords. I humbly entreat you, as you desire the success of our just and honourable cause, that you would endeavour to root out our Lieutenant Colonel; for, if we march further under his command, we fear, upon sufficient grounds, we are all but dead men. . . .

Before leaving Buckinghamshire the Roundheads poached some venison from the deer park at Hillesden House, the home of Sir Edmund Verney's Royalist brother-in-law Sir Alexander Denton. In a letter from Coventry on 26 August, in which he thanks his master for helping to get the unpopular Lieutenant-Colonel Brideman cashiered, Wharton mentions the incident: 'I departed hence and gathered a complete file of my own men about the country, and marched to Sir Alexander Denton's park, who is a malignant fellow, and killed a fat buck, fastened his head upon my halbert, and commanded two of my pickets to bring the body after me to Buckingham, with a guard of musketeers coming thither. With part of it I feasted my captain, Captain Parker, Captain Beacon, and Colonel Hampden's son, and with the rest several lieutenants, ensigns and serjeants, and had much thanks for my pains.'

From Northampton on 3 September Wharton wrote with more news. A postman called Thomas Weedon collected letters for the army at the Saracen's Head in Carter Lane and delivered them once a week, carrying back the replies to London in his saddle-bags. At Coventry 'we officers wet our halberds with a

Opposite The title page of another account of the Civil War, decorated with scenes of plunder, violence and destruction. The clash of arms at Edgehill, the first major battle, is vividly depicted.

barrel of strong beer called "old Hum" which we gave to our soldiers'. A whore who followed the army from London was taken by the soldiers and first led about the city, then set in the pillory, after in the cage, then ducked in a river and at last banished from the vicinity. He tells of more pillagings as the army marched on, often with nothing but 'stinking water' to drink. In one village all the inhabitants who had already been raided by the Cavaliers ran away from them and hid in ditches and cornfields. At Northampton the redcoats demanded a monthly bonus of five shillings which they said had been promised to them. One of them purloined three pounds from Wharton's coat. Such crimes were doubtless the work of 'the ruder sort of soldiers, whose society, blessed be God, I hate and avoid'. Essex had yet to join the army and it lacked firm martial laws. Quarrels soon broke out: 'I was informed by a countryman of a base priest, six miles distant, which had set out horse for the Commission of Array and had arms in his house, and I immediately got twenty musketeers and marched out to search the house. The countryman I clothed with a soldier's red coat, gave him arms, and made him my guide. But having marched two miles, certain gentlemen of the country informed me that Justice Edmons, a man of good conversation, but since I hear of the Array, was plundered by the base blue coats of Colonel Cholmley's regiment, and bereaved of his very beads, whereupon I immediately divided my men into three squadrons, surrounded them, and forced them to bring their pillage upon their own backs unto the house again. For which service I was welcomed with the best varieties in the house, and had given me a scarlet coat lined with plush, and several excellent books in folio of my own choosing; but returning, a troop of horse belonging unto Colonel Fiennes met me, pillaged me of all, and robbed me of my very sword, for which cause I told them I would either have my sword or die in the field, commanded my men to charge with bullet, and by divisions to fire upon them, which made them with shame return me my sword, and it being towards night I returned to Northampton, threatening revenge upon the base troopers. This night and the day following our company by lot watched the south gate, where I searched every horseman of that troop to the skin, took from them a fat buck, a venison pasty ready baked, but lost my own goods. . . .'

The soldiers, however, did not want spirit. Upon news that Prince Rupert, 'that diabolical Cavalier', had summoned Leicester they 'were even mad to be at them'. Earlier he had described the enthusiastic but unblooded soldiers as 'cannibals in arms, ready to encounter the enemy, crying out for a dish of Cavaliers to supper'. On Sundays they heard two sermons, morning and afternoon, from Puritan divines such as Obadiah Sedgwick who served as chaplain: 'These with their sermons have already subdued and satisfied more malignant spirits amongst us than a thousand armed men could have done, so that we have great hope of a blessed union. Monday morning I received your letter, dated September the 8th, with my mistress's scarf and Mr Molloyne's hatband, both which came very seasonably, for I had gathered a little money together, and had this day made me a soldier's suit for winter, edged with gold and silver lace. These gifts I am unworthy of. I have nothing to tender you for them but humble and hearty thanks. I will wear them for your sakes, and I hope I shall never stain them but in the blood of a Cavalier. Your letter, being a pithy, solid, brief and real relation, I presented to my captain and all the captains of our regiment together at dinner with Mr Obadiah Sedgwick, who rejoiced at the news and gave me much thanks. My captain greets you with his best respects.'

The army resumed its march and entered Warwickshire where they heard news that all the Royalists were gathering at Worcester. The regiment of Denzil Holles did not fare well in the sharing out of quarters, resting for several days at Burford: 'It is very poor, for many of our soldiers can get neither beds, bread, nor water, which makes them grow very strong, for backbiters have been seen to march upon some of them six on breast and eight deep at their open order, and I fear I shall be in the same condition e'er long, for we can get no carriage for officers, so that my trunk is more slighted than any other, which is occasioned, as I conceive, partly by the false informations of Lieutenant-Colonel Brideman and our late Serjeant-Major-General Ballard, profane wretches; but chiefly for want of our Colonel, who should be one of the Council of War, at which Council we have none to plead for us or remove false aspersions cast upon us, in so much that I have heard some of our captains repent their coming forth, and all for want of a Colonel. Thursday morning we marched in the front four miles towards Worcester, where we met one riding post from Worcester, informing us that our troops and the cavaliers were there in fight; but it was false, only to haste the captains from Warwick. Upon this report our whole regiment ran shouting for two miles together, and crying 'To Worcester! To Worcester!' and desired to march all night: but after we had marched two miles further we were commanded to stand until our forces passed by. . . .'

On Friday, 25 September the regiment marched four more miles towards Worcester in such foul weather 'that before I had marched one mile I was wet to the skin'. On the eve of entering Worcester the Parliamentarian horse encountered Prince Rupert and a thousand of his followers.

While reconnoitring between the Severn and the Teme, near the village of Powick, Rupert observed that a party of enemy horse, roughly a thousand strong, had crossed the Teme by Powick Bridge in their rear intending to cut off his retreat. Their officers led these troops down a lane under harassing musket fire from the Royalist dragoons and then attempted to fan them out into some sort of order. But Prince Rupert led his regiments at the gallop against them. The Roundhead horse, firing their carbines and pistols, stood their ground and received the charge. The troop of Captain Nathaniel Fiennes, son of Lord Saye and Sele, fought exceptionally well. But within minutes the Roundheads broke and crowded back over the bridge. The fugitives fled towards Worcester 'with drawn swords and many without hats', crying that the enemy was hotly pursuing

Mireveldt's fine portrait of Nathaniel Fiennes, whose troop of horse fought heroically on the Roundhead side at Powick Bridge before being beaten by Prince Rupert's cavalry. His armour, which includes a piece to protect his bridle arm, is painted black to prevent rust. Over the shoulder of his yellow buff coat he is wearing the orange sash of a Parliamentarian officer. Fiennes was later court-martialled for surrendering Bristol in 1643.

them. The Earl of Essex's inexperienced troop of Life Guards made ready to second them. Edmund Ludlow, who served in the troop, describes their discomfiture: 'But our captain Sir Philip Stapleton not being then with us, his Lieutenant one Bainham, an old soldier (a generation of men much cried up at that time) drawing us into a field, where he pretended we might more advantageously charge if there should be occasion, commanded us to wheel about; but our gentlemen not yet well understanding the difference between wheeling about, and shifting for themselves, their backs being now towards the enemy, whom they thought to be close in the rear, retired . . . in a very dishonourable manner, and the next morning rallied at the head-quarters, where we received but cold welcome from the general, as we well deserved.'

When Richard Baxter heard that a party of the Earl of Essex's army lay in a meadow near Powick, 'I had a great mind to go and see them, having never seen any part of an army'. He witnessed their rout after the skirmish. 'Though the enemy pursued them no further than the village, yet fled they in grievous terror to Parthore, and the Earl of Essex's Life Guard lying there took the alarm that the enemy was following them, and away they went. This sight quickly told me the vanity of armies, and how little confidence is to be placed in them.'

The news of this reverse at Powick Bridge spread like wildfire throughout the Parliamentarian army. It elated the Cavaliers. 'They boast wonderfully and swear most hellishly,' wrote Wharton, 'that the next time they meet us they will make but a mouthful of us. But I am persuaded the Lord has given them this small victory, that they may, in the day of battle, come on more presumptuously to their own destruction, in which battle, though I and many thousand more may be cut off, yet I am confident the Lord of Hosts will in the end triumph gloriously over these horses and all their cursed riders.' The flight of the Lord General's troop of gentlemen, added Wharton, 'is such a blot upon them as nothing but some desperate exploit will wipe off'. That night the redcoats dined off apples and pears gathered from the orchards, and sang psalms as they warmed themselves by good fires of hedgewood, fences and gates. Next morning, as the rain continued to pelt down, they marched ankle deep down muddy lanes until they entered the city gates at about four o'clock. Enraged by the reported barbarisms of the Cavaliers, Wharton and his men promised that the coming pitched battle would be 'very hot'.

At the end of September Wharton joined a commanded party, fifteen men from every company in the army, to march to secure Hereford. The weather was so bitterly cold, with rain and sleet driving into their faces, that a soldier died by the way. Wharton was more impressed by the city than by its inhabitants: '. . . which is well situated, and seated upon the river Wye, environed with a strong wall, better than any I have seen before; with five gates, and a strong stone bridge of six arches over the river, surpassing Worcester. In the city there is the stateliest market place in the kingdom, built with columns, after the manner of the Exchange. The Minster every way exceeding that of Worcester, but the city in circuit not so large. The inhabitants are totally ignorant in the ways of God, and much addicted to drunkenness and other vices, but principally unto swearing, so that the children that have scarce learned to speak do universally swear stoutly. Many here speak Welsh.

'This day, our companies exercising in the fields at Worcester, one of the Lord General's soldiers shot at random, and, with a brace of bullets, shot one of his fellow soldiers through the head, who immediately died. Sabbath day, about the time of morning prayer, we went to the Minster, when the pipes played and the puppets sang so sweetly, that some of our soldiers could not forbear dancing in the holy quire; whereat the Baalists were sore displeased. The anthem ended, they fell to prayer, and prayed devoutly for the King, the bishops, etc.; and one of our soldiers, with a loud voice, said, "What! never a bit for the Parliament?" which offended them much more. Not satisfied with this human service, we went to divine; and, passing by, found shops open, and men at work, to whom we gave some plain exhortations; and went to hear Mr Sedgwick, who gave us two famous sermons, which much affected the poor inhabitants, who, wondering, said they never heard the like before; and I believe them.'

By mid-October both armies began their marches towards London. Essex had less distance to cover, but his train of heavy artillery slowed him down and the King overtook him without either of them being aware of it. Late in the evening of Saturday, 22 October, when the Royalist army quartered in villages north of Banbury, news came that the bulk of the Parliamentarian army had stopped for the night at Kineton a few miles behind. The King resolved to give battle. Before sunrise the first regiments of Prince Rupert's horse moved back and occupied Edgehill, the heights that looked down on Kineton, where they were joined by the rest of the army. The Earl of Essex heard the news on his way to church and at once drew out his own army to face the enemy. As the Lord General had detached a brigade to protect the train, still some miles away, his forces amounted to about 14,000 men, about the same numbers as the King could command. Sir Richard Bulstrode, who served at Edgehill in the Earl of Northampton's troop in the Prince of Wales' regiment of horse, gives this account of the ensuing battle.

Our whole army was drawn up in a body, the horse three deep in each wing, and the foot in the centre six deep. The Prince of Wales' regiment was on the right wing, which was commanded by Prince Rupert, and Colonel Washington was with his dragoons upon our right. In the centre was the infantry, commanded in chief by General Ruthven, and under him, by Sir Jacob Astley. The Earl of Lindsey marched on foot, in the head of the regiment of the royal foot guards, with his son, the Lord Willoughby, and Sir Edmund Verney carried the Royal Standard. The left wing of our horse was commanded by Commissary-General Wilmot, with Lieutenant-Colonel Edward Fielding and some other principal officers; and Lieutenant-Colonel George Lisle, with Lieutenant-Colonel John Ennis were in the left wing, with a regiment of dragoons, to defend the briars on that side, and we had a body of reserve, of six hundred horse, commanded by the Earl of Carnarvon. When our army was drawn up at the foot of the hill and ready to march, all the generals went to the King (who intended to march with the army) and desired he would retire to a rising ground, some distance from thence, on the right, with the Prince of Wales and the Duke of York (having his guard of Pensioners on horseback with him) from whence he might see the issue of the battle and be out of danger, and that otherwise the army would not advance towards the enemy. To which the King (very unwillingly) was at last persuaded.

Just before we began our march, Prince Rupert passed from one wing to the other, giving positive orders to the horse, to march as close as was possible, keeping their ranks with sword in hand, to receive the enemy's shot, without firing either carbine or pistol, till we broke in amongst the enemy, and then to make use of our firearms as need should require, which order was punctually observed.

The enemy stayed to receive us in the same posture as was formerly declared; and when we came within cannon shot of the enemy, they discharged at us three pieces of cannon from their left wing, commanded by Sir James Ramsey; which cannon mounted

Opposite Van Dyck's portrait of Prince Rupert beautifully conveys his dashing good looks, and perhaps something of that impetuous over-confidence which was his fatal flaw as a commander.

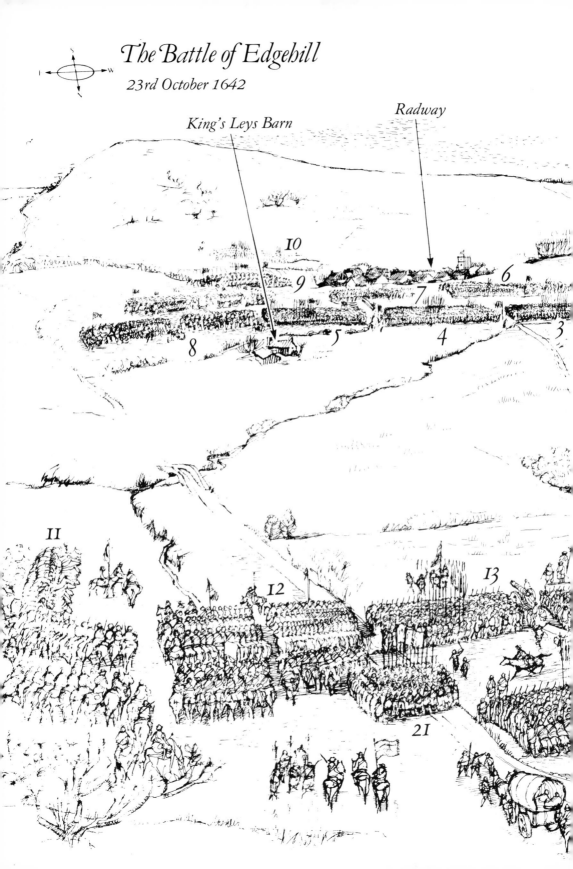

The Battle of Edgehill
23rd October 1642

King's Leys Barn

Radway

THE ROYALIST ARMY **1** Dragoons; **2** the horse regiments of Lord Wilmot, Lord Grandison, Earl of Carnarvon, Lord Digby and Sir Thomas Aston; **3** Henry Wentworth's Regiment; **4** Richard Fielding's Regiment; **5** Charles Gerard's Regiment; **6** Sir Nicholas Byron's Regiment; **7** John Belasyse's Regiment; **8** the regiments of Prince Rupert, the Prince of Wales and Sir John Byron, and the King's Lifeguard; **9** Gentlemen Pensioners; **10** William Legge's Firelocks.

THE PARLIAMENTARIAN ARMY **11** Dragoons; **12** Sir James Ramsey's Wing; **13** Charles Essex's Brigade; **14** Sir John Meldrum's Brigade; **15** Lord Fielding's Regiment; **16** Dragoons and musketeers; **17** Sir William Fairfax's Regiment; **18** Sir Philip Stapleton's Regiment; **19** Sir William Balfour's Regiment; **20** Thomas Ballard's Brigade; **21** Denzil Holles's Regiment.

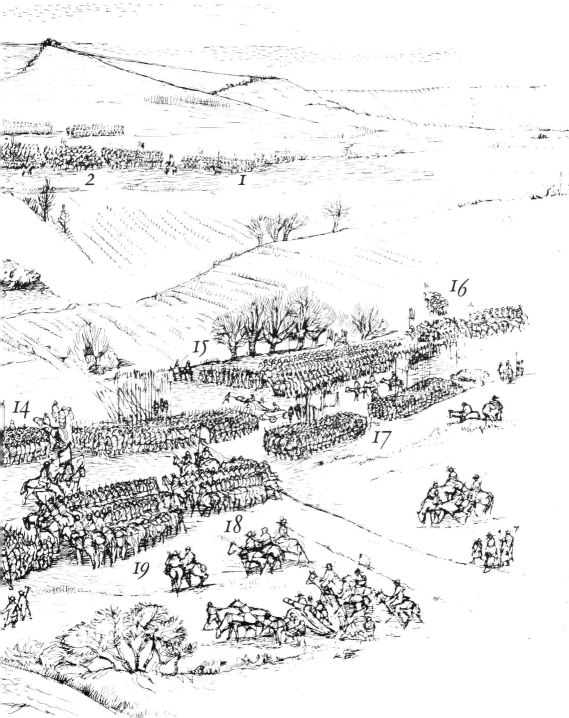

over our troops, without doing any hurt, except that their second shot killed a quarter-master in the rear of the Duke of York's troop. We soon after engaged each other, and our dragoons on our right beat the enemy from the briars, and Prince Rupert led on our right wing so furiously, that, after a small resistance, we forced their left wing, and were masters of their cannon; and the Prince being extremely eager of this advantage (which he better knew how to take than to keep) was not content with their cannon, and keeping their ground, but eagerly pursued the enemy, who fled on the other side of Kineton towards Warwick. And we of the Prince of Wales' regiment (who were all scattered) pursued also, till we met with two foot regiments of Hampden and Holles, and with a regiment of horse coming from Warwick to their army, which made us hasten as fast back as we had pursued.

In this pursuit I was wounded in the head by a person who turned upon me and struck me with his pole-axe, and was seconding his blow, when Sir Thomas Byron being near, he shot him dead with his pistol, by which means I came back. In fine, by meeting these three regiments, we were obliged to return back to our army and then found our great error, in leaving our foot naked who were rudely handled by the enemy's horse and foot together in our absence, who fell principally upon the King's royal regiment of foot guards, who lost eleven of thirteen colours, the King's Standard-Bearer, Sir Edmund Verney, killed, and the Royal Standard taken, which was presently retaken by Captain John Smith, who was knighted for it that night by the King, under the Standard Royal and made a banneret with the usual ceremonies; and had afterwards a large medal of gold given him, with the King's picture on the one side, and the banner on the other, which he always wore to his dying day, in a large green watered ribband, cross his shoulders. . . .

Now, when we returned from following the enemy, the night came soon upon us, whereas, in all probability, we had gained the victory, and made an end of the war, if we had only kept our ground after we had beaten the enemy, and not left our foot naked to their horse and foot. And, to add to our misfortune, a careless soldier, in fetching powder (where a magazine was) clapt his hand carelessly into a barrel of powder, with his match lighted betwixt his fingers, whereby much powder was blown up and many kill'd. . . .

On Monday morning, being next after the battle, several parties were sent down to view the dead, the greatest part of the enemy having retired in the night to the town of Kineton, which was near them; and Mr Adrian Scroop having seen his father fall (being much wounded) desired the Duke of Lennox to speak to the King, that one of his coaches might go with him, to bring up his father's body; which being granted, he found his father stripped, with several very dangerous wounds, and that he was alive. Whereupon he lap'd him up in his cloak, and brought him in the coach, where he was presently dressed by the King's chirurgeons, and by their care and skill was cured, and lived many years after, tho' he had seventeen wounds, and had died upon the place, but that the coldness of the weather stopp'd the bleeding of his wounds, which saved also several other men's lives that were wounded.

Opposite A window in Farndon parish Church, Cheshire, showing the Royalist soldiers of Colonel Sir Francis Gamul's regiment of foot. The colonel's portrait is next to a musket bandolier and bullet mould. Captain William Barnston's partisan and gorget are in effect his badges of rank.

W. fec: 1644

King Charles I mounted on his charger upon the battlefield, drawn by Wenceslaus Hollar.
His imperturbable demeanour under fire was much admired. Behind him is the finest
contemporary representation of a Civil War army drawn up for battle that we have today, depicted
by the accurate pen of the celebrated Bohemian engraver who was taken prisoner at Basing
House in 1645.

Many men on both sides had cause to remember that cold October night after Edgehill fight. Many had not eaten since dawn; some had wounds; all had experienced the mental shocks of actual battle. They were drained by the day's emotions of fear, excitement and elation. Edmund Ludlow in Essex's Life-guard was so loaded with his cuirassier's arms and armour that he could not without great difficulty get back on his horse after being dismounted during the day. 'The night after the battle our army quartered upon the same ground that the enemy fought on the day before. No man nor horse got any meat that night, and I had touched none since the Saturday before, neither could I find my servant who had my cloak, so that having nothing to keep me warm but a suit of iron, I was obliged to walk about all night, which proved very cold by reason of a sharp frost.' The following evening the countrymen brought in provisions for the army, 'but when I got meat I could scarcely eat it,' wrote Ludlow, 'my jaws for want of use having almost lost their natural faculty'.

Dr William Harvey, the celebrated discoverer of the circulation of the blood, served at Edgehill in the King's army as a surgeon. John Aubrey met him at Oxford shortly afterwards, but not until much later did he relate to him the inaccurate story that he had charge of the royal children, Prince Charles and the Duke of York that day. 'He told me,' wrote Aubrey, 'that he withdrew with them under a hedge, and took out of his pocket a book and read. But he had not read long before a bullet of a great gun grazed the ground near him, which made him remove his station. He told me that Sir Adrian Scrope was dangerously wounded there, and left for dead amongst the dead men, stripped, which happened to be the saving of his life. It was cold, clear weather, and a frost that night, which staunched his bleeding, and about midnight, or some hours after his hurt, he awaked, and was fain to draw a dead body upon him for warmth's sake.'

After reviewing the situation the Royalist council resolved that the King should hasten to London and make an end of the war. Parliament for its part ordered Essex to make all possible haste with his army to London to protect the capital. But the King trifled away his time in taking Banbury and Broughton Castle, the home of Lord Saye, and other places of no consequence, and so marched very slowly towards London. Coming straight down Watling Street the Earl of Essex reached the capital first. The King approached it from the west, by way of Oxford, Reading, Windsor and Colnbrook. Despite some promising peace negotiations that had just opened a fierce clash occurred at Brentford when Prince Rupert fell upon two Parliament regiments of foot under cover of a very thick mist.

The redcoats of Denzil Holles and the purplecoats of Lord Brooke, 'all butchers and dyers' as one Cavalier sneered, fought stoutly as they were driven slowly out of the village. Then Colonel John Hampden arrived at the head of his greencoats to stand in the breach. Captain John Stiles, one of the many homespun poets in arms, praised his Colonel in verse:

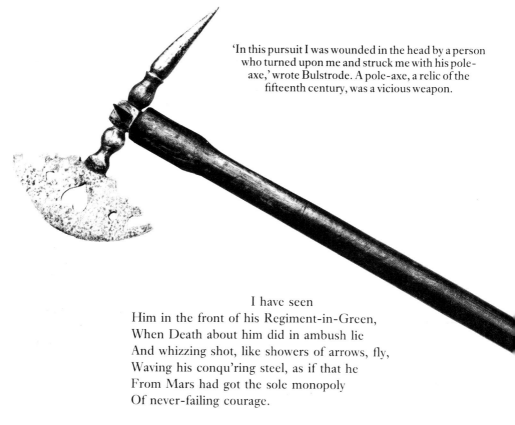

'In this pursuit I was wounded in the head by a person who turned upon me and struck me with his pole-axe,' wrote Bulstrode. A pole-axe, a relic of the fifteenth century, was a vicious weapon.

I have seen
Him in the front of his Regiment-in-Green,
When Death about him did in ambush lie
And whizzing shot, like showers of arrows, fly,
Waving his conqu'ring steel, as if that he
From Mars had got the sole monopoly
Of never-failing courage.

Essex heard the noise of battle in the House of Lords as his fellow peers were debating whether or not to order a cessation of hostilities. Having galloped across Hyde Park he sent more regiments to support Hampden and so checked the Royalists. Why Prince Rupert had launched this surprise attack remains something of a mystery. The most charitable interpretation is that he believed Essex's army was preparing to fall upon him.

Next day the Royalist commanders marched their men towards London. A mile beyond Brentford they caught sight of the full armed might of both Parliament and the City of London, a solid wall of some 24,000 soldiers who had been standing in battle order on Turnham Green. Resplendent in their burnished armour, with drums beating and colours flying, the Londoners – many of them apprentices – had marched about nine miles that day, 'very cheerfully' thanks to Sergeant-Major-General Philip Skipton's inspiring leadership. For he went all the way along with the soldiers talking to them, sometimes to one company and sometimes to another; and the soldiers seemed to be more taken with his informal words than a set formal oration. 'Come on, my boys, my brave boys!' he said, 'let us pray heartily and fight heartily. I will run the same hazards with you. Remember the cause is for God and for the defence of yourselves, your wives and children. Come, my honest brave boys, pray heartily and fight heartily, and God will bless us.'

The Earl of Holland, who was the field marshal that day, drew up the twenty-four thousand men, wisely interleaving City regiments with those of the army. Horse stood on both wings, and the regiments of Sir Philip Stapleton and Arthur Goodwin took their station forward in the van. The guns waited in a lane near Hammersmith, with a strongly-guarded wagon park in a field nearby. As the Lord General rode from regiment to regiment the soldiers threw up their caps and shouted, 'Hey for old Robin!'

As the day passed the armies stood on their guard and looked at each other. Every time the Royalists stirred, a crowd of spectators who had ridden out from the City were seen to gallop off in alarm, and then return somewhat sheepishly. Cartloads of provisions, wine and ale, were sent out of London to the army, but towards late afternoon some of the citizen-soldiers began to slip off home-wards. Leaving a body of horse to face the enemy between the two Brentfords, the King drew back his main army to Kingston-on-Thames and he rested for a night at Hampton Court. Next day he gave orders for all his forces to pull back to Reading, where he left a garrison of over two thousand foot and a regiment of horse under the command of Sir Arthur Aston. With the rest of the army he marched to Oxford, which became the Royalist capital for the rest of the war.

4
The Verneys of Claydon House

The news of Sir Edmund Verney's death at Edgehill came as a terrible blow to his ten children, relatives and friends. Sir Edward Sydenham, who had fought on the King's side and succeeded Sir Edmund as Knight-Marshal, sent a letter by hand to Ralph a few days after the battle:

For all our great victory I have had the greatest loss by the death of your noble father that ever any friend did . . . he himself killed two with his own hands, whereof one of them had killed poor Jason [Sir Edmund's servant], and broke the point of his standard at push of pike before he fell, which was the last account I could receive of any of our own side of him. . . . The battle was bloody on your side, for your horse ran away at the first charge and our men had the execution of them for three miles. It began at three o'clock and ended at six. The King is a man of the least fear and the greatest resolution and mercy that I ever saw, and had he not been in the field we might have suffered. . . .

God in mercy send us peace, and although your loss is as great as a son can lose in a father, yet God's children must bear with patience what affliction soever he shall please to lay upon them. You have a great trial. God in mercy give you grace to make a sanctified use of this great burden with patience. My humble service to your sad wife. God in his infinite mercy comfort you both which shall be the prayers of your friend and servant . . .

From his London house in Covent Garden Ralph wrote to tell Eleanor, Lady Sussex, about 'this saddest and deepest affliction that ever befell any poor distressed man'. He had sent three messengers to both armies to confirm his father's death, for the corpse had not been identified among the hundreds of naked dead buried after the battle. 'If he is gone, I have no friend in this world but yourself.' His letter crossed with one written by Lady Sussex from Chelsea that same day with 'the saddest heart and deepest wounded soul that ever creature had'. She asked to see him before leaving for Gorhambury, near St Albans, Lord Bacon's former country house which she and her husband rented, 'for you are all the joy I have left me now. I am in so miserable condition that I cannot express my thoughts. My eyes are so full that I cannot say no more, but that I am your most sorrowful and most afflicted friend, Eleanor Sussex'.

As Eleanor came herself from a family divided by the sword – the Wortleys of Yorkshire – she could understand the peculiar agony of bereavement mixed with guilt which Ralph experienced. She had married first Sir Henry Lee of Ditchley in Oxfordshire. Ditchley was a timbered manor-house with a pretty bowling green not twenty-five miles from Claydon. The Lees and Verneys were hereditary friends, acting as trustees, guardians, godfathers, executors and advisers to each other. As the Lees were short-lived, this one family created a great deal of business for Sir Edmund and Sir Ralph. After Sir Henry's death his widow married the sixth Earl of Sussex, a somewhat infirm old man, and after them the Earls of Warwick and Manchester, becoming in Ralph's words 'the old man's wife'. Although 'the sad retired life' she led with Sussex at Gorhambury during the war years was not much to her taste she did her duty to 'my old Lord' and had a genuine affection for him.

Eleanor's first remarriage did not lessen the flow of her warm, nearly illiterate letters to Sir Ralph and his father. She trusted them to make arrangements concerning her will, to order carpets and curtains, and even clothes and gowns for her, to find a husband for her daughter 'Nan', and to send her the political news of the day. She loved Ralph dearly and stood godmother to his eldest child, Edmund. She had sung Ralph's praises to Sir Edmund, and told Ralph so when she wrote on the birth of his daughter Margaret.

None was more gladder than myself to hear of your wife's safe delivery and that you have so brave a sweet baby, which I pray God may live long to be a comfort to you both. My prayers for my sweet godson is that he may make as discrete and good a man as his father, and then I am sure he will give joy enough to his friends. I must ever challenge an interest in him, for believe me I love and wish as much good to you and yours as any can do. . . . I was telling your father how happy he was in you and he said he was so indeed, for no man had a better child, and many more good words he said about you, which pleased me very much to know you was upon so dear and kind terms.

In June 1639 her only son, Sir Henry Lee, had joined the King's army at York on the eve of the Scots war. Mother and son were not on good terms: 'he promised to come this way as he went north, he has failed me,' she laments. Sick with smallpox, he returned to the Lee's house at Chelsea where his mother helped to nurse him until he died. Eleanor's brother, Sir Francis Wortley, had organised the first loyal demonstration by the Yorkshire Royalists. 'I am sorry to hear my brother Wortley has carried himself so foolishly,' she informed Ralph. 'An unfortunate man he is every way – your Parliament sure will lay heavy punishment upon him. I cannot but have some sense of him as he is my brother, but I may speak it to you, he had never much of my heart for I thought him ever full of vanity, though believe me he has many good parts had he wisdom to have managed them.'

Eleanor was not without a touch of that family vanity herself. In 1639 Sir Edmund asked her to sit for a portrait by Vandyke. She took much pains over her dress and appearance, applying myrrh water to her face: 'I have long used it and find it very safe,' she informed Ralph's wife. ''Tis good for the head and to make one look young. I only wet a fine cloth and wipe my face over at night with it.' On her behalf Ralph asked Vandyke to make some alterations to the finished

portrait. 'I am glad you have prevailed with Sir Vandyke to make my picture leaner, for truly it was too fat. If he made it fairer it will be for my credit. I see you will make him trim it for my advantage every way.' But the finished painting, delivered at Gorhambury, did not please her overmuch. 'Sweet Mr Verney, the picture came very well. Many hearty thanks to you for it. The frame is a little hurt, the gilt being rubbed off. The picture is very ill-favoured, makes me quite out of love with myself. The face is so big and so fat that it pleases me not at all. It looks like one of the winds puffing, but truly I think it is like the original. If ever I come to London before Sir Vandyke goes, I will get him to mend my picture, for though I be ill-favoured I think that makes me worse than I am.'

Later, when she sought to buy the portrait from him for her next husband, Ralph would not part with it. For she had heard his lonely *cri de coeur*. At twenty-nine he found himself head of a large and divided family. His three brothers were all close to him in age and they were not accustomed to defer to him. His five unmarried sisters living at Claydon came under his protection and clamoured for his attention. In addition, he had to provide for his wife Mary and three children of his own, not to mention obligations inherited from his father for a host of friends, neighbours, kinsfolk and servants.

To these cares must be added the burden of family dissension over politics. All of his three brothers followed their father's lead and fought for the King. Tom, aged twenty-seven, was the black sheep of the family. At his father's expense he had tried to become a settler in Virginia, but that did not suit. Then he served as a volunteer on a warship and as a restless soldier in France and Sweden, leaving a trail of debts, duels and quarrels in his wake. Back in England once more, Tom promised yet again to make a new start in exchange for just one more loan. Soon he was asking his brother Edmund to second him in a duel: 'If you are willing, I pray send me by the porter my russet shoes and my greyest pair of worsted stockings with garters and ribbons to them, and laced band and cuffs if they need be done; if not, a plain band to put on tomorrow.'

Sent to Claydon House by Sir Edmund to keep him out of trouble, Tom found himself miserable 'at living like a hermit or country fellow', and in order to escape 'would go anywhere, to the West Indies or some unknown place in the world'. He bombarded his father and elder brother with his resolutions, and requests for money and clothes on the strength of them. Presently he broke out again with a characteristic threat. 'Rather than lead this hellish life, I will take a rope and make an end of myself, and then neither father, mother, brother, nor sister, nor any friends else shall take any more care of me.' Financed by his father, he set off to acquire a plantation in Barbados, but he was home again in the summer of 1642 and offered his services in the King's army.

Tom, a self-centred and embittered young man, made no mention of his young sisters or Ralph's children who had been left in the nursery in the competent care of Nan Fudd, the nurse at Claydon. But Edmund, aged twenty-six, had inherited his father's courtly grace – a contemporary had

Opposite Van Dyck's portrait of Sir Edmund Verney, the King's standard-bearer, 'a ready and complete man for the pleasure of the ladies', who met a noble death at Edgehill.

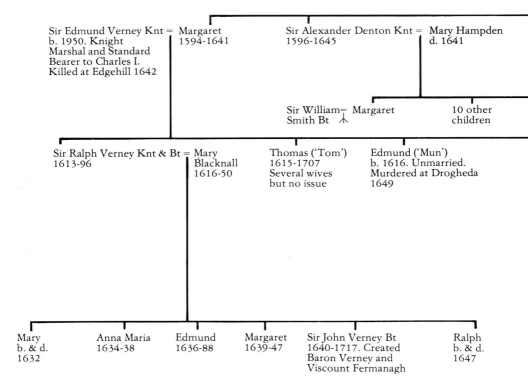

Sir Edmund Verney Knt = Margaret
b. 1950. Knight | 1594-1641
Marshal and Standard
Bearer to Charles I.
Killed at Edgehill 1642

Sir Alexander Denton Knt = Mary Hampden
1596-1645 | d. 1641

Sir William = Margaret   10 other
Smith Bt   children

Sir Ralph Verney Knt & Bt = Mary   Thomas ('Tom')   Edmund ('Mun')
1613-96   Blacknall   1615-1707   b. 1616. Unmarried.
                            1616-50   Several wives   Murdered at Drogheda
                                   but no issue   1649

Mary   Anna Maria   Edmund   Margaret   Sir John Verney Bt   Ralph
b. & d.   1634-38   1636-88   1639-47   1640-1717. Created   b. & d.
1632   Baron Verney and   1647
                                               Viscount Fermanagh

described Sir Edmund as a 'ready and complete man for the pleasure of the ladies'. After service in the Scots war under the approving eye of his father, Edmund spent some time at Claydon with his sisters. The girls mercilessly teased 'Mun', as he playfully complained to Ralph: 'I never yet saw such double diligence used in the tormenting a poor man. . . . I cannot live long if these thunderclaps continue.' He hoped that Cary would soon recover from an illness, 'for truly I am much troubled to see her as she is; she desires to have me much with her'. Pen calls him 'my dearest companion the cashiered Captain'. His cousin Doll Leeke was also very fond of him and writes to Lady Verney: 'I find my cousin Mun that he is gone; he writes me word that he has left with a ring of his hair. Beshrew him for his conceit, it seems so like a legacy that it has put a sadness into me; it is a fault to be superstitious, and therefore if I can I will forget it.' Mun joined an English regiment in the Dutch service, but returned to England in 1641 and enlisted that autumn in the army sent to Ireland. A Royalist like his father, the spirited and gallant young man felt a hot indignation against Ralph for siding against them.

Henry was not yet twenty-five when his father fell at Edgehill. Sir Edmund intended him for a military career and sent him to the Palatinate to learn his

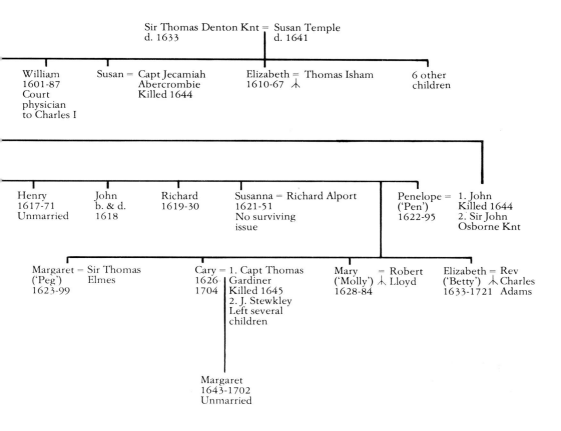

Sir Thomas Denton Knt = Susan Temple
d. 1633   d. 1641

William 1601-87 Court physician to Charles I

Susan = Capt Jecamiah Abercrombie Killed 1644

Elizabeth = Thomas Isham 1610-67

6 other children

Henry 1617-71 Unmarried

John b. & d. 1618

Richard 1619-30

Susanna = Richard Alport 1621-51 No surviving issue

Penelope ('Pen') 1622-95 = 1. John Killed 1644 2. Sir John Osborne Knt

Margaret ('Peg') 1623-99 = Sir Thomas Elmes

Cary 1626-1704 = 1. Capt Thomas Gardiner Killed 1645 2. J. Stewkley Left several children

Mary ('Molly') 1628-84 = Robert Lloyd

Elizabeth ('Betty') 1633-1721 = Rev Charles Adams

Margaret 1643-1702 Unmarried

trade. There he developed a passion for horse-racing. 'I do not at all wonder,' wrote Edmund at this time, 'at brother Henry liking a soldier's life, since he can follow that and horse matches too.' At Claydon he made at least one especial friend in that garrison of children. When Ralph's daughter Anna Maria died, not quite four years old, he wrote to Henry in the Netherlands: 'You shall herewithal receive a ring filled with my dear girl's hair; she was fond of you and you loved her, therefore I now send you this to keep for her sake.' In February 1643 Henry returned home with Queen Henrietta Maria, and through the good offices of Sir Edward Sydenham received a commission as major of horse in Sir Ralph Dutton's regiment. 'The King's hand I have kissed. He looked earnestly upon me, but spoke not to me. In time, if the war goes on, I hope to be known to him. . . .' Surely a cold reception for Charles to give to the son of his faithful servant, slain in his service not four months before.

Sir Edmund Verney had married his 'she darling' Cary to the son of a fiery old Royalist called Sir Thomas Gardiner, the Solicitor-General. Her parents-in-law made Cary welcome in their house at Cuddesdon, near Oxford. Shortly after his marriage Captain Gardiner had joined the King's army in the Scots war and she told Ralph's wife she had not seen him for four months: 'He is two hundred miles distance from me. Think what a trouble it is to me which has so good a husband. I do pray for a happy meeting of us all.' Young Thomas Gardiner sided with the King, but he wrote in a gallant vein to his brother-in-law's wife. He thanked her for her letter 'wherein every line was pleasant to me save only one, and that was, you say, you never had more cause to be sad than now. Think you, Madam, that God has outlawed you and put you out of his protection? I am confident your goodness will not let you think so. Or do you suppose there is an army of wild beasts, such as lions or tigers, come to invade the land? For if you are to deal with men endued with rational souls, your virtues will be a sufficient sanctuary from any violence.

'Besides, I believe that neither King nor Parliament have any quarrel against women, who never did either hurt save only with their tongues. And, which is most of all, if in earnest we have any wars in the Kingdom, which I hope God will prevent, yet I dare proclaim you safe and immovable in despite of fortune. . . . You have a father to defend you on the one side and a husband that will do the like on the other. These things considered, your sadness is to be envied, not to be pitied, and you should rather bless God that has so well provided for your safety in these troublesome times, than be sad and drooping.

'For my own part, come what may, I shall make sorrow a stranger to me as often as I call to mind that I hold some part in your account and love. This honour is an antidote unto me against any affliction, and I shall never esteem myself miserable so long as you conceive a good opinion of me.'

The shifting fortunes of war certainly made friends on the other side an asset. In 1643 Captain Thomas Gardiner was taken prisoner near Windsor and imprisoned in the Castle. Sir Ralph appealed successfully to the Parliamentarian commander for his release and Thomas wrote warm letters of thanks to him and Lady Verney: 'I hope God that has preserved me hitherto will yet give me life that I may face to face express to you. . . .' Alas, his prayer was not answered. In July 1645 the young soldier lost his life in a skirmish some four or five miles from Aylesbury. He left 'a sad, disconsolate widow great with child'. Ralph wrote gently to her: 'Sweetheart, I hear of your misfortune and suffer with you. I feel in a higher degree than either I can or will express. But at God's decree we must not repine. The best go first, and 'tis a mercy to be taken away from the evil to come. . . .'

In October Cary's baby was born. It was a girl, much 'to all our griefs' wrote her brother Henry, for a boy would have kept her in favour with the Gardiners. The sickly baby, the comfort and grief of its mother, had weak eyes and became almost blind in later years. The kindness of the Gardiners evaporated: they grudged her even a room and board at Cuddesdon, and then raised questions about her settlement. The forlorn young widow of eighteen and her baby went home to Claydon.

Tom also appealed to Ralph for help when he was taken prisoner at the surrender of Chichester to Sir William Waller on 5 January 1643, and like the

Sir Ralph Verney, portrayed here as he was at the time of the Civil War. He bore a heavy responsibility as head of a large and divided family after his father's death, but despite his tribulations he lived to be 83.

other officers was 'plundered of all except the clothes we wore'. Five days later he wrote from the Fleet to Ralph, who had already visited him twice with a change of clothes and forty shillings. Tom demanded instant release and 'that £10 may be paid to Mr Page who does detain my clothes'. When no pardon or money arrived, Tom became angrier, reproaching his brother and threatening him: 'Brother, it will be a wonder to see me in print. Yet I fear what with my unjust imprisonment and your uncharitable affections will move me to it, which if it does I shall then make my loyal and true-hearted affections towards my King and country known to God and to all good Christians.' He asked to be fitted out for the Barbados once more. Lady Sussex warned Ralph, who was inclined to be over-conscientious, not to take the matter too much to heart: 'I am truly sorry to hear your naughty brother gives so much trouble with you. . . . I wish he were in the forefront of the next skirmish. For God's sake be more

Tom Verney, the black sheep of the Verney family. This portrait aptly conveys his difficult and truculent nature.

wise than to afflict yourself for anything of unkindness that can come from him. He gave much trouble to his good father and so he will do to you I fear . . . you have done nothing of ill, but good to them all.'

Not long after Ralph secured Tom's release from the Fleet prison Henry, now a Colonel, wrote to him that he had been captured and taken to Portsmouth. According to Henry's version of the story, 'he was so courteous to Lady Trencher in Dorsetshire, although his quarters were four or five miles off, he with only ten or twelve soldiers lay at her house to guard it'. At midnight they were surprised by a strong party of Roundheads. But an anonymous correspondent, probably Henry's manservant, informed William Roades, the steward at Claydon, of the likely truth. Henry had a difference with his major. An innkeeper, a friend of the major, was there and 'perhaps gave ill language to Henry, who shot him with a pistol, when he died. Fearing he should be cashiered he was advised by a friend to go out upon a parley, and suffer himself to be taken prisoner . . .'

Ralph wrote to the Governor of Portsmouth promising to supply his brother's wants as soon as possible. 'In the meantime I know you are so noble that he shall have all necessary accommodations fit for a gentleman.' To Henry, who wrote to beg for £20, he said: 'I know restraint is grievous to your nature, yet you were happy to fall into such good hands.' Of course Henry had no intention of being exchanged, nor did the Royalists show any signs of wanting him back. In November 1643 he was asking Ralph to intercede on his behalf with Parliament. After being released Henry settled in London to live 'like a wandering Jew', sponging off relatives and quarrelling with his brothers about money. As Mary Verney said, 'I find that he is all for his own ends'.

By this time Ralph had almost lost his influence with Parliament. As part of the treaty which brought Scotland into the war on Parliament's side, the Solemn League and Covenant, members of both Houses were required to promise that England would accept the Presbyterian system of church government. Ralph Verney, like his father, seems to have believed that a reformed episcopacy was the best order for the Church of England, and he refused to take the Covenant on grounds of conscience. That autumn he made plans to go into exile on the continent.

The safety of Claydon House preoccupied him much during the weeks while he and Mary packed a mass of trunks with their belongings and attended to his business. They decided to leave their little son John, aged three, at Claydon with five of Ralph's sisters – Pen, Peg, Molly, Cary and Betty, who was only ten years old. Sue, his eldest sister, was already boarded out with some Irish relatives who had taken a house nearby. The remaining garrison of children came under the care of William Roades and Frances Alcock, the housekeeper at Claydon, with Nan Fudd minding the nursery. Ralph had obtained a protection for Claydon House from the King and another from Parliament. In addition he could count upon occasional visits from uncles and aunts at Hillesden House, three miles away, where a large party of the Dentons and Ishams was living. High-spirited Peg and Pen were already quarrelling, having been asked to share a maid between them. 'I am to entreat a favour,' Pen wrote to Ralph, 'which is if you can let Nan Fudd have so much time as to comb my hair, for I do hear that Bess Coleman cannot do it, and . . . my head is so tender, and to smooth some of my upper lining, by reason that Bess Coleman cannot do them, but I hope in time to bring her to it. My sister Margaret will take my sister better to her, and her maid shall dress her and hear her book and teach her work.' Her aunt, Mrs Elizabeth Isham, who came over from Hillesden, told Peg plainly that 'now their father and mother was dead, they should be the helper one of the other . . . but all would not do'.

'Sweet Hillesden' had been a second home to the Verneys. After Sir Edmund first married Margaret Denton they had lived as boarders for four years at Hillesden, for Claydon was then leased out to another family. Eight of their twelve children (two died in infancy) were born there. Sir Alexander,

Margaret's brother, married Mary Hampden, a cousin of John Hampden, but the Dentons were strongly Royalist: his brother served King Charles as a physician and his son, John, rose to be a colonel in the King's army. His Royalist sisters, Mrs Elizabeth Isham and Susan Denton, were living with him.

Early in 1644 the owner of Hillesden found himself occupying a house in an important strategic position between the Royalists in Oxford and the Parliamentary garrison of Newport Pagnell (where the young John Bunyan trailed his pike as a common soldier). Sir Alexander decided to fortify his house for the King. A young officer called Colonel William Smith arrived from Oxford to take command of the place, building barns and stabling for the garrison's horses and digging a trench half a mile in circumference to enclose the house and the large parish church.

Forage parties from both sides swept the country in all directions. One day a body of troopers carried off a herd of cattle, with money and other valuables, belonging to a certain tenant of John Hampden's. Major Amnion, 'an uncommon frenzy man', claimed all the horses and a large share of the plunder for his troop, which led to a bitter quarrel among the soldiers. The owner ransomed his cattle and then promptly claimed compensation for his losses from the Parliamentarians at Aylesbury. Sir Samuel Luke, a Bedfordshire man who served as governor of Newport Pagnell, decided upon action. When a surprise attack on Hillesden by a small force of Roundheads failed, he mustered some two thousand men from as far afield as the Eastern Association for a siege. One half of them marched under the command of Colonel Oliver Cromwell to Steeple Claydon, where they encamped in the Verney's fields for the night of 2 March.

In the meantime the Royalist garrison of some two hundred men had been hard at work at Hillesden. While nearly a thousand country people laboured to strengthen the earth rampart and build a gun platform they improvised a wooden cannon from a hollow elm tree, stoutly hooped with iron, together with five smaller brass guns obtained from Oxford. The stone church next to the house served as their magazine. When the Roundhead force appeared they sent out a flag of truce. Finding, however, that they could obtain no terms but unconditional surrender, Colonel Smith made ready to defend Hillesden with his blood.

As the surrounding ditch was still only knee deep in places the Parliamentarian pikemen and musketeers easily stormed across it, driving the defenders back from the earthworks to the house and church. As the bullet holes in the old oak door still testify, the church was not taken without a fight. Soon nineteen

Left Sir Alexander Denton, the owner and defender of Hillesden. *Below* The door of the fine old church at Hillesden, still riddled with the holes of musket bullets fired during the storming.

men on both sides lay dead on the grass. Seeing that the struggle was hopeless Colonel Smith surrendered on promise of quarter. All the prisoners, including Sir Alexander Denton and Captain Thomas Verney 'that came only to see his sisters', were marched off to Padbury, three miles away, 'where they passed the night in great discomfort'. Next day they were escorted to Newport Pagnell.

The Roundheads pillaged the house, taking away all the cattle and emptying the cellars of beer and wine. The morning after the surrender a trooper cracked a piece of panelling in one of the rooms and discovered a large bag of money. His fellows searched the house high and low, finding some more treasure concealed under the lead roof. Later that day, upon news of a Royalist advance from Oxford, the Parliamentarian commanders ordered a withdrawal; the house was set on fire and burnt almost to the ground. Upon hearing the news, an undaunted Sir Alexander wrote to his steward:

Blagrove, I would have you send me by Tyler that bag of silver which Berney left with you long since and seal it up. Let him bring it to me. Bid him also take a view of the house that was burnt upon Tuesday, that I may have some certain information of what destruction is fallen upon me, and whether it be possible to rebuild those walls that are standing if the distraction of the times should settle. I thank God I am yet in health notwithstanding these many misfortunes are fallen upon me, and my comfort is I know myself not guilty of any fault.

From the Tower of London, where he was committed in March, Sir Alexander wrote to Sir Ralph estimating the damage done at £16,000, a staggering loss for a man already heavily in debt. His children and the Verney girls, who were in the house during the storming, had been 'not fairly used yet no immodest action'. The residue of his family now took refuge with the Verneys at Claydon. Pen Verney wrote to her brother: 'When it pleased God to lay that great affliction on my uncle, I was more concerned for him, but I did stand so great a loss in my own particular that it has been a half undoing to me. We were not shamefully used in any way by the soldiers, but they took everything and I was not left scarce the clothes on my back.'

Ralph, doubtless seized with guilt at his absence, wrote to his Royalist brother Edmund in Ireland on the same day: 'Suffer me to tell you how much I am afflicted for the ruin of sweet Hillesden and the distresses that happened to my aunt and sisters. God knows what is become of my unhappy brother that was there taken. . . . I know all that side hates him and I fear they will make him feel the weight of their displeasure, from which God in mercy keep you and poor Harry – my dear brother farewell.' Tom was a prisoner for many weeks, sending his customary begging letters to Ralph. This time his wife's family raised the ransom money and he was set free.

The tragedy at Hillesden was relieved by two romantic stories. Susan Denton had caught the eye of an active Parliamentarian commander named Captain Jecamiah Abercrombie. He had occupied Hillesden House for a few

One of the succession of begging letters Tom Verney wrote to Ralph after he was imprisoned in the Fleet prison in 1643. It contains the usual request for money and a veiled threat to do away with himself. In the event Tom lived to be 92.

Above Portraits by Van Dyck
of Colonel Arthur Goodwin
(*left*), John Hampden's friend,
and (*right*) his daughter Jane,
Lady Wharton. *Right* Ann
Fanshawe, who wrote a vivid
account of life in Oxford during
the Royalist occupation, in a
miniature by John Hoskins
painted in 1657.

72

weeks in January, before the Royalists tightened their grip on it. Less than a month later he was captured, but not before he had proposed to Susan and been accepted. Upon his release he resumed soldiering. 'My sister Susan's marriage is to be accomplished very suddenly if her captain be not killed,' wrote Mrs Isham; 'it 'tis him as did first plunder Hillesden.' At least he was not penniless, as Mrs Isham wrote again to Ralph: 'The captain's land is in Ireland; he is half Scots, half Irish. I think few of her friends like it, but if she has not him she will never have any, it is gone so far.' It was a brief wartime marriage, a stolen happiness. For next year Jecamiah was killed in a skirmish near Royalist-held Boarstall House in Buckinghamshire, and his body was brought back at Susan's insistence to be buried at Hillesden beside the Dentons.

Sir Alexander never regained his liberty. In August his son Colonel John lost his life gallantly leading an attack on Waller's forces at Abingdon. Meanwhile Colonel William Smith, who shared Sir Alexander's confinement in the Tower, courted his daughter Margaret and married her that month. Later Smith made his escape; Mrs Isham and Sue Verney were among those imprisoned for eight days on suspicion of aiding and abetting him. Mrs Isham reported to Ralph their safe release after paying a fine; 'much engaged we be to your brother Thomas and his wife, for they did more for us than all our friends beside' – about the only praise Tom Verney received from Ralph's correspondents.

Early in 1645 Sir Alexander, who was only forty-eight, died of a fever. Ralph wrote about 'the sad news of the death of my poor uncle, who within eight or nine months last past did me more courtesies and expressed more friendship and affection to me, than in all his life before. . . . I have such unkind (nay, I may say unnatural) letters from some so near to me, that truly, did I not see it under their own hands. . . . I could not have credited that such a total decay of friendship and common honesty could possibly have been amongst those that profess Christianity'.

Ralph's own bitter experience lay behind these words. For refusing the Covenant he lost his seat in the House of Commons, and Parliament sequestered his estates. Mary, his wife, after many weary journeys and much soliciting, had that order countermanded, but she died, aged thirty-four, after rejoining her husband on the continent. For his part, Edmund came to England and fought at the first battle of Newbury. He was knighted in 1644 and made Lieutenant-Governor of Chester, where he served during two sieges and won high praises from Lord Byron and other commanders. After the surrender of Chester he rejoined the Marquess of Ormond in Paris and together they returned to Ireland and took part in the last fierce struggle against Cromwell. Mun had made his peace with Ralph, which was timely. For he survived the horrors of Cromwell's assault upon Drogheda in 1649 and the massacre of its inhabitants, only to be enticed from Cromwell's presence and run through by a common soldier in the blood-lust of the hour. It was a tragic end for this noble son of Sir Edmund Verney.

5
Cavaliers in Oxford

In August 1642 war fever gripped the younger members of the University of Oxford. The acting Vice-Chancellor, hearing a rumour that Parliament's soldiers had marched into the county, ordered a show of men and weapons in the public schools. Anthony Wood, the antiquarian, was then a schoolboy of ten or eleven, at New College School, which was in the cloister of that college. As a day-boy he lived with his parents in a house opposite Merton College. Much later Wood wrote his autobiography, mostly in the third person, in which he succeeds in capturing a schoolboy's view of the Civil War in Oxford and later at Thame, twelve miles east of the city. Anthony recalled the first effects of these musters held for drill.

Mr Wood's father had then armour or furniture for one man, namely a helmet, a back and breastpiece, a pike and a musket, and other appurtenances: and the eldest of his men-servants (for he had then three at least) named Thomas Burnham did appear in those arms, when the scholars and privileged men trained; and when he could not train, as being taken up with business, the next servant did train: and much ado there was to keep Thomas Wood, the eldest son, then a student of Christ Church and a youth of about 18 years of age, from putting on the said armour and to train among the scholars. The said scholars and privileged men did sometimes train in New College quadrangle, in the eye of Dr Robert Pink, the deputy Vice-Chancellor, then Warden of the said college. And it being a novel matter, there was no holding of the school-boys in their school in the cloister from seeing and following them. And Mr Wood remembered well, that some of them were so besotted with the training and activity and gaiety therein of some young scholars, as being in a longing condition to be one of the train, that they could never be brought to their books again. It was a great disturbance to the youth of the city, and Mr Wood's father foresaw that if his sons were not removed from Oxford they would be spoil'd.

Thomas Wood later left his gown at the town's end, ran to Edgehill and did the King good service there. He returned on horse-back, well armed and equipped, and became a 'rude and boisterous soldier' in the Royalist army. Many other spirited young men were swept away from Oxford by the same enthusiasm, as Anthony Cooper recalled in verse:

> When first I went to Oxford, fully there intent
> To study learned science I went.

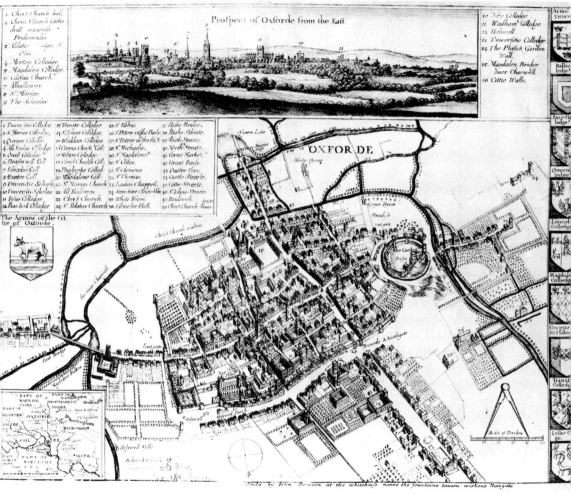

Wenceslaus Hollar's plan of Oxford at the time of the Civil War.

Instead of Logic, Physic, school converse
I did attend the armed troops of Mars.
Instead of books I sword, horse, pistols bought
And on the field I for degrees then fought.

Wood interleaved his autobiography at this point with another eyewitness account of events in Oxford at this time which he acquired from the papers of Brian Twine, the University's archivist. On Sunday, 28 August a troop of Royalist horse under Sir John Byron suddenly entered the town under cover of darkness, surprising the guard of scholars and 'put both the University and Town in a great fright' until it was clear on whose side they came. The

University, much influenced by the reforming zeal of its Chancellor, Archbishop Laud, supported the King, but a Puritan majority among the townsmen sided with Parliament. Next week the town trained band, four hundred strong, marched out with drums beating to prevent Byron's troopers and a party from the University's equally strong new militia from knocking a hole in Osney bridge in order to insert a drawbridge there. On 10 September Byron left Oxford, taking with him some of the college fellows and scholars as volunteers.

Two days later Colonel Arthur Goodwin, Hampden's fellow member of Parliament for Buckinghamshire, and some troops of horse briefly quartered in the town, off-saddling their mounts in Christ Church meadow for the night. Then Lord Saye and Sele, Lord Lieutenant of Oxfordshire and High Steward of the University, arrived in his coach-and-six from Broughton Castle and established Parliament's authority in the town. A drummer went up and down the town beating up for volunteers to serve in Lord Oliver St John's regiment. Musketeers disarmed four colleges and discovered Christ Church's hidden silver plate. A London regiment of bluecoats, about 450 strong, marched in one afternoon on their way to Edgehill; most of the rank-and-file were 'very young and but meanly apparelled and very inexpert in their arms'. Apart from mutinying for that five shillings bonus promised them in London, these youthful bluecoats drank too much in the Oxford taverns and fought with naked swords in the High Street against the russet-coated soldiers of another newly-arrived regiment of foot. Soon both regiments, their ranks thinned by desertion, marched off to fight at Edgehill on 23 October.

A week later King Charles made a triumphal entry into Oxford on horseback with his two sons and two nephews, preceded by soldiers bearing as trophies the sixty or seventy Parliamentarian colours captured at Edgehill. While the royal party lodged at Christ Church, the army dispersed to its quarters in and about Oxford. Twenty guns from the train of artillery and their carriages were parked in Magdalen College grove; the Law and Logic Schools became granaries. The mint was established in New Inn Hall, where the celebrated Oxford crown piece was executed by Rawlins in 1644. *Mercurius Aulicus*, which can claim to be England's first regular newspaper, was printed by the University Press (and reprinted in London) almost throughout the war. Production suffered from lack of materials: after Edgehill Sir John Denham's poem *Cowper's Hill* was 'printed at Oxford, in a sort of brown paper, for then they could get no better'. A powder mill was set up in the ruins of Osney Abbey and a sword factory established at Wolvercote. The castle served as a prison for Parliamentarian prisoners. Most of the 1,100 prisoners taken at Cirencester early in 1643 joined the Royalist army, but the remainder – the castle's first inmates – claimed that they were 'used like dogs rather than Christians' in their medieval prison. In the Music and Astronomy Schools tailors cut and stitched away making blue, red, yellow and purple coats for the soldiers, using cloth plundered from the rich clothing areas of nearby Gloucestershire. The great quadrangle of Christ Church became the home of 'a drove of fat oxen and almost three hundred sheep' until they were slaughtered for meat.

Anthony Wood and his fellow pupils were moved from their school, which was filled with barrels of gunpowder, to the choristers' robing chamber at the east end of the common hall – 'a dark nasty room and very unfit for such a purpose', recalled Wood, 'which made the scholars often complain but in vain'. Wood's father's house was occupied by Lord Colepepper, Master of the Rolls, and his parents removed to a little cottage at the back of it.

Work now resumed on the earthwork ramparts and trenches, redoubts and sconces which would soon encircle Oxford at the cost of £30,000 or more. Those townsmen who remained after the Puritans among them had withdrawn to the safety of Abingdon, grudgingly paid their share of the cost but failed to work diligently with pick and shovel when ordered to do so. The King was forced to insist upon one day's work a week from all able-bodied citizens on pain of a fine. An appeal to citizens to bring in their brass in April 1643 produced a response from only forty tradesmen with a mere seven hundredweight of the useful metal. Soon the sights and sounds of a garrison town became familiar to schoolboys and young scholars in Oxford: the comings and goings of Cavalier troops, the incessant beating of drums and clatter of horses' hooves, a deserter's corpse swaying on the gibbet at Carfax, the sudden glad peal of bells at news of some victory, prisoners brought in bound and led by matchcord amid much hooting and booing, the hushed silence the day after a defeat and solemn military funerals of notables fallen in battle.

The presence of so many soldiers in the town meant constant trouble. One Royalist recorded in his diary: 'Sir Arthur Aston wounded in the side in the dark, by a scuffle in the street.' A Parliamentarian spy sent into Oxford by the Earl of Essex's Scout-Master-General, Sir Samuel Luke, reported 'that at Court two gentlemen fell out and fought for a horse that was given between them, and one of them run the horse through, and that Prince Rupert came forth with a poleaxe and parted them'. Such duels were common. Richard Atkyns, a Gloucestershire Royalist, describes the etiquette which more formal encounters required:

In Oxford a knight provoked me with so ill language that I could not forbear striking of him; and being very angry, I took his periwig off from his head and trampled it under my feet. The next morning he sent me a challenge by his second, a person of quality, who found me in bed. I desired him to stay a little, and I would send for my second, to go along with him to his friend, which he did; when I sent my servant for my second, I also commanded him to secure a good charging horse by the way (intending to fight him on horseback). In less than half an hour, my second and servant came to me, and then (having the privilege to choose time, place and weapon) I told him I would meet his friend and himself, with this gentleman my second, on horseback in Bullington Green, between two and three of the clock that afternoon, with sword and pistols, and without arms, and showed him my sword and pistols; saying withal, I would not except against any his friend should bring; which he desired me to send in writing, and I did it by mine own second, who brought me word back, that all was well accepted. We all dined together with other company (as we used to do) without any suspicion of a quarrel, that I know of; after dinner, my second and I mounted, and as we passed by Magdalen College (which was the way to the place appointed) the second on the other side called to my second desiring to speak with him, his business was to persuade me to alight and treat of the matter in his chamber there; they both entreated me to alight, assuring me 'twas not dishonourable, . . . but I not convinced by their arguments, utterly refused, unless the principal himself would come and desire it, and absolve me from my promise of meeting him at the place appointed; which he did, and then we went up together to his second's chamber, where we found an earl (whose sister the knight had married) who also pretended friendship to me; he urged how much I was beforehand with his brother, and proposed . . . that I should declare I was sorry for it, which I desired to be excused in. At last he offered that if I would say I was sorry for what I had done, he should say he was sorry for giving the occasion; which was acknowledged on both sides, and so we were made friends.

At Trinity College the future antiquary John Aubrey, aged sixteen, was still in his first year when the Royalists occupied Oxford. He left an affectionate portrait of the President of Trinity at the time, one Ralph Kettle, Doctor of Divinity. The President made it his practice to walk around the college peeping in at keyholes to see if the boys were studying or idling their time away, like one of Aubrey's fellow students called Bathurst, in mending old doublets or breeches. In a campaign against 'hairy scalps', as Kettle called them, he carried scissors in the muff he wore against the coldness of the medieval college, which he whipped out to cut any long hair he saw as he prowled about the hall. Once, wrote Aubrey, 'I remember he cut Mr Radford's hair with a knife that chips the bread on the buttery hatch'. When Lord Saye came to inspect the college chapel for signs of new popery, the Doctor – 'a right Church of England man' – limped along beside him and dismissed two painted altar screens in his wheezing voice with a wave of the hand: 'Truly, Sir, we regard them no more than a dirty dish-cloth.'

The Royalists interrupted life in the college in other ways. One day Aubrey remembered a foot soldier running into the college hall where Dr Kettle had been lecturing, and breaking the hour-glass he used to time his lectures. Cavalier ladies and their gallants would meet in New College grove, and many times Isabella Lady Thynne made her entrance there with a lute played before her. 'I have heard her play on it in the grove myself, which she did rarely,' mused Aubrey in his old age. Lady Thynne and her close friend, fine Mrs Fanshawe, came to Trinity chapel in the mornings 'half dressed like angels'. Once, for a frolic, they visited the President. 'The old Doctor quickly perceived that they came to abuse him; he addressed his discourse to Mrs Fanshawe saying, "Madam, your husband and father I bred up here, and I knew your grandfather; I know you to be a gentlewoman, I will not say you are a whore but get you gone for a very woman". The dissoluteness of the times, as I have said, grieving the good old Doctor, his days were shortened.' So, too, were Aubrey's days at Oxford. In 1643 he hurriedly left the city to escape a smallpox epidemic and for a few years led what he called 'a sad life in the country'.

For the overcrowded city of Oxford experienced frequent outbreaks of smallpox, plague and the epidemical disease which contemporaries called *morbus campestris* or camp fever. Edward Greaves, an Oxford surgeon, blamed the presence of the soldiers, 'it being seldom or never known that an army where there is so much filth and nastiness of diet, worse lodging, unshifted apparel, etc., should long continue without contagious disease'. Luke's spies reported in July 1643 'that there dies about forty a week of plague in Oxford besides many of other diseases'. The accounts of St Martin's Church in Carfax record frequent payments for shrouds and grave-digging, as annually about four times the number of burials took place there than in earlier years. In 1644 the churchwardens paid 'for frankinsense and other fumes' to safeguard against infection and to drown the stench from corpses buried too near the surface.

Many years later Ann Fanshawe, one of Aubrey's dubious heroines, wrote her own account of those days in Cavalier Oxford for the benefit of her only surviving son. She prefaced this memoir by narrating the family history, including her birth as daughter to one of the wealthiest men in England, the customs-farmer Sir John Harrison. Her education included needlework, learning French, playing the lute and virginals, and dancing. 'Yet was I wild to that degree that the hours of my beloved recreation took up too much of my time, for I loved reading in the first place, and running, and all active times; and in fine I was that which we graver people call a hoyting girl,' – that is, noisy, mirthful or frolicsome. In 1643 Ann exchanged a carefree and comfortable life at her father's Montague House in Bishopgate Street and his country manor in Hertfordshire for the crowded, provincial streets of the King's new capital.

My father commanded my sister and myself to come to him to Oxford where the court then was; but we, that had till that hour lived in great plenty and great order, found ourselves like fishes out of the water and the scene so changed that we knew not at all how to act any part but obedience; for from as good houses as any gentleman of England had we come to a baker's house in an obscure street, and from rooms well furnished to lie in a very bad bed in a garret, to one dish of meat and that not the best ordered: no money, for we were as poor as Job, nor clothes more than a man or two brought in their cloak bags. We had the perpetual discourse of losing and gaining of towns and men; at the windows the sad spectacle of war, sometimes plague, sometimes sicknesses of other kind, by reason of so many people being packed together, as I believe there never was before of that quality; always want, yet I must needs say that most bore it with a martyr-like cheerfulness. For my own part I began to think we should all like Abraham live in tents all the days of our lives.

Her second brother William Harrison died at Oxford with a bruise on his side caused by a fall from his horse, which was shot under him in a skirmish with some Parliamentarian cavalry. She and her family buried him in Exeter College Chapel. On hearing of his death the King called him 'a very good and gallant young man'.

On 18 May 1644 at Wolvercot Church just outside Oxford Ann married Sir Richard Fanshawe, a diplomat who had just been appointed Secretary of the Council of War to the Prince of Wales. Ann was nineteen and her husband nearly thirty-six. After a year Richard left Bristol with the Prince, leaving his wife pregnant with their first child behind. Sadly, her baby died two days after his birth. On the day that Ann left her bedroom she went to church. After the service a gentleman handed her a letter from Sir Richard, together with a purse of fifty gold pieces. 'I opened first my letter and rid those unexpressable joys that most overcame me, for he told me that I should the Thursday following come to him, and to that purpose he had sent me that money, and would find two of his men with horse and all accommodation both for myself, my father, and sister, and that Lady Capel and Lady Brentford would meet me on the way. But that gold your father sent me when I was ready to perish did not so much revive me as his summons. I went immediately to walk, or at least to sit, in the air (being very weak) in the garden of St John's College, and there with my good father communicated my joy, who took great pleasure to hear of my husband's good success and likewise of his journey to him.

'We all of my household being present heard drums beat in the high way under the garden wall. My father asked me if I would go up upon the mount and see the soldiers march, for it was Sir Charles Lee's company of foot, an acquaintance of ours. I said yes, and went up, leaning my back to a tree that grew on the mount. The commander, seeing us there, in compliment gave us a volley of shot, and one of their muskets being loaded shot a brace of bullets not two inches above my head as I leaned to the tree; for which mercy and deliverance I praise God.'

When Ann Fanshawe travelled westwards to join her husband in May 1645, young Anthony Wood had spent a year at the grammar school at Thame, where John Hampden, Arthur Goodwin and Edmund Waller had studied before him.

In 1643 some regiments from the inactive Earl of Essex's army had billeted themselves in Thame. One evening in June Prince Rupert sallied out from Oxford at the head of a column of Cavaliers to beat up some enemy quarters in the Chilterns, and to seize a waggon-train loaded with chests of money for Essex's men. On his way home next day Rupert scattered some Roundhead troops of horse and dragoons who had followed him on to Chalgrove Field. In

John Hampden's spur is a moving relic of the great Parliamentarian who died at Chalgrove Field.

the fight John Hampden was fatally wounded when an overloaded pistol exploded in his hand. Hampden made his way back to Thame where he died a few days later. His friend Arthur Goodwin, who followed him to the grave within weeks, wrote this moving letter on 26 June to his daughter Jane Lady Wharton:

I am here at Hampden in doing the last duty for the deceased owner of it, of whom every honest man has a share in the loss, and therefore will likewise in the sorrow. In the loss of such a friend to my own particular, I have no cause of discontent, but rather to bless God that he has not according to my deserts bereft me of you and all the comforts dearest to me. All his thoughts and endeavours of his life was zealously in this cause of God's, which he continued in all his sickness, even to his death. For all I can hear the last words he spake was to me, though he lived six or seven hours after I came away as in a sleep. Truly, Jenny, (and I know you may easily be persuaded to it), he was a gallant man, an honest man, an able man, and take all, I know not to any man living second. God now in mercy has rewarded him. I have written to London for a black suit. I pray let me beg of you a broad black ribbon to hang about my standard. I would we all lay it to heart, that God takes away the best amongst us. I pray the Lord to bless you. Your ever, dear Jenny, most affectionate father,

Arthur Goodwin

A year later, when Anthony Wood's widowed mother sent him and his brother Christopher to Thame, people still talked about the loss of Hampden.

81

The boys, who were sent from Oxford to avoid the siege threatened by Essex and Waller that summer, as well as an outbreak of infection, were lodged in the vicarage on the north side of the church. The Wood boys escaped the plague and smallpox at Thame, although their studies continued to be disturbed by soldiers. For Thame lay within reach of Parliament's forces at Aylesbury and from the King's outlying garrisons at Wallingford Castle and Boarstall House. By September 1645 three hundred Parliamentarian troopers, many of them officers without employment known as 'reformadoes', garrisoned the town. Among their commanders was a Dutchman called Puide.

One of the first of these interruptions happened on 27 January 1644. Colonel Thomas Blagge, the governor of Wallingford, was a Royalist from Suffolk as were five other officers in his regiment of foot. He was roving about early that day at the head of his troop of horse when, at Long Crendon, about two miles north-west of Thame, he encountered a strong party of Colonel Crawford's Roundheads from Aylesbury garrison. Outnumbered by about three to one, the Cavaliers soon turned their horses' heads for home. But Blagge and his major, Robert Walters, stood their ground manfully, and fought a rearguard action against Crawford's troopers, slashing and beating with their swords against a swarm of rebels. Soon Colonel Blagge was cut over the face and had some other fleshwounds. Anthony Wood caught a glimpse of him:

After the action was concluded at Crendon, and Blagge and his men forced to fly homeward, they took part of Thame in their way. And A.W. and his fellow-sojourners being all then at dinner in the parlour with some strangers there, of whom their master Burt and his wife were of the number, they were all alarm'd with their approach: and by that time they could run out of the house into the backside to look over the pale that parts it from the common road, they saw a great number of horsemen posting towards Thame over Crendon bridge, about a stone's cast from their house (being the out and only house on that road before you come into Thame) and in the head of them was Blagge with a bloody face, and his party with Captain Walters following him. The number, as was then guessed by A.W. and those of the family, was 50 or more, and they all rode under the said pale and close by the house. They did not ride in order, but each made shift to be foremost; and one of them riding upon a shelving ground opposite to the door, his horse slip'd, fell upon one side, and threw the rider (a lusty man) in A. Wood's sight. Colonel Crawford, who was well hors'd and at a pretty distance before his men in pursuit, held a pistol to him; but the trooper crying 'Quarter!', the rebels came up, rifled him, and took him and his horse away with them. Crawford rode on without touching him, and ever or anon he would be discharging his pistol at some of the fag-end of Blagge's horse, who rode through the west end of Thame, called Priest-end, leading towards Ricot. Whether Crawford and his men followed them beyond Thame, in truth I cannot now tell; but I think they did not, but went into the town, and refreshed themselves, and so went to Aylesbury. . . .

Another alarm and onset was made by the Cavaliers from Oxford about break of day on Sunday morning September 7, before any of the rebels were stirring. But by the alarm taken from the sentinel that stood at that end of the town leading to Oxford, many of them came out of their beds into the market place without their doublets; whereof Adjutant-General Puide was one who fought in his shirt. Some that were quarter'd near the church, as in Vincent Barry's house between it and the school and those in the vicar's house (wherein A.W. then sojourn'd) fled into the church (some with their horses also) and going to the top of the tower, would be peeping thence to see the Cavaliers run into the houses where they quarter'd, to fetch away their goods.

There were about six of the Parliament soldiers (troopers) that quarter'd in the vicar's house; and one being slow and careless, was airing and warming his boots, while they were fighting in the town: and no sooner he was withdrawn, into the garden I think, but some of the Cavaliers who were retiring with their spoil towards Boarstall (for they had separated themselves from those that went to Oxford) ran into the vicar's house, and seized on cloaks and goods of the rebels, while some of the said rebels (who had lock'd themselves up in the church) were beholding out of the church windows what they were doing.

On the day before (Saturday) some of the said rebels that lodg'd in the said house had been progging for venison, in Thame park I think; and one or two pasties of it were made, and newly put into the oven before the Cavaliers entered into the house. But so it was, that none of the said rebels were left at eleven of the clock to eat the said pasties, so their share fell among the schoolboys that were sojournours in the said house.

As for the beforemention'd Adjutant-General Puide, he had leave, within three days after he was brought to Oxford, to depart upon his parole; yet wanted the civility either to return himself or to release the gentleman (or any other) that he had promised in exchange for him. Such and no better is the faith and humanity of the rebels.

Besides these here set down, were other alarms and skirmishes, which being frequent and of little concern – yet much to the schoolboys who were interrupted thereby – I shall forbear the recital of them. They had also several times troopers from Boarstall, who would watch and be upon the guard in the vicarage house (the out-house northward from Thame, as I have before told you) and continue there a whole night together, while some of their party were upon London road eastward from the town to lay in wait for provision or wine that came from London towards Aylesbury, or to any persons thereabouts that took part with the rebels. Some of these troopers would discourse with the schoolboys that lived in the house (being of the number of six or sometimes more) while they were making their exercise in the hall against the next day. Some of them A.W. found to have grammar learning in them, as by the questions they proposed to the boys; and others having been or lived, in Oxford, knew the relations of A.W., which would make them show kindness to him and his brother. But that which A.W. observ'd was that the vicar and his wife were always more kind to the Parliament soldiers or rebels than to the Cavaliers, as his master W. Burt and his wife were, having been always acquainted with and obliged to the families of the Ingoldesbys and Hampdens in Buckinghamshire, and other puritanical and factious families in the said county; who, while young, had been mostly bred in the said school of Thame, and had sojourned either with the vicar or master. But as for the usher David Thomas, a proper stout Welshman, A.W. always took him to be a good loyalist, as indeed he was.

On June 10, Wednesday, the garrison of Boarstall was surrendered for the use of the Parliament. The schoolboys were allowed by their master a free liberty that day, and many of them went thither (four miles distant) about 8 or 9 of the clock in the morning to see the form of surrender, the strength of the garrison, and the soldiers of each party. They, and particularly A.W., had instructions given to them before they went, that not one of them should either taste any liquor or eat any provision in the garrison; and the reason was, for fear the royal party who were to march out thence should mix poison among the liquor or provision that they should leave there. But as A.W. remembered, he could not get into the garrison, but stood, as hundreds did, without the works, where he saw the governor, Sir William Campion, a little man, who upon some occasion or other laid flat upon the ground on his belly to write a letter or bill or the form of a pass, or some such thing.

June 24, Wednesday and Midsummer day, the garrison of Oxford which was the chiefest hold the King had, and wherein he had mostly resided while the civil war continued, was surrendered for the use of Parliament, as most of his garrisons were this year, occasion'd by the fatal battle of Naseby which happened in the last year, wherein the King and his party were in a woeful manner worsted. In the evening of the said day many of the King's foot party that belonged to the said garrison came into Thame, and laid down their arms there, being then a wet season. Some of whom continuing there the next day, A.W. went into the town to see them. He knew some of their faces and they his, but he being a boy and having no money, he could not then relieve them, or make them drink: yet he talked with them about Oxford and his relations and acquaintance there; for the doing of which he was check'd when he came home.

6

Western Wonders

On 16 May 1643 Sir Ralph Hopton and his Cornish Royalist army revenged an earlier defeat at the hands of the Cornish and Devon Parliamentarians by gaining a great victory at Stratton. Parliament's general in the west, the Earl of Stamford, fled into Exeter leaving behind him three hundred dead, seventeen hundred prisoners, thirteen brass guns and seventy barrels of powder and stores of provisions. At Launceston, which he occupied after the battle, Hopton heard that the Marquess of Hertford and Rupert's brother Prince Maurice were marching westwards to join him. Although Plymouth and Exeter were still in the hands of the Roundheads, he advanced without delay and met them at Chard in Somerset on 4 June. The Cavalier poet, Sir John Denham, conveys the jubilant mood in the Royalist camp in his lines:

> Do you not know, not a fortnight ago,
> How they bragg'd of a western wonder?
> When a hundred and ten slew five thousand men
> With the help of lightning and thunder?
>
> But now on which side was this miracle try'd,
> I hope we at last are even;
> For Sir Ralph and his knaves are risen from their graves
> To cudgel the clowns of Devon.

Denham had himself made the acquaintance of Hopton's next opponent, Sir William Waller, who was Parliament's commander in the Severn Valley. In November 1642 Sir John had refused to surrender Farnham Castle to Waller. During the storm Waller led the assault in person, sword in hand. The Royalists had no right to quarter, but they were all spared on Waller's orders. This story of kindness would not have surprised Sir Ralph Hopton, for he had known Waller intimately for more than twenty years.

In November 1620 Queen Elizabeth of Bohemia fled from Prague towards Frankfurt-on-the-Oder through the winter snows, leaving behind her scenes of confusion and defeat as the Imperial Army under Tilly closed in upon the city. Escorting the coach of the 'Winter Queen' rode a troop of sixty young English volunteers, among them 22-year-old William Waller from Kent, and 25-year-old Ralph Hopton from Somerset. Waller had already risked his life in a skirmish with the Cossacks in Bohemia: his horse was shot under him, and with his foot tangled in a stirrup he was dragged through them, a pistol bullet grazing his head. When deep snows halted the coaches, Ralph Hopton carried the Queen behind him on his horse for forty miles. It is possible that her infant son, Prince Rupert, was mounted behind William Waller. Not long afterwards Waller and Hopton, now firm friends, returned to England.

The two young men shared much the same social background. As hereditary Chief Butler of England William enjoyed a sizeable income from a tax on wine imports. He spent a year or two at Magdalen Hall in Oxford, the most Puritan of all the colleges, and then travelled abroad. In Paris he learned to manage a military charger, the 'great horse', and then moved on to Italy, where he completed a grand tour fraught with minor dangers: over-turning boats, epidemics of sickness and the unwelcome attentions of the Inquisition. He served for some months in the mercenary forces of the Republic of Venice, then at war on its northern borders with the Holy Roman Empire. 'At the leaguer before Rubia,' he wrote, 'I escaped several very near shot; one grazing at my foot, another lighting between Sir John Vere and me, as we sat close together by the battery. . . .' In 1620 he volunteered for service with Sir Horace Vere, who had been commissioned by King James to secure the possessions of his son-in-law, Frederick, Elector Palatine, and the life of his daughter, the young and beautiful Elizabeth, that 'queen of women, the Queen of Bohemia', as Waller called her, who had accompanied her husband when he rashly accepted the Bohemian crown.

Ralph Hopton, born at Witham Friary in Somerset in 1596, came from a family which had made its fortune in that county through the dissolution of the monasteries. After his service with Elizabeth of Bohemia, who was exactly his own age, Hopton spent a further five years in the Low Countries, becoming a lieutenant-colonel in Sir Charles Rich's regiment of foot by 1624 under the command of the celebrated mercenary Count Mansfeldt. In the Long Parliament he followed the lead of Hyde and Falkland in opposing the unconstitutional aspects of the King's personal rule. For example, he voted for the attainder of the Earl of Strafford in April 1641. But he was essentially a reformer of the old order, not a harbinger of a new one. In particular he wished to see the episcopacy reformed but not abolished.

In December 1641 Hopton led the delegation that presented the Grand Remonstrance to the King, the most important single act in his career as a Member of Parliament, but events soon exposed his fundamental loyalty to the Crown. He even defended the King's attempted arrest of the Five Members in January 1642, and went on to 'contradict everything without scruple' that the majority of the House of Commons resolved thereafter, so much so that the House imprisoned him for two weeks in the Tower of London. As soon as Hopton was released in March he returned to Somerset, where he was the first to implement the King's Commissions of Array, designed to secure the royal control of the militia.

A rare contemporary painting of a seventeenth-century battle scene. The musketeer is seen guarding a general's tent. In the rear cavalry are charging furiously against some regiments of foot.

At the time of Hopton's imprisonment in the Tower, Waller had not even entered the House of Commons as a member, although he did so the following month, April 1642, sitting for Andover. Nor had he been nearly as active as Hopton in national or local government, preferring the quiet life of a country gentleman at Forde House in Devon, which he eventually inherited from his wife's father, Sir Thomas Reynell. Jane, the bride he had married in 1623, died in 1637 and William brought his only surviving child, Margaret, to London in order to find a step-mother for her. After a time his choice fell upon Lady Anne Finch, daughter of the Lord Keeper. Lady Anne, a forceful Puritan lady, and her husband received the grant of Winchester Castle, and set about renovating this imposing residence. Possibly through Lady Anne's influence, Waller came into Pym's circle and became a passionate adherent of Parliament's cause.

In the late summer and autumn of 1642, Waller distinguished himself by capturing Portsmouth, Farnham, Winchester, Arundel and Chichester. At Edgehill, although his regiment was scattered in Prince Rupert's first charge, Waller escaped in the confusion. In February 1643 he was appointed Major-General of the associated counties of Worcestershire, Somersetshire, Gloucestershire, Wiltshire and Shropshire, one of the first of the county associations which both sides brought into being as the war progressed.

In a series of swift marches Waller secured the lower Severn Valley for Parliament that spring. But his brilliant successes were soon marred by the rivalries and incompetence of local Parliamentarian commanders. Sir Edward Hungerford and Sir Edward Baynton in Wiltshire, for instance, fought like stags to control the county. After each had imprisoned the other, Parliament intervened in favour of Hungerford. After Waller had captured Malmesbury he left Hungerford to garrison it. But the irresponsible governor soon left for Bath.

On 25 March his soldiers abandoned the town and Prince Rupert's Cavaliers re-occupied it next day without striking a blow. For his part Hungerford sought to vindicate himself in print by blaming 'the backwardness of the country to come in to bear arms or to assist with money (who seemed very forward whilst Sir William Waller was present, but altered their minds so soon as they did see him with his army to be departed from them); my soldiers generally discontented that they had no pillage as others who took less pains (as they thought) and lost no blood, overburdened with duties, being but a few in number and hourly raised with alarms; the captains at odds amongst themselves, Major Trayle that should have reconciled all, not so careful as he ought, Major Clifton that was sent to join him gone away from thence to Bath, these two being the able commanders especially entrusted for the defence of the town'.

Further south Waller had to contend with a month's truce which the Cornish Royalists and Devon Parliamentarians under the Earl of Stamford had concluded and kept extending for further periods. At the time there was a rash of such treaties of temporary or even permanent neutrality in the counties most divided by the sword. Waller courteously acknowledged a letter from the Devon commissioners informing him of the second extension, and then plainly but courteously declared his own mind:

I am still of the same opinion that besides the distaste given thereby to Parliament there can be nothing more destructive to the Kingdom and to your own county than these treaties. The Kingdom will lose by this neutrality that strength which might have been derived from your county, and in this way, whilst this and that county shall sit down and think to save their own stakes, leaving the burden of the war upon a few shoulders, his Majesty will with the more ease subdue our party in the field, and that done (being Master of the field) march with ease through every corner of the Kingdom, and then all the privilege those poor countries shall obtain that sat down first will be to be devoured last.

I am confident the Cornish party has no real intention to embrace a peace, and I have some informations that give me an assurance of it. I presume not to write any thing by way of advice; I know very well your judgements and my own weakness. I only represent my own apprehensions which I humbly submit to you. The happiness I have enjoyed in your country, and the extreme obligation I have received from it, bind me to desire and endeavour the welfare thereof.

As this unwelcome truce, which brought the war to a standstill in Somerset and Dorset as well as in Devon, would not expire until 22 April Waller decided to exploit the victory he had secured over Lord Herbert's Welsh levies near Gloucester by reducing South Wales. After marching about that hostile country Waller's small Western army entered Chepstow 'very weary of the Welsh ways over the mountains'. Here Waller learned that Prince Maurice in command of a strong Royalist force had moved to cut him off from his base at Gloucester. Instead of joining up with Lord Herbert's local army the twenty-two-year-old Prince quartered his regiments in villages west of the Severn. As Waller approached by night – the Royalists had by now nicknamed him 'the Night Owl' – Prince Maurice concentrated his two thousand horse, foot and dragoons at Little Dean.

Present at Little Dean fight on 11 April was Captain Richard Atkyns in Prince Maurice's own regiment of horse, a young Gloucestershire Cavalier of good family. After two years at Balliol College, however, Atkyns could not 'read a Greek or Latin author with pleasure'. He accompanied the son of Lord Arundel of Wardour to France but returned home when this youth died from getting 'a heat and a cold at tennis'. When he was twenty-one, in 1636, his father died and left him an income of £800 a year. 'After the days of mourning were accomplished,' he wrote, 'I put off my hounds, put £200 in my purse, and came to London and kept my coach.' He blamed his ill-success as a courtier on 'a blushing modesty, a flexible disposition and no great diligence'. In middle age Richard described himself as 'fat, sweaty and gouty', while his aunt, Lady Atkyns, called him a great swearer and a drunkard. But in 1643 Atkyns had not fallen to such depths; indeed he had a reputation a Puritan captain might envy. After Atkyns joined the Royalist army with his troop of horse, twenty of them gentlemen like himself, 'the swearing captains put the name of the "Praying Captain" upon me, having seen me sometimes upon my knees'. At Little Dean he was given command of the forlorn-hope.

No sooner had I received the word of command, but my charging horse fell as trembling and quaking that he could not be kept upon his legs; so that I must lose my honour by an excuse, or borrow another horse; which with much ado I did of the Lord Chandos' gentleman of the horse, leaving twice as much as he was worth with him. The charge was seemingly as desperate as any I was ever in, it being to beat the enemy from a wall which was a strong breastwork with a gate in the middle, possessed by about 200 musketeers besides horse. We were to charge down a steep plain hill, of above twelve score yards in length, as good a mark as they could wish. Our party consisting of between two and three hundred horse. Not a man of them would follow us, so the officers, about ten or twelve of us, agreed to gallop down in as good order as we could and make a desperate charge upon them.

The enemy seeing our resolution never fired at us at all, but ran away and we (like young soldiers) after them doing execution upon them. But one Captain Hanmer, being better horsed than myself, in pursuit fell upon their ambuscade and was killed horse and man. I had only time enough to turn my horse and run for my life. This party of ours, that would not be drawn on at first, by this time seeing our success came into the town after us and stopped our retreat. And, finding that we were pursued by the enemy, the horse in the front fell back upon the rear and they were so wedged together that they routed themselves, so as there was no passage for a long time. All this while the enemy were upon me, cutting my coat upon my armour in several places and discharging pistols as they got up to me, being the outermost man, which Major Sheldon declared to

For the marching postures of the Dragoone, they are like the 23. and 24. Figures in the Booke of Cavalrie; I could wish they might have growne little in experience or valour, onely in pride and covetousnesse, to defraud: and I dare boldly say, such will, never be souldiers, &c.

(a) I am perswaded there be many that I have beene abroad have growne little in experience or valour, onely in pride and covetousnesse, to defraud: and I dare boldly say, such will, never be souldiers, &c.

(b) First, firing of the Musketier on horse-backe by introduction, which I am of opinion is not over-balanced with danger, but the properest, one of them upon such an occasion: but I leave it to the judgement of others, according to my request at the end, &c.

The second firing of the Musketier on horse-backe.
3. The Dragoone to fire on foot, if that he shall see occasion, and after fire given, to mount, &c.
4. The Dragoone service in a siege, and how he is to, behave himselfe, and to fire, &c.

Fellow-Souldiers,

HAving upon some occasions viewed and looked upon some part of the Booke of *Military Instructi* *Cavalry*, &c. and finding it to speake so disrespectively of the Books of Infantrie, withou ons, and for that he saith, the Dragoone, or Musquetier, must exercise himselfe to give fire on ho the Harquebusier, &c. as you may read in his 31.Cap.pag.44. and yet leaveth him to be direct by the Infantry, I shall here take occasion to speake somewhat for the complete and perfect met *Young Artillerie Man*, set forth by my honoured fellow-souldier and acquaintance, Lievt. Colon which for its sufficiency, and plainnnesse, to speak truly, I think as yet unparalleld in any langua being perfectly apprehended and understood, will furnish the Partie that shall understand it, in ments (God giving him courage to performe and act it sufficiently) in most things. But I would souldiers to make use of, and store up experimentall (a) knowledge: for as this war differeth much warres, so doth the severall skirmishings, and occasions (therein:) and resolution goeth very far be grounded upon judgment, and produceth many faire effects, through Gods blessing.

For the exercise of the Dragoone, firing on horse-back, I will recite somewhat, I have seen, the more confused manner and way, and give some directions to performe the same.

Suppose the enemy retreating, and their horse facing while they draw off their great guns, and baggage, marching away with thei they losing ground, retreat entire, together, with their Cornets on the head of their Troups, they being on a hill, having a deep and dale, to friend, fit to lay Ambuscadoes, besides the night approaching to help them, &c.

Here Dragoones may do better service, firing on horse-back, then the Curasier, the way being dubitable,&c. by advancing slowly following them about musket shot, the Curasier being withing such distance as is needfull, to relieve them, if that the enemy shoul charge, or attempt it: for the better performance thereof, they are to fire by (b) introduction, on horse-back; which is a passing thro tween the Files, the files being at open Order: the first rank having given fire, by the Commanders direction, let the bringer-up pa the Files, which is commonly to the left, placing themselves before their Leaders, in the Front, and then giving fire, the rest of the R the same successively, till such time as they shall receive Order to the contrary, or to close their Files. I am loath to forme their plac upon such occasions, but the Van, or Flanks, is most advantagious, and necessary for them, because from thence they can command, a theft, and make the best use, to line the hedges, or to beat up their Ambuscadoes, if need require: but not knowing the scituation o or the forme of the enemy, which they may pursue, I leave it to the wisdome of the Commander, &c.

Secondly, a party of Dragoones may fire retreating, on horse-back, and do good execution, they riding such a pace, as their occ reth, or the ground will permit, the last rank somtimes facing about, and firing upon the enemie, then wheeling off to the right, or ground best affords. I would advise them (herein) to keep their Files close, and place themselves before their Leaders in the Front, ceive order to the contrary. The Dragoons having been sent forth for the taking some bridge, or stopping some passage, the enemy sessed himselfe of it before them, and advancing towards their Quarters, whether in field or garrison, and being too strong for them with, having retreated as before to their Quarters, or some place of advantage, where they may secure their horses in the way, the quainted therwith before, and what Scouts the enemy hath out, may give the enemy an unexpected volley of shot from some secret a cted place, which may offer it selfe to their view, which having performed, to mount suddenly againe, for better and sooner expediti

For service to be performed by the Dragoone in a Siege, it is commonly on Foot, wherefore I leave the direction thereof in firin verall and speciall occasions, as they shall arise, and their Commanders give directions, further certifying, that by the skilfull, and t it is sooner formed in field, then described by the pen, onely finding the Cavalrie Booke so full of good language and learning, and t being made a part thereof, and left to anothers direction, I could do no lesse then vindicate my deceased fellow-souldiers book, ut sup testimonie of my love to the School of War I was bred in, and my reall and hearty affections to my Countrey, offer this my mite in furie, with my humble prayers to the Almighty, to convert us all unto him in his good time, and to send peace in this distracted Kin

Postscript.

Gentle Reader, accept of these lines in love, and correct them in love, so shall I be ingaged hereafter, further to publish such thin find occasion, for thy benefit, onely for the present, I have commended to the Cutters, or Ingravers of Copper, and so to the Presse, f ding of the young Artillerie-mans request, the Motions of the Posture for the Musket and Pike in their severall Garbes and Portrai the Postures of the halfe Pike joyned with the Musket, being at this time required either for Musketier or Dragoone: but the pres calling upon this (as I conceive) hath caused me to set this forth alone: wherefore expect the other as soon as it can be finished. Va

From the Hermit at Wapping,
June 5. 1644.

Your Friend, *Nathana*

Published according to Order.

During the Civil War there was much demand from the amateur military commanders of all ranks for drill manuals, like this one by Nathaniel Burt.

my very great advantage. But, when they pursued us to the town, Major Leighton had made good a stone house and so prepared for them with musketeers that one volley of shot made them retreat. They were so near me that a musket bullet from one of our own men took off one of the bars of my cap I charged with and went through my hair and did me no hurt. But this was only a forlorn party of their army to face us, whilst the rest of their army marched to Gloucester.

A few days later Waller suffered a reverse near Tewkesbury on Ripple Field at the hands of Prince Maurice. Yet his pressing need for money did not choke Waller's chivalry. On 4 June, when he could not have been more busy with preparations for the coming campaign, he found leisure to write to the wife of one of the Royalist prisoners he captured at Hereford in late April. Lady Scudamore had complained to him about damage done by his soldiers to some property near Gloucester, and the loss of her income.

Noble Lady,
I shall ever take it a great honour to receive your commands, and I shall with a ready obedience entertain them. In obedience to your Ladyship's letter, I sent for Alderman Pury and questioned him what waste had been committed upon your Ladyship's house or grounds. I find some trees have been felled and I have given order there shall be no more touched; but I am assured nothing about the house has been defaced, only a tower of an old chapel adjoining thereunto was pulled down in regard it might have been some annoyance to the works. For your Ladyship's rents, I have given order the sequestration should not be executed; so that, Madam, they are still at your command. If there be any thing else wherein I may advance your Ladyship's service, I humbly beg the favour to be commanded, that I may have opportunity to give some demonstration with what passion, I am, Madam,

Your devoted humble servant,
Gloucester, June 4, 1643.   William Waller
For the Right Honourable the Lady Scudamore
at Homelacy, humbly present these.

In common with most of the country folk in the border counties, the inhabitants of Herefordshire could be described by John Corbet as 'a people naturally malignant, that were dashed at present but did flourish again in the wake of the King's army'. Only a decisive victory against the Royalists in the field could secure these regions for Parliament. In April the cause of Parliament in the Severn Valley had reached its zenith. Bristol, Gloucester, Tewkesbury, Cirencester, Malmesbury, all contained Roundhead garrisons. In the West Sir William had become 'a commander-in-chief upon whom the hearts of the people could fasten'.

Whilst laying siege to Worcester in May, Waller heard the news of the joining of the two Royalist armies at Chard and he made haste southwards to give them battle. While the rival armies lay some miles apart, Waller at Bath and Hopton at Wells, the latter either suggested a meeting or wrote urging his old friend to change sides, possibly mentioning Waller's former major, Colonel Horatio Carey, who deserted some time during that June. Waller replied with a letter that reveals not only his deep affection for Hopton but also the spirit with which he had espoused the cause of Parliament.

To my noble friend Sir Ralph Hopton at Wells
Sir,
  The experience I have had of your worth and the happiness I have enjoyed in your friendship are wounding considerations when I look upon this present distance between us. Certainly my affections to you are so unchangeable that hostility itself cannot violate my friendship to your person, but I must be true to the cause wherein I serve. The old limitation *usque ad aras* holds still, and where my conscience is interested all other obligations are swallowed up. I should most gladly wait on you according to your desire, but that I look upon you as you are engaged in that party beyond a possibility of retreat and consequently incapable of being wrought upon by any persuasion. And I know the conference could never be so close between us, but that it would take wind and receive a construction to my dishonour. That great God which is the searcher of my heart, knows with what a sad sense I go upon this service and with what a perfect hatred I detest this war without an enemy, but I look upon it as *opus domini*, which is enough to silence all passion in me. The God of peace in his good time send us peace and in the meantime fit us to receive it. We are both upon the stage and must act those parts that are assigned us in this tragedy. Let us do it in a way of honour and without personal animosities. Whatsoever the issue be, I shall never willingly relinquish the dear title of
your most affectionate friend and faithful servant,
William Waller

Bath, 16 June 1643.

At the ensuing battle of Lansdown (5 July) Waller occupied a fine defensive position on the brow of the long down north of Bath. With a remarkable boldness he unleashed his cavalry and dragoons to attack the combined Royalist armies as they marched towards him from the north. Having cleared the fields at the foot of Lansdown, Hopton's Cornish foot clamoured to advance into the flashing muzzles of Waller's guns, crying out 'Let us fetch those cannon!' They were given their wish. The main column marched up the steep incline in the centre, while two bodies of musketeers moved round on the wings to occupy the woods at each end of Waller's ridge.

Richard Atkyns received orders to lead some troops of horse held in reserve to support the hard-pressed Cornish foot. 'As I went up the hill, which was very steep and hollow, I met several dead and wounded officers brought off, besides several running away, that I had much ado to get up by them. When I came to the top of the hill I saw Sir Bevil Grenville's stand of pikes, which certainly preserved our army from a total rout with the loss of his most precious life. They

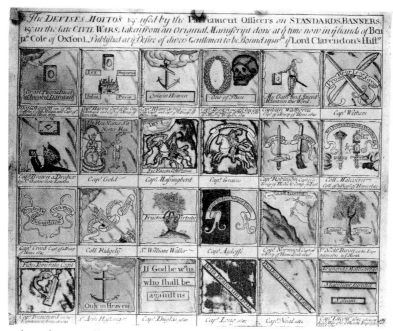

Commanders of troops of horse on both sides in the Civil War carried personal banners. These often incorporated, as well as the family arms, a propaganda slogan or motto. Waller's banner is in the fourth row, and Sir Arthur Heselrige's in the fifth.

stood as upon the eaves of an house for steepness, but as unmovable as a rock. On which side of this stand of pikes our horse were, I could not discover, for the air was so darkened by the smoke of the powder that for a quarter of an hour together (I dare say) there was no light seen, but what the fire of the volleys of shot gave; and 'twas the greatest storm that ever I saw, in which though I knew not whither to go, nor what to do, my horse had two or three musket bullets in him immediately, which made him tremble under me at the rate, and I could hardly with spurs keep him from lying down; but he did me the service to carry me off to a led horse and then died.

'By that time I came up to the hill again, the heat of the battle was over and the sun set, but still pelting at one another half musket shot off. The enemy had a huge advantage of ground upon our men, for their foot were in a large sheep-cot, which had a stone wall about it as good a defence against any thing but cannon as could be, and ours upon the edge of the hill, so steep that they could hardly draw up. 'Tis true there were shelves near the place like Romish works where we quartered that night, but so shallow that my horse had a bullet in his neck. We pelted at one another till half an hour before day, and then we heard not any noise, but saw light matches upon the wall, which our commanders observing, sent one to discover whether they had quit the field or not, who brought news that they were gone.'

Another Royalist eyewitness on Lansdown that day, Lieutenant-Colonel Walter Slingsby, described the end of the battle thus: 'The rebels' foot took example by their horse and quit their breastworks retiring behind a long stone wall that runs across the down. Our foot leaps into their breastworks; our horse draws up upon their ground. Our two wings that were sent to fall into the two woods had done their business and were upon the hill as soon as the rest.

'The enemy, observing our front to enlarge itself upon the hill and our cannon appearing there likewise, began to suspect himself and drew his whole strength behind that wall, which he lined well with musketeers and in several places broke down breaches very broad that his horse might charge if there were occasion, which breaches were guarded by his cannon and bodies of pikes.

'Thus stood the two armies taking breath looking upon each other, our cannon on both sides playing without ceasing till it was dark, legs and arms flying apace, the two armies being within musket shot. After it was dark there was great silence on both sides, at which time our right wing of shot got much nearer their army lodging themselves amongst the many little pits betwixt the wall and the wood from whence we galled them cruelly.

'About 11 of the clock we receiv'd a very great volley of small shot but not mix't with cannon by which some of us judg'd that he was retreating and gave this at his expiring. But the general apprehension through our army was that the enemy had intention to try a push in the night for their ground, which they had so dishonourably lost. For we were then seated like a heavy stone upon the very brow of the hill, which with one lusty charge might well have been roll'd to the bottom.

'It was not long before we knew certainly that they were gone. At their departure they left all their light matches upon the wall and whole bodies of pikes standing upright in order within the wall as if men had held them. We were glad they were gone for if they had not I know who had within an hour. But indeed had our horse been as good as the enemy's the rebels had never gone off the field unruin'd.'

Meanwhile Sir Bevil Grenville lay dying. Before the war he had been one of Waller's close friends. Once Waller had taken Grenville's undergraduate son Dick out to dinner in Oxford. On another occasion Grenville obtained a horse for Waller, 'the best I can get in all this county', and would not hear of payment. 'I beseech you name not money between you and me; it is a thing so much beneath my thoughts and under the respect I owe you, my noblest friend, as it is not considerable with me.' Nothing could more epitomize the tragedy of 'this war without an enemy' than the death of Sir Bevil Grenville at the hands of his old friend's army. On 20 July Sir John Trevelyan wrote to his widow Grace: 'Madam, he is gone his journey but a little while before us. We must march after when it shall please God, for your Ladyship knows that none fall without his Providence which is as great in the thickest shower of bullets as in the bed.'

Sir Ralph Hopton also came near to losing his life at Lansdown by means of an accident, as Atkyns relates: 'The next morning was very clear, and about half an hour after sun rising, we rendezvoused our horse and foot. ... Major

Sheldon and myself went towards Lord Hopton, who was then viewing the prisoners taken, some of which were carried upon a cart wherein was our ammunition; and (as I heard) had match to light their tobacco. The Major desired me to go back to the regiment whilst he received orders of his Lordship. I had no sooner turned my horse and was gone three horses lengths from him, but the ammunition was blown up and the prisoners in the cart with it together with the Lord Hopton, Major Sheldon, and Cornet Washnage, who was near the cart on horseback and several others.

'It made a very great noise and darkened the air for a time, and the hurt men made lamentable screeches. As soon as the air was clear, I went to see what the matter was. There I found his Lordship miserably burnt, his horse singed like parched leather, and Thomas Sheldon (that was a horse's length further from the blast) complaining that the fire was got within his breeches, which I tore off as soon as I could, and from as long a flaxen head of hair as ever I saw, in the twinkling of an eye, his head was like a blackamoor. His horse was hurt and run away like mad, so that I put him upon my horse and got two troopers to hold him up on both sides and bring him to the headquarters, whilst I marched after with the regiment.'

The Royalists carried Hopton in the Marquess of Hertford's coach to Devizes, and he had recovered sufficiently to take command of the town while the bulk of the Cavalier horse rode off to Oxford to get reinforcements. Under the command of Lord Wilmot and Sir John Byron a strong body of Cavaliers returned to Devizes and inflicted a shattering defeat on Waller at Roundway Down (13 July). Atkyns took part in this exhausting enterprise.

At about midnight our horse marched, or rather made an escape out of town, leaving the foot behind us. . . . At the break of day we were at least eight miles from Devizes and free from all enemies between that and Oxford. Prince Maurice and several of the officers galloped to Oxford to be there as soon as they could. But my horse had cast two shoes and I was forced to stay behind to set them at Lambourne where, leaning against a post, I was so sleepy that I fell down like a log of wood and could not be awakened for half an hour. 'Twas impossible then to overtake them, so I went to Farringdon, being not able to reach Oxford that night. I fell off my horse back twice upon the downs before I came to Farringdon, where I reeled upon my horse so extremely that the people of the town took me to be dead drunk. When I came to my house (for there I sometimes lived) I despatched a man and horse immediately to the Prince to receive orders, and desired my wife's aunt to provide a bed for me. The good woman took me to be drunk too, and provided a bed for me immediately, where I slept at least fourteen hours together without waking.

The next morning I had orders that the rendezvous was about Marlborough, whither I went with several horse quartered at Farringdon, and came timely thither. The Lord Wilmot was sent with a recruit of horse from Oxford, and I suppose all the horse at that rendezvous were about eighteen hundred and two small pieces of cannon.

Sir John Byron, a commander in the Cavalier army that so completely routed Waller's army at Roundway Down.

We lost no time but marched towards the enemy, who stood towards the top of the hill; the foot in the middle between two wings of horse, and the cannon before the foot. . . . The charge was so sudden that I had hardly time to put on my arms. We advanced at a full trot three deep and kept in order. The enemy kept their station and their right wing of horse, being cuirassiers, were I'm sure five if not six deep, in so close order that Punchinello himself, had he been there, could not have gotten in to them.

All the horse on the left hand of Prince Maurice's regiment, had none to charge; we charging the very utmost man of their right wing. I cannot better compare the figure of both armies than to the map of the fight at sea, between the English and Spanish Armadas, only there was no half-moon, for though they were above twice our numbers – they being six deep in close order and we but three deep and open by reason of our sudden charge – we were without them at both ends. The cannoneers seeing our resolution did not fire their cannon. No men ever charged better than ours did that day, especially the Oxford horse, for ours were tired and scattered, yet those that were there did their best.

'Twas my fortune in a direct line to charge their General of Horse which I supposed to be so by his place. He discharged his carbine first but at a distance not to hurt us, and afterwards one of his pistols, before I came up to him and missed with both. I then immediately struck into him, and touched him before I discharged mine; and I'm sure I hit him, for he staggered and presently wheeled off from his party and ran. . . .

I pursued him, and had not gone twenty yards after him, but I heard a voice saying, ''Tis Sir Arthur Heselrige – Follow him!' But from which party the voice came I knew not, they being joined, nor never did know till about seven years since. But follow him I did and in six score yards I came up to him, and discharged the other pistol at him, and I'm sure I hit his head for I touched it before I gave fire and it amazed him at that present, but he was too well armed all over for a pistol bullet to do him any hurt, having a coat of mail over his arms and a headpiece (I am confident) musket proof, his sword had two edges and a ridge in the middle, and mine was a strong tuck. After I had slackened my pace a little, he was gone twenty yards from me, riding three quarters speed and down the side of a hill, his posture was waving his sword on the right and left hand of his horse, not looking back to see whether he were pursued or not, (as I conceive) to daunt any horse that should come up to him.

In about six score more yards I came up to him again (having a very swift horse that Cornet Washnage gave me) and stuck by him a good while, and tried him from head to the saddle and could not penetrate him nor do him any hurt. But in this attempt he cut my horse's nose, that you might put your finger in the wound, and gave me such a blow on the inside of my arm amongst the veins that I could hardly hold my sword. He went on as before and I slackened my pace again and found my horse got up to him again, thinking to have pulled him off his horse. But he having now found the way, struck my horse upon the cheek, and cut off half the headstall of my bridle; but falling off from him, I ran his horse into the body and resolved to attempt nothing further than to kill his horse; all this time we were together hand to fist.

In this nick of time came up Cornet Holmes to my assistance (who never failed me in time of danger), and went up to him with great resolution, and felt him before he discharged his pistol, and though I saw him hit him, 'twas but a flea-biting to him. Whilst he charged him, I employed myself in killing his horse, and ran him into several places, and upon the faltering of his horse his headpiece opened behind, and I gave him a prick in the neck, and I had run him through the head if my horse had not stumbled at the same place. Then came in Captain Buck, a gentleman of my troop, and discharged his pistol upon him also, but with the same success as before, and being a very strong man, and charging with a mighty sword, stormed him and amazed him, but he fell off again. By this time his horse began to be faint with bleeding, and fell off from his rate, at which said Sir Arthur, 'What good will it do you to kill a poor man?' Said I 'Take quarter then', with that he stopped his horse and I came up to him, and bid him deliver his sword, which he was loathe to do. And being tied twice about his wrist, he was fumbling a great while before he would part with it. But before he delivered it, there was a runaway troop of theirs that had espied him in hold. Says one of them 'My Lord General is taken prisoner!'; says another, 'Sir Arthur Heselrige is taken prisoner! Face about and charge!' With that they rallied and charged us, and rescued him; wherein I received a shot with a pistol, which only took off the skin upon the blade bone of my shoulder.

This story being related to the King at a second or third hand, his answer was, 'Had he been victualled as well as fortified, he might have endured a siege of seven years'. His horse died in the place, and they horsed him upon another and went away together. . . .

When we came back to the army (which in so confused a field was difficult to do) we found the enemy's foot still in a close body, their muskets lined with pikes and fronting every way, expecting their horse to rally and come to their relief. In the meantime our horse charged them, but to no purpose; they could not get into them. At last, when they saw our foot march from Devizes and come within a mile of them, they asked quarter, and threw down their arms in a moment. . . .

When I alighted I found my horse had done bleeding, his cuts being upon the gristly part of his nose, and the cheek near the bone. I bade my groom have a great care of him, and go into quarters immediately; but instead this rogue went directly to Oxford, left my hurt horse at Marlborough with a farrier, and sold another horse of mine at Oxford and carried my portmanteau with him into the North which had all my clothes and linen in it, and other things worth above £100, and I never saw him more. My charging horse I had again and some money for my other, which was bought at an under value, being no good title. But for want of a shift (my wound having bloodied my linen) I became so lousy in three or four days that I could not tell what to do with myself. And when I had got a shift, which was not till we took Bath, my blood and the sweat of my body had so worn it, that it fell off into lint. . . .

After we were refreshed in our quarters, we marched to Bath, which town the enemy had newly quitted, and marched or rather retreated to Bristol. There I found my Lieutenant Thomas Sandys, formerly taken prisoner, recovering of his wounds but not well able to go abroad. We were very glad to see each other, and I desired him to tell me the manner of his being taken. He told me he pursued the enemy too near their body, and they sent out fresh horse upon him and took him and gave him quarter without asking. But after he was their prisoner, a Scot shot him into the body with two pistol bullets, which were still in him so that he was very near death.

When he was brought to the town, Sir William Waller enquiring what prisoners were taken, heard of his name, and came to see him. He seemed exceeding angry at the inhumane action that befell him, and sent for his own chirurgeon presently, and saw him dressed before he went away. He gave the innkeeper charge that he should have whatever he called for, and he would see him paid; that whatsoever woman he sent for to attend him, should be admitted, and lent him ten broad pieces for his own private expenses; and before he marched to Bristol, he came to see him again, and finding him not able to march, took his parole to render himself a true prisoner to him at Bristol when he was able to ride; which I found (for his word sake) he was inclinable to do. To which I answered that he was now made free by as good authority as took him prisoner, and that I expected he should return to his command; upon which we struck a heat and at last referred the business to the Lord Carnarvon to determine.

The case was agreed to be 'whether a prisoner upon his parole to render himself to the enemy, being afterwards redeemed by his own party, ought to keep his parole or not'. His Lordship heard arguments on both sides; at last said thus, that there had been lately a precedent in the Council of War in a case of like nature, wherein it was resolved, that if the prisoner (being redeemed by a martial power without any consent of his own) shall afterwards refuse the command he was in before and attempt to render himself prisoner to the enemy, he shall be taken as an enemy, and be kept prisoner by his own party; the reason seems very strong because he may be prevailed upon by the enemy to betray his own party; and the freeing of his person, gives him as it were a new election; and if he choose rather to be a prisoner than a free man; it demonstrates his affection to be there. But this did not satisfy my Lieutenant, for he would not take his place as before but marched along with the troop as my prisoner, till the taking of Bristol (the place where he promised to render himself) and then he thought he was fully absolved from his parole, and betook himself to his employment again.

On 15 July Captain Edward Harley wrote an account of the campaign as seen from a Parliamentarian saddle to his father, Sir Robert Harley, at Westminster. With his brother Robert as Lieutenant he commanded a troop in Waller's own regiment of horse. At Lansdown he saw Sir Arthur Heselrige's regiment receive 'a push in the thigh with a pike' as they tried to break up the Cornish regiments. 'Our regiment charged twice, and in the second charge my bay horse was shot under me, but I thank God brought me off well in this hot service.' On Roundway Down his troop was drawn up on the side of the hill facing the direction of the expected advance.

As soon as ever we came there were a very great body of the enemy, which we found afterward to be between forty and fifty colours besides dragoons. But at the very first charge all our horse run away and left our foot, who behaved themselves very bravely as long as they were able to defend themselves, and then shifted for themselves. We have not lost many men, considering what a miserable rout we were in. All our cannon, baggage and ammunition are lost and very many arms. We must needs look upon this as the hand of our God, mightily against us for 'twas he only that made us fly. We had very much self-confidence, and I trust the Lord has only brought this upon us to make us look more to him, whom I am confident, when we are weakest, will show himself a glorious God over the enemies of his Truth. So this time nothing has been gained by us with multitudes, and I beseech the Lord give us faith to live by that, and then I doubt not but our broken bones shall prevail over the enemy's mighty strength.

Postscript – Sir, I lost ten horses, and two men in the fight last week and this last time I have lost five or six more so that my troop is now very weak.

Sir Arthur Heselrige is hurt in three places, but not mortal. My brother Robert humbly begs your blessing. I thank God we are both well, having the mercies of our God very great to us in preserving us safe. I beseech you pardon this scribbling for I have not been in a bed these twelve nights before.

7

London's Brave Boys

Elation swept through Cavalier Oxford, as the bells of victory rang out joyfully in the summer of 1643. Waller was beaten at Roundway Down and the Fairfaxes at Adwalton Moor within days of each other. On 26 July Prince Rupert stormed and took Bristol. Except for some strongholds the entire West and North lay in Royalist hands. Essex's army, the shield of London, was slowly rotting away through inaction, disease and desertion. Hampden was slain at Chalgrove Field. In these dire straits Pym and his supporters turned for aid to the Scots. But the price of Scottish help was an undertaking to replace episcopacy with the presbyterian system: it was the Bishops War in reverse. Although Sir Henry Vane fudged the wording as best he could, such an attempt was fundamentally divisive. For the Puritans were far from agreed about the merits of presbyteries. Like John Milton, many of them believed that 'new presbyter is but old priest writ large'. Some of these English Puritans preferred some form of loose bonding of independent congregations in the national church; hence their name Independents. This was more or less the system established in New England. Others pressed for a separation of Church and State, with religious toleration for all Protestants. Faced with this potential disunity Parliament's leaders played for time. They appointed an assembly of Puritan divines to meet with some of their own number in Westminster in order to thrash out the whole question of church doctrine and government. The Westminster Assembly proceeded to do so in a series of gratifyingly long debates. Meanwhile Pym, already suffering from cancer of the bowel which would kill him in December, applied himself to saving the military situation.

King Charles made that daunting task rather easier for him by failing to follow up his triumph at Bristol. Instead of marching with all speed on London, he divided his army: one part would besiege Exeter, while he led the other part towards Gloucester, the one remaining Parliamentarian stronghold in the Severn Valley. Gloucester was governed by Colonel Edward Massey, a young professional soldier who had served as Lieutenant-Colonel of the Earl of Stamford's bluecoats and then inherited command of them. Together with another regiment of foot raised within the city, and some dragoons and horse, these soldiers formed a garrison of about fifteen hundred men. On 10 August 1643 two messengers from the city rejected the King's summons to surrender. The King received their reply with his customary imperturbability, confidently telling them 'Waller is extinct and Essex cannot come'.

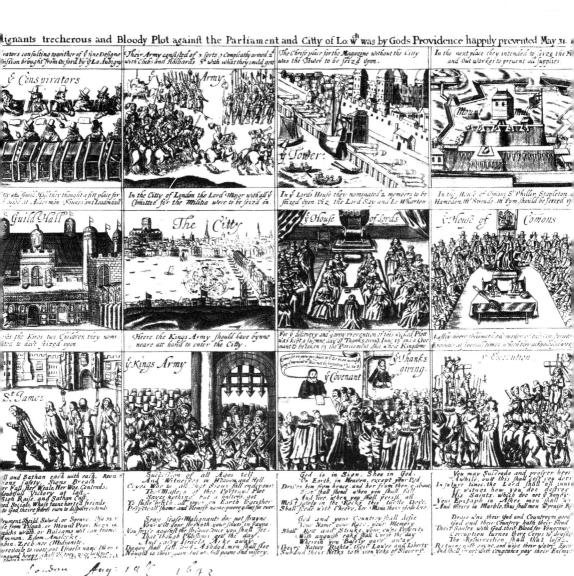

A Parliamentarian strip-cartoon account of the Royalist plot to seize power in London in 1643, which was successfully foiled. Edmund Waller, the celebrated poet, was a principal conspirator, and narrowly avoided execution during the aftermath.

Within hours the Royalist skirmishers advanced into the suburbs, which soon blazed with fires. Next day a crackle of musket fire came from the besiegers' mushrooming earthworks. For King Charles had decided upon a siege in order to save the lives of his infantry rather than to storm the place. Colonel Massey countered with frequent sallies to harass the enemy and to retard their siege works. When the large Royalist battery in a square redoubt on the south side smashed a breach in the old city wall, Massey's men promptly blocked it with wool-packs and cannon baskets. A few sixty-pounder mortar-bombs with sizzling fuses fell into the streets, but most of them flew harmlessly over the city. Thanks to Massey's powers of leadership and his active policy of attack as the best form of defence, morale among the soldiers remained high. His Puritan chaplain, John Corbet, observed that the civilians also remained cheerful as the siege became more intense. Having told the story of the various sorties Corbet continues:

Certainly the care of a higher Providence preserved and brought off those many several parties, when the vanquishing of any one of them must needs run the city upon extreme hazard; for our whole strength remained upon the works day and night except the reserve of a hundred and twenty men at the main guard. One rare and slender rank were to receive the storm without seconds, yet the safety of the whole did require those frequent sallies, a desperate remedy to a despairing city, not only to cast back the enemy's preparations but to amaze them, that the soldiers should be held up in such height of resolution and cause them to expect more hot service from within the works. Our men likewise were to be kept in the heat of action to prevent the fainting of the spirits; their hands also imbrued in blood did the more enrage them. Nor by safer means could they overcome the terror which by the reputation of the King's army might possess their minds. The enemy were kept waking by continual alarms to waste and weary them. And it was the care of the Governor to cause a perpetual noise, that whensoever their cannon had been silent for a while, one or two of our guns gave fire to disturb the calm and signify to the country that we were yet alive. For the besiegers ever and anon scattered reports of the taking of the town with a purpose to prevent our relief. All things within did presage a deliverance.

The sadness of the times did not cloud the countenance of the people. They beheld their fortunes with a clear brow, and were deliberate and cheerful in the endeavours of safety. No great complainings were heard in our streets; no discontent seized on the soldiers, at other times prone to mutiny; men of suspected fidelity did not fail in action; every valuable person was active in his own place. The usual outcries of women were not then heard, the weakness of whose sex was not overcome by the terrible engines of war. And our becalmed spirits did implore divine assistance without confusion. The Governor personally performed, ready at every turning of affairs, and gracing the business with speech and gesture. Upon the least intimation of diffidence he pretended rational hopes of success, adding withal that our late yielding could not mollify the King's army; and if in the close we must needs be lost, no surer means of safety than by the utmost gallantry to constrain honourable conditions.

The enemy still prepared for a general storm, meanwhile seeking to waste our magazine, which they knew must needs suddenly fail, expended their own store, and daily acted to the terror of the inhabitants; shooting grenades, fire-balls, and great stones out of their mortar-pieces, and had now planted a battery on the southside westward, unto which the lower part of the town was open. Thence in one night they shot above twenty fiery melting hot iron bullets, some eighteen pound weight, others two-and-twenty pound weight, which were seen to fly through the air like the shooting of a star. They passed through stables, and ricks of hay, where the fire by the swiftness of the motion did not catch, and falling on the tops of houses, presently melted the leads, and sunk through; but all the skill and industry of the enemy could not set one house on fire.

They still played their great shot against the walls, and wrought hard in filling up the moat with faggots and earth at the place where they battered, where also they built a gallery over the head of the trench, the breadth of four abreast; in the shelter whereof they had almost worked themselves over the moat. Then we found that they had sunk a mine under the east gate; whereupon the governor commanded a counter-mine in two places, but finding the springs, left off, conceiving for the same reason the endeavour of the enemy to no purpose. To discover or interrupt this work, a sergeant with five daring men were put forth at a port hole in the dungeon at the east gate, came close to the mouth of their mine, took off the board that covered it, and for a while viewed the miners. One of these cast in a hand-grenade amongst them, whilst the four musketeers played upon them as they ran forth, and with the noise of our men from the walls gave the whole league a strong alarm, and crept in at the port-hole without harm. Wherefore discovering that the enemy notwithstanding the springs, went on with their mine, we renewed our countermine; for they had sunk a great depth under the moat, and extremely toiled in drawing up the spring water, till at length they had gotten under the gate that our miners could hear them work under them and did expect to spoil them by pouring in water or stealing out their powder. . . .

As the soldiers within were heated with their own performance, so the enemy without being wasted in a lingering design before the hour of service came, grew feeble in their own thoughts and to us contemptible. Our common soldiers took to themselves a liberty to revile, prevented and confounded the enemy with the self-same language in which they were wont to abuse and scorn our party; which contumely, though it begets a more deadly hatred and desire of revenge in generous minds, at that time did deject exceedingly and debase the spirits of their private soldiers, who had never performed one gallant achievement and to whom the sturdiness of our men was well known. The slowness of their design in that form of a leaguer, proceeded from the desire of saving their foot, with this presumption, that there was no power to raise the siege; which confidence deceived them, till too late; for their foot after those many knocks, and the first fury spent, were not so capable of the service, without the help of many tedious preparations. Wherefore besides their mine and battery, they framed great store of those unperfect and troublesome engines to assault the lower parts of the city. Those engines ran upon wheels, with planks musket proof placed on the axle-tree, with holes for musketshot and a bridge before it, the end whereof (the wheels falling into the ditch) was to rest upon our breast works.

While the Royalists experimented with these siege-engines, suggested by Roman models in antiquity, a Parliamentarian army was drawing ever closer to them. In order that the Earl of Essex might march westwards on this service London provided him with five regiments of trained bands and the City's regiment of horse in their redcoats. Sergeant Henry Foster, who served in the Red regiment, wrote an account of their marchings which was printed that autumn. They set out on Wednesday evening, 25 August, and reached Brentford at one o'clock next morning, 'from whence the next day many of our citizens, who seemed very forward and willing at the first to march with us, yet upon some pretences and fair excuses returned home again, hiring others to go in their room'.

Apart from the usual fatal accidents with muskets, cold nights spent on guard, false alarms, and some skirmishes with Prince Rupert's Cavaliers, the march to Gloucester was uneventful. On Prestbury Hill they caught sight of Gloucester, and Essex ordered four or five great guns to be fired. Having marched for the last six days with very little provision the Red regiment huddled in their wet coats, hungry and thirsty, for a long night on the brow of the hill, 'it being a most terrible tempestuous night of wind and rain, as ever men lay out in, we having neither hedge nor tree for shelter'. Many of the waggons and carriages which ventured down the hill in the dark were overthrown and broken, killing six or seven horses. Next morning, 5 September, the Londoners, wet through to the skin, descended the hill but could get little or no refreshment as every house was full of soldiers. Here they heard that the enemy had raised their siege of Gloucester the previous day.

In the Royalist newspaper *Mercurius Aulicus* on 9 September the editor could report that 'many letters were this week intercepted from London, most of which are persuasory epistles from the train-band wives, labouring to recall their militant husbands who (like true Londoners) are following their leader, the Earl of Essex. Take one for all, superscribed "To her dear husband Master John Owen under Lieutenant-Colonel West in the Blue regiment"; the contents to a syllable are as follows:

'Most tender and dear heart, my kind affection remembered unto you. I am like never to see you more I fear, and if you ask the reason why, the reason is this, either I am afraid the Cavaliers will kill you or death will deprive you of me, being full of grief for you, which I fear will cost me my life. I do much grieve that you be so hard-hearted to me. Why could not you come home with Master Murphy on Saturday? Could not you venture as well as he? But you did it on purpose to show your hatred to me. There is none of our neighbours with you that has a wife but Master Fletcher and Master Norwood and yourself. Everybody can come but you. I have sent one to Oxford to get a pass for you to come home, but when you come you must use your wits. I am afraid if you do not come home, I shall much dishonour God more than you can honour him. Therefore if I do miscarry, you shall answer for it. Pity me for God's sake and come home. Will nothing prevail with you? My cousin Jane is now with me and prays for your speedy return. For God's sake come home. So with my prayer for you I rest your loving wife.

London September 5   Susan Owen'

BLACKWELL'S
BROAD STREET OXFORD OX1 3BQ
TEL. 01865 792792   FAX. 01865 794143
VAT REG NO. GB 532585539

DATE: 18/06/98 15:52 NO: 174863
CASHIER: Customer Service   TILL: 002

DESCRIPTION	QTY	PRICE	TOTAL
BY THE SWORD DIVIDED			
0750918586	1 @	10.99	10.99

TOTAL SALE	10.99

PAYMENT METHOD

CASH	20.00
CHANGE	9.01

TOTAL NO. OF ITEMS   1

Please retain your receipt as proof of
purchase will be required in the event
of any query.

BLACKWELL VOUCHERS
THE IDEAL GIFT FOR BOOK LOVERS

A nineteenth-century view, by C. W. Cope, of the scene in London as the trained bands set out to raise the siege of Gloucester in 1643. Many historians regard this success as the turning point of the Civil War.

Harried by Prince Rupert's horse and dragoons, Essex's army made but slow progress homebound towards London. The weather continued wet and cold; food and beer were once again in short supply. After leaving Hungerford, moreover, the Roundheads learned that the King's army had stolen a march upon them and occupied their next quarter, the town of Newbury. This forced march exhausted the Cavaliers. 'We were like to drop down every step we made with want of sleep,' wrote Captain John Gwyn, 'yet, notwithstandingly, we marched on still, until the evening we overtook the enemy's army at Newbury town's end; then our quarter-masters, with their party, beat their quarter-masters and their parties of horse out of the town.' Therefore Essex's whole army had to spend the night in the open fields, eating what little everyone had in his knapsack. During the night the Royalists took up a strong position on a hill to the south of Newbury, with their right flank protected by the river Kennet. Sergeant Henry Foster's men had little sleep.

The next morning, September 20, very early before day, we had drawn up all our army in their several regiments and marched away by break of day; and then advancing

A heroic portrait of the Earl of Essex as the victor at the first battle of Newbury.

towards the enemy with most cheerful and courageous spirits. The Lord Robartes'
soldiers had begun to skirmish with them before we came up to the enemy; which we
hearing, put us to a running march till we sweat again, hastening to their relief and
succour.

When we were come up into the field, our two regiments of the trained bands were
placed in open campania [level country] upon the right wing of the whole army. The
enemy had there planted eight pieces of ordnance, and stood in a great body of horse
and foot, we being placed right opposite against them and far less than twice musket
shot distance from them. They began their battery against us with their great guns,
above half an hour before we could get any of our guns up to us. Our gunners dealt very

ill with us, delaying to come up to us. Our noble Colonel Tucker fired one piece of ordnance against the enemy, and aiming to give fire the second time was shot in the head with a cannon bullet from the enemy. The Blue regiment of the trained bands stood upon our right wing, and behaved themselves most gallantly. Two regiments of the King's horse which stood upon their right flank afar off, came fiercely upon them and charged them two or three times, but were beat back with their musketeers, who gave them a most desperate charge and made them fly.

This day our whole army wore green boughs in their hats to distinguish us from our enemies; which they perceiving one regiment of their horse had got green boughs and rid up to our regiments crying, 'Friends! friends!' but we let fly at them and made many of them and their horses tumble, making them fly with a vengeance. The enemy's cannon did play most against the Red regiment of trained bands; they did some execution amongst us at the first, and were somewhat dreadful when men's bowels and brains flew in our faces. But blessed be God that gave us courage, so that we kept our ground and after a while feared them not. Our ordnance did very good execution upon them, for we stood at so near a distance upon a plain field that we could not lightly miss one another. We were not much above half our regiments in this place; for we had sixty files of musketeers drawn off for the forlorn hope, who were engaged against the enemy in the field upon our left flank.

Where most of the regiments of the army were in fight they had some small shelter of the hedges and banks, yet had a very hot fight with the enemy and did good execution, and stood to it as bravely as ever men did. When our two regiments of the trained bands had thus played against the enemy for the space of three hours, or thereabouts, our Red regiment joined to the Blue which stood a little distance from us upon our left flank, where we gained the advantage of a little hill, which we maintained against the enemy half an hour. Two regiments of the enemy's foot fought against us all this while to gain the hill, but could not. Then two regiments of the enemy's horse, which stood upon our right flank, came fiercely upon us and so surrounded us that we were forced to charge upon them in the front and rear, and both flanks, which was performed by us with a great deal of courage and undauntedness of spirit, insomuch that we made a great slaughter among them and forced them to retreat. But presently the two regiments of the enemy's foot in this time gained the hill, and came upon us before we could well recover ourselves, that we were glad to retreat a little way into the field, till we had rallied up our men and put them into their former posture, and then came on again.

If I should speak any thing in the praise and high commendations of these two regiments of the trained bands, I should rather obscure and darken the glory of that courage and valour God gave unto them this day. They stood like so many stakes against the shot of the cannon, quitting themselves like men of undaunted spirits, even our enemies themselves being judges. It might be expected that something should be spoken of the noble and valiant service performed by the rest of the regiments of the army both horse and foot; but their courage and valour itself speaks, which was performed by them that day, our men fighting like lions in every place, the great slaughter made amongst the enemies testifies.

My noble and valiant Captain George Massie, who was with the forlorn hope, received a shot in the back from the enemy, of which wound he is since dead. This 20 September we lost about sixty or seventy men in our Red regiment of the trained bands, besides wounded men, we having the hottest charge from the enemy's cannon of any regiment in the army. Also that worthy and valiant gentleman Captain Hunt was slain in this battle, whose death is much lamented. These two poor regiments were the very objects of the enemy's battery that day and they have since made their boast of it. It is conjectured by most, that the enemy lost four for one. Seventy chief commanders were slain on their side. This is most certain, that they did acknowledge themselves to be beaten. It is credibly informed by those that were this day in the King's army, that the King himself brought up a regiment of foot and another of horse into the field, and gave fire to two pieces of ordnance, riding up and down all that day in a soldier's grey coat.

The next day I viewed the dead bodies. There lay about one hundred stripped naked in that field where our two regiments stood in battalia. This night the enemy conveyed away about thirty cart loads of maimed and dead men, as the town-people credibly reported to us, and I think they might have carried away twenty cart loads more of their dead men the next morning. They buried thirty in one pit. Fourteen lay dead in one ditch. This battle continued long. It begun about six o'clock in the morning and continued till past twelve o'clock at night. In the night the enemy retreated to the town of Newbury and drew away all their ordnance. We were in great distress for water or any accommodation to refresh our poor soldiers, yet the Lord himself sustained us that we did not faint under it. We were right glad to drink in the same water where our horses did drink, wandering up and down to seek for it. Our word this day was 'Religion', their's was 'Queen Mary' in the field.

Most of the casualties in the Red regiment which was 'bang'd at Newbury' came from the cannon fire of eight guns in the main Royalist battery. Captain Gwyn saw the effects of that fire at close range: '. . . a wing of Essex's horse moving gently towards us, made leave our execution upon the enemy and retreat gently into the next field, where were several gaps to get to it but not direct in my way; yet, with the colours in my hand, I jumped over hedge and ditch, or I had died by multitude of hands. We kept this field until midnight and until some intelligence came that Essex was marching away with a great part of his army, and that he had buried a great many of his great guns by two of the clock in the afternoon. Near unto this field, upon the heath, lay a whole file of men, six deep, with their heads all struck off with one cannon shot of ours. We pursued Essex in his retreat, took Reading without opposition, made it a garrison and Sir Jacob Astley governor.'

The principal casualties on the Royalist side were the Earl of Carnarvon, the Earl of Sunderland and Viscount Falkland, the King's principal Secretary of State. Clarendon records that Falkland had grown weary of the war and exposed himself to needless danger at the siege of Gloucester to get himself shot dead. At Newbury he fought as a volunteer in Sir John Byron's regiment, having 'in the morning of the battle called for a clean shirt, saying that if he were slain they should not find his body in foul linen. Some of his friends they dissuaded him from venturing himself as having no call to it, being no military officer. But he replied that he was weary of the times, and foresaw much misery to his own country, and did believe he should be out of it before night'. In the thick of the fighting he spurred his horse forwards into a gap in a hedge and fell dead in a storm of bullets.

The celebrated gossip John Aubrey offers a different version of Falkland's motives for throwing away his life at Newbury. He says that Falkland was overcome by remorse for advising King Charles to besiege Gloucester, which so weakened the army that it proved to be the turning point of the war. Grief for the 'death of Mrs Moray, who was his mistress, and whom he loved above all creation', also spurred him forwards. His corpse was stripped, trod upon and mangled, but was recognised by a mole on the neck. Aubrey adds that Falkland was a little man of no great strength of body, with black eyes and black hair rather 'flaggy'.

After burying their dead the Parliamentarian army next day resumed their march to London. The Cavaliers fell upon their rear in a narrow lane about a mile from Aldermaston. The Roundhead rearguard of horse panicked and fled, galloping wildly into the lane, routing their own foot and trampling many down, crying out 'Away! Away! Every man shift for his life! You are all dead men!' As Foster recalled, this 'caused a most strange confusion amongst us. We fired ten or twelve drakes at the enemy, but they came upon us very fiercely, having their foot on the other side of the hedges. Many of our waggons were overthrown and broken. Others cut their traces and horse-harness, and run away with their horses, leaving their waggons and carriages behind them. Our foot fired upon the enemy's horse very bravely and slew many of them. Some report above one hundred and not ten of ours. Some that we took prisoners our men were so enraged at them that they knocked out their brains with the butt end of their muskets. In this great distraction and rout a waggon of powder lying in the way overthrown, some spark of fire or match fell among it, which did much hurt: seven men burnt and two kill'd. The enemy had got two of our drakes in the rear, had not our foot played the men and recovered them again. This was about four or five o'clock at night. Many of our men lost their horses and other things which they threw away in haste.'

After refreshing themselves for three days in Reading, where they celebrated a thanksgiving on Sunday, 24 September, the Londoners marched home to a heroes' welcome: 'The Lord Mayor together with the aldermen of the City met us at Temple-bar and entertained us joyfully, many thousands bidding us welcome home and blessing God for our safe return. Thus God that called us forth to do his work brought us through many straits, delivered us from the rage and insolency of our adversaries, made them turn their backs with shame, giving us victory, and causing us to return home joyfully.'

Not every citizen took to the streets to hail the return of London's 'brave boys'. Apart from those merchants and tradesmen who remained loyal to the King there were a number of Royalist gentlemen residing in the city. They seem to have been able to indulge in their customary style of living with little interruption. Such men as Sir Henry Blount, who fought with the Gentlemen Pensioners at Edgehill, were reluctant to remain far from the fleshpots of London. 'He was pretty wild when young, especially addicted to common wenches,' and advancing years did not diminish his desires. Probably at forty-two Blount felt past soldiering. He returned to London after Edgehill and resumed his former life, dining most commonly at Heycock's near the Palsgrave-Head tavern. According to Aubrey, who knew him well, Blount won a wager with a friend that the local whores would choose him if he balanced a twenty shilling piece on his bald head rather than his friend's handsome body offered for nothing. 'Drunkenness he much exclaimed against, but he allowed wenching,' added Aubrey. 'He was wont to say that he did not care to have his servants go to church for there servants infected one another to go to the alehouse and learn debauchery; but he bid them go to see the executions at Tyburn, which works more upon them than all the oratory in sermons.'

Sir Humphrey Mildmay was another Royalist who managed to live a jolly life in wartime London. His family history, incidentally, illustrates the social mobility that existed in England. For his great-grandfather was an Essex yeoman who apprenticed one son to a London mercer and left to another the 'one stall in which I used to stand every Wednesday' in Chelmsford market. Yet his youngest son rose to be Chancellor of the Exchequer under Queen Elizabeth. By then the family had acquired its full share of the confiscated monastic lands, the making of many Tudor fortunes. A Puritan by persuasion, this son Sir Walter Mildmay founded Emmanuel College in 1584. When the Queen taxed him with this Puritan foundation, Mildmay made a famous reply: 'I have set an acorn, which when it becomes an oak, God alone knows what will be the fruit of it.' What a harvest it proved to be! No other college produced more Puritan leaders on both sides of the Atlantic. But Sir Humphrey Mildmay, his eldest grandson, who studied at Emmanuel College with his four brothers, was not among its fruits. With regard to religion or personal morality he shared little in common with that Puritan grandfather whose manors at Danbury in Essex and Queen Camel in Somerset he had inherited.

Mildmay was fifty years old and married with fifteen children when war broke out. According to his diary, begun in 1633, he had tasted the pleasures of life in London to the full. Mildmay liked to spend much of his mornings 'abroad' from his house in Clerkenwell when the weather allowed. He shopped in Newgate Market with his wife or met friends in the Royal Exchange at Cornhill or bought books in Duck Lane. Often he ate dinner in a tavern with friends and spent the afternoon drinking wine. One Sunday evening at home, graced with 'much company', sees them all at night 'mad, merry and late also'.

The 2 of May. 1643. y Croſſe in Cheapeſide was pulled downe, a Troope of Horſe & 2 Companies of foote wayted to garde it & at y fall of y tope Croſſe droñes beat trū-pets blew & multitudes of Capes warre throwne in y Ayre, & a greate Shoute of People with ioy, y 2 of May the Almaṇa ke ſaeth, was y invention of the Croſſe, & 6 day at night was the Leaden Popes burnt, in the pla- ce where it ſtood with ringinge of Bells, & a greate Acclamation & no hurt done in all theſe actions.

10 of May the Boocke of Sportes vpon the Lords day was ba-rnt by the Hangman in the place where the Croſſe ſtood, & at Exhange

Puritan demonstrations in London in May 1643 included the pulling down of the old cross at Cheapside by cheering crowds.

His brothers, Sir Henry and Captain Anthony, both adherents of Parliament for self-seeking reasons, frequently accompanied him in drinking bouts. Mild-may continued to attend plays at such theatres as the Cockpit, the Globe and Blackfriars even when the London trained bands were on their march home from Gloucester.

Although his diary is eclipsed by that of Samuel Pepys, Mildmay reveals the same human foibles. He writes of his particular distaste for 'sour' and 'dirty' weather, in which people 'stir not out of doors', such as one November morning's 'frost, dry and hard, with a great mist for the thieves'. He chafed when he was kept 'at home in a sad day of rain all day'; such weather could make him feel melancholy. Hangovers sometimes caused these depressions:

Not well, having bibbed sack the night before.
I fooled and abused my health all day and came home drunk and sick to bed.
I am sick: God amend me each way.

Gloom did not usually persist very long, for he was a jolly, sociable man. Although he retired one night 'with sorrow my full at home', the morrow brought 'much mirth and good company' and the day's end 'bed in peace, I bless God'.

'To Mrs Mayne's to supper, where I laughed and kissed the wenches exceedingly.' Like Pepys after him, Sir Humphrey had an admiring eye for 'pretty' women of any social standing. One May afternoon he confesses to have spent 'a-playing the fool with two punks on the Thames till towards night'. His account book recorded payments for these illicit pleasures, such as sums to 'the wanton nurse at Mrs Langhorne's' and 'two bawds', to a 'she friend' or 'to wine etc., in a place of wantonness'. Whores received from ten shillings upwards, but Mrs Langhorne's nurse was evidently cheap as well as wanton – one shilling suffices for her. His wife Jane, Lady Mildmay, kept him company in London and ignored his amorous adventures, though he makes such occasional comments as 'My wife was sullen at night, without a cause' which suggest that she was not impervious to them. She remained at Danbury for much of that year, which is not surprising when we learn that it took a coach, two carts, six men, and fifteen horses besides the coach horses to move the family to and fro. When one of his men brings an 'angry letter' from her at Danbury, Sir Humphrey hastens to return a message 'to stop all faults'. A few days later she responds with 'two cold pies and a kind letter'.

Some of Mildmay's drinking companions were Royalist clergymen of the Church of England. He attended the services of that church habitually, often during 1643 in the chapels of Ely House and Lord Petre's house in Aldersgate Street. Christmas day, 1643, was pleasantly remembered: 'To Ely House to church. Dr [William] Fuller preached, and Dr Martin gave the blessed sacrament to me. I dined there and there remained until supper.' Mildmay also made a point of observing 'his Majesty's fast' on Fridays by eating fish. He is shocked when his sister Mary serves him 'a dinner of flesh, like a Puritan' on a Friday. Conversely he scorned the fast days appointed by Parliament: '(21 July, 1643, Friday) This day Mr Pym kept fast. I dined with Sir John at the "Cocks" and supped at home.'

He amused himself by inventing epithets for these rival days: 'The fast of Master Pym and the five good ones. The dog's fast. The damned fast.' His aversion to the Puritans crops up repeatedly; he refers to one of his beasts as 'the Puritan horse'.

In October 1643 he dined with one of his most constant companions, Sir John Curzon, a Royalist captured in 1642 while trying to execute the King's commission of array. He found Sir John 'much afflicted for the death of his son at Worcester'. But Curzon found a place for himself in Parliament's service shortly afterwards. Sir Humphrey's own son Nompee was also wounded while in battle the next year while serving as a cornet in the regiment of his Cavalier uncle, the Earl of Cleveland. Early in 1644, for reasons he did not explain, Sir Humphrey decided to leave London and visit his Somerset estates which lay in Royalist territory. By this time all the talk in London was about the campaign of Mildmay's kinsman Lord Hopton to the south of the capital. In Hampshire Hopton found himself opposed by his old friend and foe Sir William Waller.

Fresh brigades of London trained-bands marched out to take up the cause which Sergeant Henry Foster and his companions had upheld so valiantly at Newbury and all London waited to hear news of their fate.

The Citie Trained Bands, and the brave Sea-men with Barges and Long-boates adorn'd with streamers drums & trumpets, and furnisht with Ship-guns, & other Warrlike instruments, quard the Lords & Commons safely to Parl: by land & water.

The Countie of Buckingham cometh to London the very same day of the Lords & Comons so quarded, with their Petition to the Parl: Carrying the Protestation on their staves on horseback, and the Counties of Essex, Hertford, Barkshire, Surrey, & others, followed them, in like maner, shortly after.

More scenes of turbulence in London.

8

Hopton and Waller

On 29 September 1643 Lord Hopton of Stratton, for so he had become, had attended a meeting at Oriel College in Oxford and received the King's directions 'that being reasonably well recovered of his hurts' he should take the field again with a new army in order to secure Dorset, Wiltshire and Hampshire, 'and so point forward as far as he could go towards London'. By this move the King's council of war clearly planned to bring pressure to bear upon the capital from the south, while the main Cavalier army approached it from Oxford and joined forces with the Earl of Newcastle's army from the north. By hindsight it seems an over-optimistic strategy, but the reverses at Gloucester and Newbury had not robbed the Royalist generals of the military initiative.

To counter this new threat Parliament had secured the appointment of Sir William Waller as commander of the forces of the four associated counties of Kent, Sussex, Surrey and Hampshire. For Waller this commission was something of a consolation prize. Upon his return from 'my dismal defeat at Roundway Down' the more hawkish citizens of London and the 'vehement' party in the House of Commons had pressed for him to be made general of a new 'flying army' of twenty regiments, which would be independent from the Earl of Essex. The Lord General had truculently signed his commission but after the relief of Gloucester had renewed his flagging popularity, he promptly withdrew it. If Waller is to be believed, he did not entirely regret this turn of events. For the newly-hatched Independents were the chief patrons of this new army. In effect, as Waller perceived, they wanted their own new model army, officered by godly men chosen by themselves. Waller compromised on the latter point, but henceforth 'I trusted not them nor they me, and so we agreed'.

After Waller mustered his small army on 1 November at Farnham Castle he marched towards Basing House, believing it to 'be a slight piece and if I could carry it it would be a great encouragement to the soldiers'. For the most part his army consisted of regiments from his old Western brigade. The four associated counties were asked to provide their quotas of horse and foot, but few companies or troops were ready to take the field. A strong London brigade made up for this deficiency. But the Westminster Liberty regiment, also known as the Red regiment on account of its colours, the Green Auxiliaries and Yellow Auxiliaries had not seen active service. Hence Waller's desire to encourage these raw young soldiers with an early success.

Basing House proved to be a tough nut to crack. The Marquess of Winches-

Sir Ralph Hopton, portrayed by an unknown artist in about 1637.

Sir William Waller – a portrait painted in 1647 by an unknown artist. Waller was then a prisoner in Windsor Castle. Like many Puritans who sat for a portrait he is wearing his best black suit, which gave rise to the later and erroneous idea that Puritans habitually dressed in black.

ter, a wealthy Roman Catholic, fortified his house within compact star-shaped earthworks and garrisoned it with two regiments of foot and a troop or two of cavalry. Apart from this strength Waller had to contend with some appalling weather: bitter cold and driving rain which turned to sleet and snow. The London brigade slept at night in the open fields, 'a very cold night and very tedious to many of our men which were never accustomed to such a lodging', wrote Lieutenant Elias Archer of the Yellow Auxiliaries.

After a preliminary bombardment Waller sent forwards a forlorn hope of five hundred musketeers to seize the farm buildings adjacent to the north garden wall, which they did with some difficulty. The Royalists promptly counter-attacked and drove them out from the burning buildings. The London brigade watched the rout from Cowdrey Down. 'This and the coldness of the night with foul weather was great discouragement to the London regiments who were not used to this hardness,' wrote Waller. Two deputations of officers told him next morning that the men were clamouring to go home, and so Waller retired the army into Basingstoke for an unearned holiday.

Upon information received from two deserters, Waller decided to have 'another fling at Basing'. On Sunday afternoon, 12 November, he mounted a three-pronged attack from the south, east and west. He led one storming force in person, but the bomb which should have blown a hole in the curtain wall was misapplied. In Basing Park the Londoners fared no better, as Archer records:

While we were thus close under the walls, the women which were upon the leads of the house threw down stones and bricks, which hurt some of our men; in the meantime, the rest of our forces continued firing against other parts of the house, and performing such other service as it was possible for men to do in such a desperate attempt, till it was dark night that we could not see their loop-holes (although we were within pistol shot of the walls) then we were drawn off into several grounds and fields near adjoining, where we quartered that night.

I know something is expected should be spoken of the loss we there sustained, I conceive our loss of men in all the three days service against the house, to be about 250 or 300, at the most in which loss Sir William's own regiment, and the regiment of Westminster trained bands to bear the greatest shares; for upon Monday being the first onset, I am certain that in all we did not lose four men slain out-right, besides what were wounded. On Tuesday (being the second day's service) Sir William's Captain-Lieutenant by an unfortunate mistake in the way to the place where he was designed to go on, went with his party which he then commanded up a lane where the enemy had planted two drakes with case-shot, which being fired slew both him and many of his men, whose loss was very much lamented being a man of undauntable courage and resolution.

And on the Sabbath day being the third and last day's service against the house, the said regiment of trained bands being designed to set upon the south-west part of the house through the park (being upon a plain level ground before the wall, without any defence or shelter) whether the fault were in their chief leader, at that present either through want of courage or discretion I know not, but their front fired before it was possible they could do any execution, and for want of intervals to turn away speedily the second and third ranks, fired upon them, and so consequently the rear fired upon their own front, and slew and wounded many of their own men, which the enemy perceiving fired a drake or two among them which did them much injury, and was a lamentable spectacle. It was told me since by a captain in that regiment that they had seventy or eighty men slain and hurt in that disorder. . . .

It is possible that Robert Rodway was killed in this unfortunate accident. A lieutenant in Hopton's army seized a letter for his wife from the bag of Robert Lewington, the Hampshire carrier, and it was printed in *Mercurius Aulicus* with the editor's comment, 'I conceive 'tis worth noting that the City of London (being awed by a garrison of insolent rebels) can produce such women, who by honest means (kind commendation and loving epistles) would withdraw their husbands from actual rebellion. If some London ladies (the Lady Waller for one) would preach the like doctrine, many men, yea and women, had now been alive . . .' Upon the outside of the letter was written the address:

To my very loving husband Robert Rodway, a
trained soldier in the Red regiment under the
command of Captain Warrin, deliver this with
speed, I pray you.

Most dear and loving husband, my king love, remember unto you hoping that you are good health as I am at the writing hereof. My little Willie has been sick this fortnight. I pray you to come home if you can come safely. I do marvel that I cannot hear from you as well other neighbours do. I do desire to hear from you as soon as you can. I pray you to send me word when you do think you shall return. You do not consider I am a lone woman. I thought you would never leave me this long together. So I rest ever praying for your safe return.

> Your loving wife
> Susan Rodway, ever
> praying for you till
> death I depart

On Tuesday it was reported that Hopton was advancing on Basingstoke. 'When the regiments were drawn out,' wrote Waller, 'as I was riding about to give orders, I was saluted with a mutinous cry among the City regiments of "Home! Home!" so that I was forced to threaten to pistol any of them that should use that base language, and an enemy in the field so near. With this they were all very well acquietted.' After consulting his council of war Waller withdrew the army to Farnham Castle.

Some days later Waller experienced a much-needed boost to his morale. 'At Farnham, God appeared wonderfully for me, when Lord Hopton drew up his whole army within demiculverin shot of me, being (with the forces of Sir Jacob Astley who was then joined to him) at the least eight thousand horse and foot; and through the mistake or neglect of my Adjutant-General and the slackness of my men in drawing to the rendezvous, I was not able to face him with two thousand. In that extremity the Lord took opportunity to show himself for me, by sending a mist all morning, that by reason thereof the enemy durst not give on.'

With the onset of winter Hopton now dispersed his army to three Hampshire towns while a fourth party crossed into Sussex and occupied Arundel. Meanwhile Waller received reinforcements at Farnham, notably Sir Arthur Heselrige's regiment of foot under Lieutenant-Colonel John Birch, with its blue colours, and Sir William Springate's whitecoats from Kent. Before the London brigade marched home he decided to employ them in a full-scale attack on the nearest Royalists at Alton. He ordered the army to concentrate in Farnham Park on Tuesday, 12 December. Elias Archer describes the part played by the London brigade in this small masterpiece in beating up enemy quarters:

In the morning most of our forces were again drawn into the park, where our men were mustered, and we remained all day, expecting to be discharged and march homewards on the morrow. And about an hour and a half before night Sir William came into the park to us and at the head of every regiment of our London Brigade, he gave us many thanks for our service past, and told us that according to his promise and our expectation we were to be discharged and march homewards on the morrow, and said he would not detain us (if we were so bent homewards that we would stay no longer). But withall he told us that yet we could not return with much honour in respect of the bad success we had in our chiefest service, certifying us withall, that at the present there was an opportunity which might much avail the States and bring honour both to God and ourselves, if we would but lend him our assistance till the Monday following, engaging himself upon his honour and credit, that we should be no longer detained. Which we considering gave our full consent to stay, for which he gave us many thanks, in a very joyful expression advising us presently to prepare for the service because delays are dangerous.

Whereupon most of our men went presently into the town to refresh and prepare themselves for the service, where although they before gave their general consent many of them stayed behind and went not with their colours. Nevertheless we advanced without them and marched all that night, pretending at the first setting forth to go towards Basing. But having marched that way about two miles, we returned to the left, and (in a remote way between the wood and hills) marched beyond Alton, and about 9 o'clock on Wednesday morning December 13 came upon the west side of the town, where we had both the wind and hill to friend.

Then Sir William's own regiment of foot, Sir Arthur Heselrige's five companies and five companies of Kentishmen went on upon the north and north-west side and gave the first onset by lining of hedges and the like, but could not (as yet) come to any perfect execution, in respect that our London regiments were not come in sight of the enemy, and therefore they bent all their force against those three regiments and lined divers houses with musketeers. Especially one great brick house near the church was full, out of which windows they fired very fast, and might have done great prejudice to those men, but that when our train of artillery came towards the foot of the hill, they made certain shot which took place upon that house and so forced them to forsake it.

In the meantime our London regiments and four companies which belong to Farnham Castle came down the hill. Then the Red regiment and the greencoats, which greencoats are the four companies of Farnham Castle, set upon a half-moon and a breast-work, which the enemy had managed, and from whence they fired very hot and desperately till the Green Auxiliaries marched on the other side of a little river into the town with their colours flying and (being in the wind of the enemy) fired a little thatched house and so blinded them, that this regiment marched forwards and coming in part behind the works, fired upon them, so that they were forced to forsake the said half-moon and breast-works, which they had no sooner left but presently the green-coats, and part of the musketeers of the Red, and our Yellow regiment entered while the rest of our regiment marched into the town with their colours flying.

Now was the enemy constrained to betake himself and all his forces to the church, churchyard, and one great work on the north side of the church; all which they kept near upon two hours very stoutly and (having made scaffolds in the church to fire out at the windows) fired very thick from every place till divers soldiers of our regiment and the Red regiment, who were gotten into the town, fired very thick upon the south-east of the churchyard, and so forced them to forsake that part of the wall, leaving their muskets standing upright, the muzzles whereof appeared above the wall as if some of the men had still lain there in ambush and our men seeing nobody appear to use those muskets, concluded that the men were gone, and consulted among themselves to enter two or three files of musketeers promising Richard Guy, one of the Captain's sergeants (who was the first man that entered the church-yard) to follow him if he would lead them. Whereupon he advanced, and coming within the church-yard door, and seeing most of the Cavaliers firing at our men, from the south and west part of the church-yard, looked behind him for the men which promised to follow him and there was only one musketeer with him. Nevertheless he flourishing his sword, told them if they would come, the church-yard was our own.

Then Simon Hutchinson, one of Lieutenant-Colonel Willoughby's sergeants, forced the musketeers and brought them up himself. Immediately upon this, one of the sergeants of the Red regiment (whose name I know not and therefore cannot nominate him as his worth deserves) brought in another division of musketeers, who together with those which were there before, caused the enemy's forces to betake themselves towards the church for safeguard. But our men followed them so close with their halberts, swords, and musket-stocks that they drove them beyond the church door, and slew about ten or twelve of them, and forced the rest to a very distracted retreat, which when the others saw who were in the great work on the north side of the church-yard, they left the work and came thinking to help their fellows, and coming in a disorderly manner to the south-west corner of the church, with their pikes in the rear, (who furiously charged on, in as disorderly a manner as the rest led them) their front was forced back upon their own pikes, which hurt and wounded many of the men, and brake the pikes in pieces.

By this time the church-yard was full of our men, laying about them stoutly, with halberts, swords, and musket-stocks, while some threw hand-grenades in the church windows, others attempting to enter the church being led on by Major Shambrooke, (a man whose worth and valour envy cannot stain) who in the entrance received a shot in the thigh (whereof he is very ill). Nevertheless our men vigorously entered and slew Colonel Bowles, their chief commander at the present, who not long before swore, 'God damn his soul if he did not run his sword through the heart of him which first called for quarter'. He being slain, they generally yielded and desired quarter, except some desperate villains which refused quarter, who were slain in the church and some others of them wounded, who afterwards were granted quarter upon their request.

They being all subdued, all the prisoners which were taken about the church were all put into a great barn which joined to the church-yard, and after the church was cleared of our men, they were all put into the church, and the rest which were taken in several houses in the town were put to them, and there they were coupled together and brought to Farnham, the number of them being 875, among whom were about 50 commanders, besides horsemen which were taken in pursuit of the Lord Crawford, who ran away from the town as soon as we gave the first assault upon their works. What service our horse did I cannot punctually relate because I saw it not; but it seems they were not idle, for (I heard) they made our number of prisoners near 1100, many of those prisoners being men of considerable respect in the King's army.

One thing I had almost forgotten (which I know is expected) that is, to speak of the loss of men either side sustained in this service: our loss was not above eight or nine men at the most, besides what were wounded; and I conceive their loss of men to be about 50 or 60, most of which were slain in the church and church-yard after we had entered.

Being returned to Farnham, we rested and refreshed ourselves for that night and the next day. And on Friday December 15 there were propositions made for us to march towards Arundel which most of our men utterly disliked and refused, as conceiving the recovery of that Castle to be a thing not to be effected. Time enough for us to be upon our march homewards before Christmas, because of the great distance between Farnham and Arundel, and the service to be done when we came thither. And therefore desired Sir William to discharge us according to his promise at our setting out to Alton; which request he granted, only appointing us to conduct those of the prisoners to London which refused the Covenant (for between 500 and 600 of them, the same day took the Covenant) and arms to serve the King and Parliament under Sir William.

'Great was my exaltation,' wrote Waller when he recalled his famous victory at Alton. Hopton experienced a corresponding depression. 'This is the first evident ill success I have had,' he admitted in a letter to Waller from Winchester on 16 December. 'I must acknowledge that I have lost many brave and gallant men. . . . God give a sudden stop to this issue of English blood.'

Waller resolved next to re-capture Arundel without the help of the London regiments. On 19 December his army reached Arundel Park and slept the night under 'the best spread trees'. Next day three columns of foot marched along the broad back of a grassy down to storm the line of earthworks on the north side of Arundel Castle. Lieutenant-Colonel Birch's secretary, who was present that day, later wrote a fulsome memoir in which he reminded his Puritan master of God's several mercies during this action:

Thus marching on, the enemy letting fly very thick, you not liking your major's pace who was marching before you on the right hand, but indeed more softly than you used to do in such a shower, you commanded the captains where you were to come on speedily, and you ran up to the major's party then about forty paces short of the enemy's line. Where, they being almost at a stand, your example drew them on instantly to enter that line, unto which your self first entered, though it was intricate to get over that steep line; but one assisting another, instantly there was near 200 entered. In which instant of time, before the rest could enter, (and the great fishpond being between our army and the place where you entered, so that the enemy saw you could not quickly be relieved) out came they with about 100 gentlemen reformadoes on horseback besides foot and other troops of horse, and gave your disordered foot at that very instant of entry such a charge, that they laid many flat to the ground, as well as yourself.

The rest went back over the line with great speed; and I think I may say truly not one man stayed within the line, except those that were slain, wounded, or prisoners, but yourself; who leaning on the line with one hand, and your halbert in the other, the enemy's horse could not fall upon you but to their great loss, bestowing some few pistols on you. But God would not have you then hit; and indeed you had never escaped so, had it not been for those musketeers, who lying near you on the top of the line kept off the horse at present, and made some few to fall; so that they were forced to draw further off, and there stand. In which place neither could they indeed long continue; for the rest of the musketeers following the example of those by you, got on top of the line and from thence fired so hot on the enemy's horse that they were glad to withdraw.

Thus God gave you possession of the enemy's ground the second time: which effected, your great care was to make way for some honest captains of horse and their train, which voluntarily came up to your assistance. Which being done, immediately whilst you were putting those horse and foot in order, whose number were both about eighteen hundred, the enemy looked upon them contemptibly; and thereupon drew forth to fall on you near the town wall, where you were between the enemy's two lines. And their horse and foot doing their utmost, at this instant was that gallant Scot slain, who had vowed that day, afore he went on, that he would never flee further from you than the length of your halbert, saying he would stick to you whilst you lived but he would be near to the intent he might examine your pockets when you fell; which God called him unto first.

At this instant, the enemy spending their shot at too great a distance, your order was to horse and foot instantly to assault the enemy; yourself with cheerful speech assuring they would not stand, which proved accordingly. For the enemy feeling the force of the shot poured on them with three ranks at a time after short time gave ground, and yourself entered the town with them, scarce knowing friend from foe; the enemy as much as they could betaking themselves to the castle; into which place your command was to enter with them. At which instant Sir William Waller's Lieutenant-Colonel, who but then you encouraged by clapping your hand on his shoulder, your hand no sooner off but he was shot dead; and yourself not gone about twenty paces further received that wonder of God's mercy, the shot in your belly, which deliverance to you was so great that I cannot speak of it without admiration; and the more at the hand of God so assisting, that though you kept in your guts, stopping the hole with your finger, yet none knew it until you had slain or taken prisoners the enemy then about you and ordered your men to draw into a body on one side the street, where the shot had not such power. And then pretending you must turn to the wall, giving a captain by you private notice, you went towards the park house, as if no such shot had been until your spirits yielded and your self sunk, and were then carried to the lodgehouse aforesaid with life in you, but supposed by all to be past cure, this being about 9 in the morning; when you were laid with many others on the floor, grovelling, and to the chirurgeons not so much probability of life appeared as to bestow a dressing.

Thus you lay until about 6 at night; at which time being as you were in the morning, the chirurgeons thought to adventure a dressing, and to bestow so much pains as to carry you up unto a bed. Thus have I presented you with God's great work, much of it carried on by your hand that day, and the great mercy in your deliverance, which I hope will never be worn out of your mind. I beseech you, remember the 17th day of December 1643. That castle in a few days after being yielded, therein was found twelve hundred men, besides those that were slain, fled and taken prisoners at the entry of the town; which number I rather mention to make more plainly appear God's hand, that these should be driven into the castle by so small a number.

The castle of Arundel withstood a siege until early in January when famine within the walls compelled the Royalists to surrender on promise that their lives would be spared. Colonel Joseph Bamfield, the young military commander of the garrison, wrote: 'I never signed the capitulation and might have been denied benefit of the articles and quarter had General Waller been cruel. Of above nine hundred officers and soldiers, horse and foot, which I retain'd before the siege, few more than two hundred marched out, the rest being either killed or dead of the bloody flux and spotted fever, with the first whereof I was myself attached . . .'

Waller left Arundel in mid-January, entrusting the town to Colonel Herbert Morley and young Sir William Springate, who soon contracted the fever, probably typhus, which had ravaged Bamfield's soldiers. His wife Mary made the hazardous journey from London to be with him, although she was at that time pregnant with their future daughter Gulielma, who would marry the Quaker William Penn. Many years later, long after she had re-married, Lady Springate wrote down for her American Quaker grandson, named Springate, the story of Sir William's life, including her last visit to him:

When we came to Arundel we met with a most dismal sight: the town being depopulated, all the windows broken with the great guns, and the soldiers making stables of all the shops and lower rooms; and there being no light in the town but what came from the light in the stables, we passed through the town towards his quarters. Within a quarter of a mile of the house the horses were at a stand, and we could not understand the reason of it, so we sent our guide down to the house for a candle and

lantern, and to come to our assistance. Upon which the report came to my husband, who told them they were mistaken, he knew I could not come I was so near my time. But they affirming that it was so, he commanded them to sit him up in his bed, 'that I may see her', said he, 'when she comes'. But the wheel of the coach being pitched in the root of a tree was some time before I could come.

It was about twelve at night when we arrived, and as soon as I put my foot into the hall (there being a pair of stairs out of the hall into his chamber) I heard his voice, 'Why will you lie to me! If she be come, let me hear her voice', which struck me so that I had hardly power to get up the stairs. But being borne up by two, he seeing me, the fever having took his head, in a manner sprang up as if he would come out of his bed, saying, 'Let me embrace you before I die. I am going to your God and my God'.

I found most of his officers attending on him with great care and signification of sorrow for the condition he was in, they greatly loving him. The purple spots came out the day before and now were struck in, and the fever got into his head, upon which they caused him to keep his bed, having not been persuaded to go to bed no day since his illness till then, which had been five days. Before his spots came out, they seeing his dangerous condition (so many Kentish men, both commanders and others having died of it in a week's time near his quarters), constrained him to keep his chamber. But such was his activeness of spirit and stoutness of his heart that he could not yield to this ill that was upon him, but covenanted with them that he would shoot birds with his cross-bow out of the windows, which he did till the fever took his head and the spots went in. And after that the fever was so violent and he so young and strong of body, and his blood so hot (being but about the age of 23) that they were forced to sit round the bed to keep him in, but he spake no evil or raving words at all, but spoke seriously about his dying to my doctor, which I brought down with me by his orders.

For two days his devoted wife watched by his bedside, cooling his lips with her own, before he died. She then accompanied his body, borne on the Kentish regiment's ammunition waggon, to Ringmer in Sussex. 'When he was dead,' she wrote, 'then I could weep.'

When spring came Hopton and Waller resumed their campaigns with much strengthened armies. Apart from two fresh London regiments Waller also received a brigade of horse under Sir William Balfour from the Lord General's army. Hopton was joined by Patrick Ruthven, Earl of Forth, with two thousand men drawn from the garrisons of Oxford and Reading. By mid-March both generals could muster about ten thousand soldiers apiece.

Hopton and Waller faced each other briefly across a valley near East Meon and then raced towards Alresford. The 'Hoptonians' occupied the town that day, Wednesday, 27 March, while Waller's men encamped near Cheriton. Captain Robert Harley, who had inherited his brother's troop of horse in Waller's regiment, wrote him a letter describing the campaign. At East Meon he had watched from his saddle the raw London lads, who had never before left their smoky city, with a countryman's amused contempt: 'Here you should have seen the Londoners run to see what manner of things cows were. Some of them would say they had all of them horns and would do great mischief with them. Then comes one of the wisest of them crying "Speak softly!". To end the confusion of their opinions they piled up a council of war and agreed it was nothing but some kind of looking glass and so marched away.'

On Thursday, 28 March rival parties of horse skirmished together on the downs around a house and two barns full of corn which they both coveted. As darkness fell a column of Royalist foot secured this farm and marched forwards to secure the high ground of East Down which commanded the quarters of the London brigade in Lambourn meadows. Robert Harley had no sleep that night, as he commanded his regiment's outguards:

In the morning before day, I sent a party of horse to discover which way the enemy did lie. They found them all drawn together on the hill upon the right hand of us. Not long after the party was returned, but the trivall [a triangle] was beaten. The trumpets sounded to horse and an alarm was struck up throughout the whole army. To some it was a trusty awaking from a cold sleep; to others it stroke more terror than the earth had done cold before. In the morning when I went to view the army, I saw such a cheerfulness in every one's countenance that it promised either victory or a willingness rather to die than lose the field. Only the citizen's silver lace began to look like copper. There was on the right hand of us – as we were now faced – a wood which we did conceive might be of great advantage to us if it were maintained. For which purpose there was a party of a thousand musketeers. Colonel Potley's regiment and the Londoner's white regiment sent thither, and three hundred horse to second them.

On the left wing of us there was hedges and a little village. We sent a very strong party of musketeers to line those hedges, whereof one party were Londoners. The enemy made no long stand but fell upon our men that were in the wood, and likewise sent a party to fall on our men at the little village. The citizens in the wood – were in the wood but they found the way how to get out – no sooner they did see that the bullets would come otherwise than they would have them but they made a foul retreat – I am confident I smelt them – with a fair pair of heels, which did so discourage the rest, that they all left their charge with a shameful retreat. Our three hundred horse which were to second our foot as soon as the enemy offered to charge came away in the same confusion on the left hand. Also the Londoners lost their ground. Now the day began to look black on our side, and if God had not wonderfully showed himself, we had lost the field. Yet I thought I did see something that promised victory. All were still willing to go on, and the soldiers put the fault on their officers and the officers on the soldiers.

The enemy being now possessed of the wood, that we might not be outdared by their horse, we drew down all our horse into a heath which stood betwixt the two hills where they did fight but under favour of the enemy's ordinance, the hills being one from another not whole culver shot – which was well known to some of the enemy's horse which were dispersed by our shot. Here my lieutenant lost his horse and a part of his foot, but I hope he will recover speedily. Their cannon did very small execution amongst us, the enemy thinking all were his own if he could but possess himself of the village and those hedges we had lined. For that intent he sent down a party of fifteen hundred commanded men to possess themselves of those places. We likewise sent down twelve hundred commanded men to second our own men. These did hold their places very near a heath; then the enemy got ground and fired the village. It was no sooner on fire but the wind turned. Our men, seeing the advantage, set them to a disordered retreat. Our horse seeing it, sent a party of a hundred horse under the command of Captain Butler to charge them, and another under the command of Colonel Norton to second them. Captain Fleming commanded another party. They all of them performed their charges so well that through God's blessing they routed them all, slew about a hundred and fifty and took a hundred and twenty prisoners with divers commanders of quality. We received not much loss, only Captain Fleming hurt in the arm with a captain's leading staff. I do not hear of any other considerable loss or hurt.

Not till now did their horse come to charge. The fight betwixt the horse continued nearly four hours. Their horse being at length discouraged, doing no good with their desperate and bold charges, made a fair retreat to the top of the hill where their foot were. Colonel James Carr and Major Strahan had so plied their business on the left of our army that they forced the enemy to draw off their ordinance, and quickly engaged all the enemy's foot on them, but they seeing their horse to retreat would no longer abide the charge of our foot and dragoons, but made a speedy retreat to a hill a little beyond the place where we did fight. When we had possessed with our horse the hill which the enemy had, we were at a stand whether we should advance on the enemy. It was once by some ordered that we should return to our stations which we had before; and I believe we should not have pursued if Colonel Weyms had not showed himself very violent for it. To him next under God does belong much of our victory. Through his persuasions it was ordered we should again fall on them and give them a general charge. This delay of ours gave them leave to draw off all their cannon and most of their carriages, but no sooner was our cannon come up and played on them awhile but they prevented our charge in commanding everyone to shift for himself, and so they proved their horses to be better than ours. They never faced about as I can hear to this day.

Now when it was too late we followed them on the spur unto Winchester walls. We took divers carriages and store of ammunition. The enemy in his flight set Alresford on fire, and for their reward we coming into the town before they well knew of it, we gave none of them any quarter. Very many Irish men were slain here. Our whole body of horse halted three miles short of Winchester; our parties went to Winchester gates. The slaughter on either side was very small, especially on ours, considering how long we did fight. I believe in all we did not lose sixty men. The enemy, I am confident, had slain three hundred men besides horse. . . .

Among those killed at Cheriton were Lieutenant-General Lord John Stuart, a kinsman of King Charles, and Major-General Sir John Smith, who had rescued the royal standard at Edgehill.

Lord John Stuart (*left*) and his foppish younger brother Lord Bernard, portrayed by Van Dyck before the war. Lord John was killed at Cheriton in 1644, and his brother died a year later at Rowton Heath.

Although Waller could not follow up his greatest victory by marching swiftly into the West, as he so ardently desired to do, he had won for Parliament an invaluable breathing space. Seen in retrospect the battle of Cheriton on 29 March 1644 marks a turning point in the struggle between King and Parliament. As the secretary of the King's council of war, Sir Edward Walker, observed, it 'necessitated his Majesty to alter the scheme of his affairs and in the place of an offensive to make a defensive war'. The King had lost the initiative.

9

The Northern Struggle

In the North William Cavendish, Earl of Newcastle, and the Fairfaxes, Ferdinando Lord Fairfax and his son Sir Thomas, struggled for the mastery. Newcastle, bred on tales of chivalry, preferred to see the war in terms of a contest between gentlemen. Some Royalist generals challenged their rivals to settle matters by personal duel. This medieval faith in 'trial by battle' could be applied to armies. Newcastle once exhorted Lord Fairfax to follow 'the examples of our heroic ancestors, who used not to spend their time in scratching one another out of holes, but in pitched fields determined their doubts'. In reply Lord Fairfax sensibly declined to fight the civil war according to 'the rules of Amadis de Gaul or the Knight of the Sun'.

The Earl of Newcastle, a man of considerable wealth, could afford to be somewhat of a dilettante. An accomplished horseman and author of a famous book on the equestrian arts, he excelled also in the indoor courtly pastimes of dancing and fencing. Clarendon wrote that 'he was amorous in poetry and music'. He enjoyed the grandeur of life at Court. Sir Philip Warwick, after paying tribute to his generosity and loyalty, speaks of his 'steady and forward courage, for he had a tincture of a romantic spirit and had the misfortune to have somewhat of the poet in him'. Samuel Pepys, who sat through two of Newcastle's plays after the Restoration, dismissed them scornfully as 'so silly a play as in all my life I never saw' and 'the most silly thing that ever came on the stage'. Critics had even less to say – if that is possible – for Newcastle's poems.

At first Newcastle threw himself wholeheartedly into the romantic role of the King's General in the North. Clarendon noted that 'he liked the pomp and absolute authority of a general well and preserved the dignity of it to the full'. But the Earl did not relish the burdens of responsibility or the sheer fatigue of being a military commander in the field. He delegated, by default, the management of his army to a professional officer, Lieutenant-General James King, who received a barony as a reward. Newcastle would sometimes withdraw for two days at a time, leaving his commanders and staff officers clamouring for decisions at his door.

The Fairfaxes, who led the Parliamentarian opposition, were men of different mettle. Although Lord Fairfax gave a lead in the field, he relied heavily upon the military talents of his thirty-year-old son. Thomas had acquired his training in the military arts in the Low Countries. He married his commander Sir Horace Vere's daughter Anne in 1637. He was knighted for leading a company of Yorkshire dragoons against the Scots in the Bishops' War. With his father he emerged as a leader of the county's politically more moderate Parliamentarians. He personally presented a petition from them to the King on Heyworth Moor on 2 June 1642, thrusting his way through a crowd of Royalist supporters to do so. He even participated in an attempt to keep Yorkshire out of the war by means of a local treaty. Once the fighting began, however, Sir Thomas Fairfax proved to be a northern Waller in the vigour and imagination he brought to the war.

Newcastle's influence as a great northern magnate enabled him to raise a complete army in those parts with remarkable speed. Having secured the port of Newcastle as his base he moved southwards in November 1642 with eight thousand horse, foot and dragoons and occupied York. In order to assemble such numbers in so short a space of time Newcastle exposed himself to the charge of 'taking, as the proverb is here, tag-rag and bob-tail, men of all sorts and conditions, especially Papists'. The Puritan propagandists made much of this 'Papist army of the North', which caused Newcastle to jest, as he watched his soldiers at work on the trenches outside Hull, 'you see that we trust not in our good works'.

The presence of Papists in Newcastle's army disturbed the more Protestant-minded Northern Royalists much as their co-religionists with the King had made Lord Spencer so uneasy before Edgehill. Captain John Fenwick, who rallied to the Earl with a troop of horse, bearing upon his colour the slogan FOR THE KING AND THE PROTESTANT RELIGION, soon deserted to Fairfax because he could no longer stomach the Catholics in the Royalist ranks. Whatever their religion the Northern Cavaliers showed their rugged qualities in many a fierce fight and became a byword for their steadfast loyalty to the King.

The Royalists in York under the Earl of Cumberland were not idle while Newcastle was assembling his army. Sir Henry Slingsby, who commanded a regiment of the city's loyal trained bands, recounts an incident at this time which illustrates the futility of war: 'My Lord Cumberland once again sent out Sir Thomas Glenham to beat up Sir Thomas Fairfax's quarters at Wetherby, commanding out a party both of horse and dragoons. He comes close up to the town undiscry'd a little before sunrise, draws his horse up before the town through a back yard as they were direct'd by a countryman; this gave an alarm through the town. Sir Thomas Fairfax then drawing on his boots to go to his father at Tadcaster, he gets on horseback, draws out some pikes and so meets our gentlemen. Everyone had his shot at him, he only making out at theirs with his sword and then retires again under the guard of his pikes. At another part of the town of York, Lieutenant-Colonel Norton enters with his dragoons. Captain Atkinson encounters him on horseback, the other being a foot; they meet; Atkinson misses with his pistol, the other pulls him off his horse by the sword belt. Being both on the ground Atkinson's soldiers come, fells Norton into the ditch with the butt end of their muskets. Then comes Norton's soldiers and

beats down Atkinson and with blows at him broke his thigh bone, whereof he died. After this scuffle they retreat'd out of the town (a sore scuffle between two that had been neighbours and intimate friends). . . .'

On 13 December 1642 Slingsby received a commission from the Earl of Newcastle to raise a regiment of volunteers, and he experienced the difficulties common to commanders on both sides: 'I caused my drum to be beaten up in York and other places, and those that came to be listed I caus'd to be billet'd amongst my tenants, and when I had gotten them up to the number of 200, I had them mustered and afterwards receiv'd their pay of the treasurer with the rest of the regiments. No little trouble I had in raising of them both in keeping the men together that I had rais'd till they might be muster'd and have pay, as also in listing of them under several captains of my regiment. For they would be changing from one [regiment] to another, and some I should entertain (that is to get other conditions and eas'd of duty) would list themselves in my service. Then, being found out, taken from me imprison'd. . . .'

Considering the superiority of his forces, Newcastle's operations against the Fairfaxes, which began that December, are not really very creditable. He had to mount three separate attacks to expel the Parliamentarians from the West Riding of Yorkshire. The first thrust ended on 23 January 1643 when Sir Thomas Fairfax recaptured Leeds. Next month Newcastle had to march to the east coast in order to meet Queen Henrietta Maria, who was due to land with arms and money for her husband. Her ship and escort of Dutch frigates, closely pursued by Parliamentarian men o'war, eventually anchored in Bridlington Bay. Henrietta landed and walked to a house overlooking the harbour. Here she came under fire from the warships in the bay. She tells her adventures to Charles in a lively letter:

Bridlington, 25 February 1643

My dear Heart,

As soon as I landed here I sent Prodgers to you but, having learned today that he was taken by the enemy, I send again by this bearer to give you an account of my arrival. Thanks to God, for just as stormy as the sea was the first time I set sail, just so calamitous was it this time till I was fifteen hours sail from Newcastle, when the wind changed to the north-west, compelling us to make for Bridlington Bay. And after two hours waiting at sea your cavalry arrived and I landed instantly, and the next day the rest of the army came.

God, who took care of me at sea, was pleased to continue his protection by land. For that night four of the Parliament's ships arrived at Bridlington without our knowledge and in the morning, about four o'clock, the alarm was given that we should send down to the harbour to secure our ammunition. But about an hour after these four ships began so furious a cannonading that they made us get out of our beds and quit the village to them – at least us women, for the soldiers behaved very resolutely in protecting the ammunition.

Opposite William Cavendish, first Duke of Newcastle, probably painted in the early years of the Civil War, when the Earl (later the Marquess) was the King's principal commissioner in the North until his defeat at Marston Moor. One of the most accomplished and magnificent men of his time, he was a friend and patron of Van Dyck and a leading authority on the art of horsemanship, to which he devoted himself during his exile in Flanders.

I must now play the Captain Bessus, and speak a little of myself. One of these ships did me the favour to flank my house, which fronted the pier, and before I was out of bed the balls whistled over me; and you may imagine I did not like the music. Dressed as I could, I went on foot some distance from the village, and got shelter in a ditch, like those we have seen about Newmarket. But before I could reach it the balls sang merrily over our heads and a sergeant was killed twenty paces from me. Under this shelter we remained two hours, the bullets flying over us, and sometimes covering us with earth. At last the Dutch admiral sent to tell them that if they did not cease he would fire upon them as enemies. This was a little late, but the admiral excused himself because of a fog which he said was there. On this the Parliament ships went off, and if they had not done so then the ebbing tide would have left them in shoal water. As soon as they were retired I ventured back to my house, not choosing that they should have the vanity to say they had made me quit the village.

At noon I set out for the town of Bridlington, and all this day they unloaded our ammunition in face of the enemy. I am told, one of the captains of the Parliament ships had been beforehand to reconnoitre where my lodging was, and I assure you it was well marked, for they always shot upon it. I can say, with truth, that by land and sea I have been in some danger, but God has preserved me, and I confide in his goodness to you, in this confidence I should dare to go to the very cannon's mouth only that we should not tempt him. I must now go and eat a morsel, for I have taken nothing today but three eggs and slept very little. Adieu, my dear Heart. As soon as I have arrived in York I will send to ascertain how I can come and join you, but I beg you not to take any resolution till you have tidings from me.

Henrietta Maria

In the late spring Newcastle and Lord George Goring, his cavalry commander, launched the second attack on the Fairfaxes. After unsuccessfully attempting Leeds the Cavaliers captured Rotherham and Sheffield in quick succession, but on 20 May Sir Thomas took Wakefield and seized his magazine. *The Rider on the White Horse* was the title of one newsbook listing Sir Thomas Fairfax's exploits, and it captures the image of leadership he conveyed. His celebrated white charger served him well at the storming of Wakefield, as he recounts: 'After an hour's dispute, the foot forced open a barricade, where I enter'd with my own troop. Colonel Alured and Captain Bright followed with theirs. The street where we entered was full of their foot. We charged them through and routed them, leaving them to the foot that followed close behind us. And presently we were charged again with horse led on by General Goring, where after a hot encounter some were slain and the General himself was taken prisoner by Colonel Alured.

'I cannot but here acknowledge God's goodness to me this day. For, being advanced a good way, single before my men, having a colonel and lieutenant-colonel who had engaged themselves to be my prisoners only with me, and many of the enemy now betwixt me and my men, I lighted upon a regiment of

Queen Henrietta Maria (*above*) coming ashore at Bridlington Bay, while under fire from Parliamentarian warships – a Victorian recreation of the dramatic incident. *Below* Van Dyck's famous portrait of her.

foot standing in the market-place. Being thus compassed and thinking what to do, I spied a lane which, I thought, would lead me back to my men again. At the end of this lane there was a corps-de-guard of the enemy's with fifteen or sixteen soldiers, who were just then quitting of it with a sergeant leading them off whom we met. And, seeing their officers, they came up to us taking no notice of me and asked them what they would have them do, for that they could keep the work no longer, the Roundheads (as they called them) came so fast upon them.

'The gentlemen who had passed their words to me to be my true prisoners said nothing. And, looking one upon another, I thought it not fit now to own them as prisoners, much less to bid the rest to render themselves to me. But, being well-mounted and seeing a place in the works where men used to go-over, I rushed from them and made my horse leap over the work. And, by a good providence, got to my men again who, before I came, had by direction of Major-General Gifford brought up a piece of ordnance and placed it in the church-yard against that body of men that stood in the market place, who presently rendered themselves. All our men being got into the town, the streets were cleared and many prisoners taken. But the horse got off almost entire.'

On 4 June, the same day that Hopton and Hertford met at Chard to oppose Waller in the West, the Queen set out from York. She reached Oxford amid much rejoicing on 14 July. Charles met her on Edgehill, a propitious place to his mind for their longed-for reunion. She brought to him three thousand foot and thirty troops of horse and dragoons raised in the North and for the most part equipped with the arms she had purchased on the continent.

The third Royalist sortie towards the Parliamentarian heartland in Yorkshire – the Puritan cloth-making towns of the West Riding – fared better for Newcastle. On 22 June 1643 he took Howley Hall, half-way between Wakefield and Leeds. Its owner, Lord Savile, had steered an uncertain course between the two sides, supporting one and now the other. As a mediator between the two, which he aspired to be, his duplicity and self-interest soon robbed him of any credibility. Finding that Savile had connived at the garrisoning of his house by some Parliamentarians under one of his kinsmen, Newcastle promptly arrested him and sent him to Oxford to await trial.

On 30 June Newcastle at last encountered the Parliamentarian army in the open battle he had sought. The two sides met on Adwalton Moor just outside Bradford. The Royalist horse under Lord Goring occupied the best tactical ground on the field, 'so that no place was left to draw up my Lord's horse but amongst some old coal pits', wrote Sir Thomas Fairfax. A great ditch and high-hedged bank pierced with narrow passages divided the two armies. Amid the crash of cannonfire and billowing smoke the more numerous Roundhead musketeers fought their way forwards slowly from hedge to hedge. Then Colonel Skirton begged Newcastle to let him take one of their unemployed clumps of pikemen and launch one charge at the enemy. These 'stout and

Opposite Sir Thomas Fairfax, Parliament's leading soldier in the North.

valiant men', especially Newcastle's 'Lambs', so-called because of their undyed white woollen coats, carried all before them. Scenting victory Cavalier horse surged across the hedge and charged home. Fairfax blamed his reserve for failing to second him, but whatever the reason he had lost the day.

This important victory led to the fall of Bradford and Leeds and the eventual flight of the Fairfaxes to the safety of Hull. John Lister, then a sixteen-year-old apprentice, remembered the townsfolk trying to protect the steeple of their church during the brief siege of Bradford by hanging wool-packs on its sides. But the Royalists 'cut the cords with their spiteful shot and shouted full loudly when the packs fell down'. After sunset on Sunday, 2 July the guns opened fire again, 'and at the first shot they killed three men sitting on a bench, and all that night it was almost as light as day with so many guns firing continually'. The Fairfaxes, who had taken refuge in the town immediately after the battle, ordered their units to break out under cover of darkness and leave the townsfolk to capitulate. Lady Fairfax, who accompanied her husband on campaign, was captured between Bradford and Leeds, riding behind an officer named William Hill. Newcastle sent her home in some style in his coach-and-six, a gallant act for which Fairfax gives him little credit. Lister's Puritan master Mr Sharpe decided to accompany Fairfax's regiments in their flight. Once free of the town he made his way to Colne in Lancashire. Lister describes the mood in Bradford and his own escape:

But oh! what a night and morning was that in which Bradford was taken! What weeping, and wringing of hands! None expecting to live any longer than till the enemies came into the town, the Earl of Newcastle having charged his men to kill all, man, woman, and child, in the town, and to give them all Bradford quarter, for the brave Earl of Newport's sake. However, God so ordered it, that before the town was taken, the Earl gave a different order, that quarter should be given to all the townsmen. . . .

Some desperate fellows wounded several persons, that died of their wounds afterwards; but I think not more than half a score were slain; and that was a wonder, considering what hatred and rage they came with against us. But we were all beholden to God, who tied their hands and saved our lives.

My master being gone, I sought for my mother, and having found her, she and I and my sister walked in the street not knowing what to do or which way to take. And as we walked up the street, we met a young gentleman called David Clarkson [a Puritan minister] leading a horse. My mother asked him where he had been with that horse. Says he, 'I made an essay to go with my brother Sharp and the army, who broke through the enemy's leaguer. But the charge was so hot I came back again and now I know not what to do.' Then I answered, and said, 'Pray mother, give me leave to go with David, for I think I can lead him a safe way.' For being born in that town I knew all the by-ways about it.

David also desired her to let me go with him, so she begged a blessing on me and sent me away, not knowing where we could be safe. So away we went and I led him to a place called the Sill-bridge, where a foot company was standing. Yet I think they did not see us, so we ran on the right hand of them, and then waded over the water. And hearing a party of horse come down the lane towards the town, we laid us down in the side of the corn and they perceived us not. It being about day-break, we stayed here as long as we durst for being discovered, it beginning to be light. Well, we got up and went in the shade of the hedge, and then looking about us and hoping to be past the danger of the leaguer, we took to the high way, intending to go to a little town called Clayton.

And having waded over the water, we met with two men that were troopers and who had left their horses in the town and hoped to get away on foot. And now they and we walked together and hoped we had escaped all danger. And all on a sudden a man on horseback from towards the beacon had espied us and came riding towards us and we, like poor affrighted sheep, seeing him come fast towards us with a drawn sword in his hand, we foolishly kept together and thought to save ourselves by running. Had we scattered from one another, he had but got one of us. We all got into a field. He crossed the field and came to us, and as it pleased God, being running by the hedgeside, I espied a thick holly tree and thought perhaps I might hide myself in this tree and escape. So I crept into it, and pulled the boughs about me and presently I heard them cry out for quarter. He wounded one of them and took them all prisoners, and said, 'There were four of you. Where is the other?' But they knew not, for I being the last and least of them was not missed. So he never looked after me more. But I have often thought since how easily we might have knocked him down had we but had courage. But alas! we had none.

Having passed this day skulking in the hedges, when it was dark I betook myself to

Ferdinando, Lord Fairfax.

travelling towards Colne, the place to which I thought my good master was gone. And there I found him and glad we were to see each other. He enquired of me (because I stayed in Bradford longer than he did) what was done and what I knew I told him. And in the conclusion he asked me if I knew the way and durst go back again to Bradford and see if I could find my dame, and bring him word where she was, and how she did and what was done in the town. 'Yes Master,' said I, 'if you please to send me, I am ready and willing to go.' So in the morning he sent me away and to Bradford I came and found some few people left, but most of them scattered and fled away. I lodged in a cellar that night, but oh! what a change was made in the town in three days time! Nothing was left to eat or drink, or lodge upon, the streets being full of chaff and feathers and meal, the enemies having emptied all the town of what was worth carrying away, and were now sat down and encamped near Bowling-Hall, and there kept a fair and sold the things that would sell.

In the morning I crept out of the poor cellar where I lay and walked in the street to enquire after my dame. At last I heard that she and my mother were both well and gone the day before to Halifax. The women were gathering meal in the streets. For when the soldiers found anything that was better than meal they emptied the sacks and put that which was better into them. So that there was good store of meal thrown out both in the houses and streets.

With only Hull remaining in Parliamentarian hands in Yorkshire the King

Two interiors at Littlecote, Wiltshire, a largely Tudor manor house which has stood almost entirely unaltered since Civil War days. Its owner Colonel Alexander Popham sided with Parliament, and the arms and equipment of his soldiers can still be seen in the great hall. The guardroom (*above*) saw many of these soldiers as they awaited their turns of duty. *Left* The chapel, with its austere woodwork and a central pulpit in place of the altar, emphasising the importance of the sermon in Puritan worship. It is the only example of a Puritan chapel in a private house which has survived to this day.

now summoned Newcastle to march into the Eastern Association. Newcastle obeyed in so far as he invaded Lincolnshire and occupied Gainsborough, but by the end of August he was back in Yorkshire besieging Hull. It was an error of judgement on his part to put local interest before the Royalist grand strategy. With Waller defeated in the West, Essex gravely weakened by disease and desertion, and the Eastern Association defended by an incomplete army, a bold thrust in that direction might well have prevented the Lord General marching to the relief of Gloucester. Be that as it may, when Newcastle retraced his steps to Hull his good fortune came to an end. Not long afterwards his field army suffered defeat at Winceby (11 October) at the hands of the Eastern Association on the same day that his forces besieging Hull were beaten as well.

Having recruited his regiments as best he could, the war-weary Marquess of Newcastle, for so he had become, marched northwards in January 1644 to oppose the Scots army which had now crossed the border in support of Parliament. But General Lesley refused to meet him in pitched battle and compelled him to fall back. Poor Newcastle! His critics at Oxford pointed to this run of misfortunes, while hostile tongues spread rumours that he wanted nothing more than to lay down his command. Alarmed at this prospect Charles wrote to him in April saying that the North would be lost if he abandoned his charge: 'Remember all courage is not in fighting; constancy in a good cause being the chief, and the despising of slanderous tongues and pens being not the least ingredient.'

But the end of the war for Newcastle was drawing near. In that very month of April the armies of Fairfax and Lesley, together with the Earl of Manchester's Eastern Association's forces, closed in upon the Marquess at York. Prince Rupert came to the rescue and raised the siege of York with a brilliant march. Misunderstanding the King's orders, the Prince pursued the retreating enemy. Contrary to Newcastle's advice Rupert then fought the battle of Marston Moor. By nightfall on 2 July some four thousand men, including the flower of Newcastle's 'Lambs', lay dead on the field.

Among the slain was Colonel Charles Towneley, a Royalist from Lancashire. His wife Mary, hearing of his fate, came next day to seek his body. Wandering around the field she met a senior officer who listened to her plea with expressions of sympathy but asked her to leave the desolate scene before some soldier molested her. She agreed, and departed on horseback behind a Roundhead trooper of whom she asked the name of the officer. It was Oliver Cromwell. He himself had lost a son earlier that year, and during the battle the son of his brother-in-law, Colonel Valentine Walton, had fallen while riding as captain in his regiment. Cromwell wrote to his father:

Sir, God has taken away your eldest son by a cannon-shot. It brake his leg. We were necessitate to have it cut off, whereof he died.

Sir, you know my own trials in this way, but the Lord supported me with this, that the Lord took him into the happiness we all pant for and live for, never to know sin or sorrow anymore. He was a gallant young man, exceedingly gracious. God give you his comfort. Before his death he was so full of comfort that to Frank Russell and myself he could not express it, it was so great above his pain. This he said to us. Indeed, it was admirable.

A little while after he said one thing lay upon his spirit. I asked him what that was? He told me it was that God had not suffered him to be any more the executioner of his enemies. At his fall, his horse being killed with the bullet, and, as I am informed, three horses more, I am told he bid them open to the right and left that he might see the rogues run. Truly he was exceedingly beloved in the army of all that knew him . . .

Newcastle had taken command of a troop of gentlemen volunteers and fought at their head during the battle. Convinced now that the war was lost he resolved to ship for the continent. In vain Prince Rupert tried to persuade him to stay and try again, but Newcastle could not face the ridicule that such a defeat would bring upon his head. 'I will not endure the laughter of the court,' he declared. Newcastle made his way to the port of Scarborough where Sir Hugh Cholmley was the Royalist governor. In his memoirs Cholmley recalled a conversation with him while he lodged in his house for two days awaiting a ship: 'At his departure, he thanked me for my entertainment, and told me, "He had some fear I should have stayed him". He said, "He gave all for lost on the King's side, and wished my departure with him", which I supposed he conceived would be some countenance to his. My answer was, "I could wish his stay. That if he had committed an error, I knew my duty so well, I was not to call him to an account but obey, he being my general. That for my own part, though the place was in no defensible posture, I meant not to surrender till I heard from the King or was forced to it". And after the Marquis's departure, most of the gentlemen of the country which came thither with him, disliking the strength of the place, procured passes either to remain at home or go to Prince Rupert, then in Westmoreland. Which gave such discouragement to the foot soldiers as many of them ran away. And indeed I was at present in a very sad condition, for the town by situation was not tenable, the castle ruinous without habitation or provisions or ammunition considerable. . . .'

Newcastle eventually settled in Antwerp. His first wife had died in 1643 and he remarried in exile. Returning to England at the Restoration he devoted himself largely to recovering his estates and rebuilding his fortunes. In 1665 King Charles II created him Duke of Newcastle, a fitting reward for his loyalty to the House of Stuart.

Civil Strife in the Midlands

'The war is like a football play, where one side does give the other a kind of overthrow and strikes up another's heels, but presently they rise and give the other as great a blow again.' These words of *Mercurius Britannicus* in 1643 aptly describe the ebb and flow of skirmishes, sieges and marches in the Midlands throughout the war. Parliament sustained an early blow when Lord Brooke, newly appointed commander of the associated counties of Warwick, Stafford, Leicester and Derby, was shot dead through the head by a sniper at Lichfield.

A fortnight later the Royalists suffered an equally grievous loss in the person of Spencer Compton, Earl of Northampton. Having captured Lichfield, Sir John Gell and his fellow Parliamentary commanders resolved to line up with Sir William Brereton's forces from Cheshire and consolidate their hold on the northern Midlands. The Staffordshire Royalists promptly summoned Northampton to their aid, who, hurrying to their side, encountered Brereton and Gell on Hopton Heath, near Stafford. Despite ground made uneven by coal pits, the Cavaliers had the better of the day, but Northampton was unhorsed. Surrounded by his enemies he killed a colonel and several others with his sword. Someone struck off his helmet with the butt of a musket. Summoned to surrender, he retorted, 'I scorn to take quarter from such base rogues and rebels as you are', and was killed by a blow on the head with a halbert. Brereton and Gell refused to return the Earl's body for burial unless the Royalists would return their captured guns. His spirited son would make no such deal, and the Cavaliers long resented what they regarded as an uncivilised proposal. Indeed when young Northampton met Brereton in a narrow lane near London after the war he at once drew his sword and challenged him. Brereton refused to fight, but before he made his somewhat undignified retreat he received several vicious slashes on his head and shoulders.

Parliament's commanders in the Midlands were not remarkable as soldiers but they worked hard. Sir William Brereton in Cheshire, for example, earned some high praise from Clarendon for exercising his command 'with notable sobriety and indefatigable industry, virtues not so well practised in the King's quarters'. Sir John Gell was an equally industrious soldier, although, if Lucy Hutchinson can be believed on this score, much of his energy was misdirected. In some venomous words she dismisses him as an ungodly and cowardly man. Apart from plundering indiscriminately, she says, he pursued his personal grudge against Sir John Stanhope to absurd ends, while sparing no expense to keep his name in the weekly newspapers.

About this time Sir John Gell, a gentleman in Derbyshire, who had been Sheriff of the county at that time when the illegal tax of Ship Money was exacted, and so violent in the prosecution of it that he starv'd Sir John Stanhope's cattle in the pound and would not suffer any person to relive them there. . . . To prevent a punishment from the Parliament he very early put himself into their service, and after the King was gone out of these countries prevented the Cavalier gentry from seizing the town of Derby, and fortified it and raised a regiment of foot, who were good, stout fighting men, but the most licentious ungovernable wretches that belonged to the Parliament. He himself, no man knows for what reason he chose that side; for he had not understanding enough to judge the equity of the cause, nor no piety or holiness, being a foul adulterer all that time he serv'd the Parliament, and so unjust that without any remorse he suffer'd his men indifferently to plunder both honest men and Cavaliers; so revengeful that he pursued his malice to Sir John Stanhope upon the foremention'd account with such barbarism after his death that he, pretending to search for arms and plate, came into the church and defac'd his monument that cost £600, breaking off the nose and other parts of it, and digg'd up a garden of flowers, the only delight of his widow, upon the same pretence. And thus woo'd that widow, who was by all the world believ'd to be the most prudent and most affectionate of womankind, but deluded by his hypocrisies, consented to marry him, and found that was the utmost point to which he could carry his revenge, his future carriage making it apparent he sought her for nothing else but to destroy the glory of her husband and his house.

This man kept the diurnal [journal] makers in pension, so that whatever was done in any of the neighbouring counties against the enemy was ascrib'd to him. And he has indirectly purchas'd himself a name in story which he never merited, who was a very bad man, to sum up all in that word, yet an instrument of service to the Parliament in those parts. . . . Some that knew him well said he was not valiant, though his men once held him up among a stand of pikes while they obtain'd a glorious victory when the Earl of Northampton was slain. Certain it is he was never by his good will in a fight, but either by chance or necessity. . . . Mr Hutchinson, on the other side, that did well for virtue's sake and not for the vain glory of it, never would give anything to buy the flatteries of those scribblers, and when one of them had once, while he was in town, made mention of something done at Nottingham with falsehood, and given Gell the glory of an action wherein he was not concern'd, Mr Hutchinson rebuk'd him for it, whereupon the man begg'd his pardon, and told him he would write as much for him the next week. But Mr Hutchinson told him he scorn'd his mercenary pen, only warn'd not to dare to lie in any of his concernments. Whereupon the fellow was awed, and he had no more abuse of that kind.

In the East Midlands the Royalists of the region garrisoned Newark at the end of 1642 and it served as their stronghold and rallying point until they surrendered it on the King's orders at the end of the war. Newark possessed great strategic importance, bestriding the road between the Royalist North and the King at Oxford. Moreover, the Royalist fortress of Newark divided the Parliamentarian garrisons of Nottingham, Derby and Leicester from the Roundheads at Lincoln when that city passed into their hands. Lastly, it could serve as a *point d'appui* for the Northern Royalist army if it came to an invasion of the Eastern Association.

The Parliamentary commanders, who saw all these strategic advantages clearly, made three attempts to take Newark by siege or storm. The second siege ended in disaster when Prince Rupert swept into view and captured most of the besieging force. His exploit took place on 21 March 1644, a few days before the expected clash of Hopton's and Waller's armies in Hampshire, and it gave the Parliamentarian generals one of their worst moments in the war. 'Truly, I tremble to think how near we were to the very precipice of destruction,' wrote the Earl of Essex in relief when he heard of Waller's victory at Cheriton.

The Royalists used Newark as a base to harry the countryside and skirmish with the Roundheads. When it came to serious encounters in the field, however, they could not boast of unbroken success. Against their victories at Grantham and Ancaster Heath must be set their black days at Gainsborough and Winceby. As Nottingham lay only fifteen miles from Newark it was inevitable that Colonel John Hutchinson should receive some visits from some boisterous Cavalier neighbours. Lucy Hutchinson describes the events in Nottingham after their scouts brought word of a Royalist advance in January 1644.

Whereupon a strong alarm was given throughout the garrison, and a foot company sent down from the Castle to the works, and the horse were there set with them to dispute the enemy's entrance into the town. But the horse, perceiving the enemy's body to be a great one, retreated to the Castle, and the foot seeing them gone, and none of the townsmen come forth to their assistance, made also an orderly retreat back to the Castle, in which there was not a man lost nor wounded. The works being unperfect and quitted were easily enter'd, though the cannon that play'd upon them from the Castle took off wholly the second file of musketeers that enter'd the gates, and kill'd them. The first was led up by Lieutenant-Colonel Cartwright, who two days before had sent to the Governor for a protection to come in and lay down arms. The enemy being enter'd possessed themselves of St Peter's Church and certain houses near the Castle, from whence they shot into the Castle yard and wounded one man and killed another, which was all the hurt that was done our men that day.

The Governor was very angry with the horse for coming up so suddenly, and stirr'd them up to such a generous shame that they dismounted, and all took muskets to serve as foot, with which they did so very good service that they exceeding well regain'd their reputations. As soon as they had taken foot arms, the Governor sent out one of his own company with part of them, and they beat the Cavaliers out of the nearest lanes and houses which they had possessed, and so made a safe way for the rest to sally out and retreat, as there should be occasion. When this was done, which was about noon, the Governor sent out all the rest of the horse and foot to beat them out of the town, where Sir Charles Lucas, who was the chief commander of all the forces there, had prepar'd a letter to send up to the Governor to demand of him the Castle; or if he would not deliver it, that then he should send down the Mayor and Aldermen, threat'ning that if they came not immediately he would sack and burn the town.

There were at that time above a thousand Cavaliers in the town, and as many in a body without the town to have beaten off Derby and Leicester forces, if they should have made any attempt to come in to the assistance of their friends in Nottingham. On the other side of the Trent were all the forces Mr Hastings could bring out from his own garrison and Belvoir and Wiverton to face the bridges. All the Cavalier forces that were about the town were about 3,000. When Sir Charles Lucas had written his letter, he could find none that would undertake to carry it to the Castle, whereupon they took the Mayor's wife and with threats compell'd her to undertake it. But just as she went out of the house from them she heard an outcry among them that 'the Roundheads were sallying forth', whereupon she flung down their letter and ran away; and they ran as fast from four hundred soldiers who furiously came upon them out of the Castle and surpris'd them while they were sure the Castle would not have made so bold an attempt. But the Governor's men chased them from street to street till they had clear'd the town of them, who ran away confusedly.

The first that went out shot their pistols into the thatched houses to have fired them, but by the mercy of God neither that, nor other endeavours they shew'd to have fired the town as they were commanded, took effect. Between thirty and forty of them were kill'd in the streets, fourscore were taken prisoners, and abundance of arms were gather'd up, which the men flung away in haste as they ran. But they put some fire into a hay barn and hay mows and to all other combustible things they could discern in their haste, but by God's mercy the town notwithstanding was preserv'd from burning. Their horse faced the town in a valley where their reserve stood, while their foot marched away, till towards evening, and then they all drew off. Many of them died in their return, and were found dead in the woods and in the towns they passed through. Many of them discouraged with this service, ran away, and many of their horses were quite spoil'd: for two miles they left a great track of blood which froze as it fell upon the snow, for it was such bitter weather that the foot had waded almost to the middle in snow as they came in, and were so numbed with the cold when they came into the town that they were fain to be rubbed to get life in them, and in that condition were more eager of fires and warm meat to refresh them than of plunder, which sav'd many men's goods, and their security, that did not believe an enemy who had unhandsomely, to speak truth, suffer'd them to enter the town without any dispute, would have durst at such great odds to have set upon driving them out.

Indeed, no one can believe but those that saw that day what a strange ebb and flow of courage and cowardice there was in both parties that day. The Cavaliers marched in with such terror to the garrison, and such gallantry, that they startled not when one of their leading files fell before them all at once, but marched boldly over the dead bodies of their friends under the mouth of their enemy's cannon, and carried such valiant dreadfulness about them as made very courageous stout men recoil, and call up all their virtuous shame to bring them back. Our horse, who ran away frightened at the sight of their foes when they had breastworks before them, and the advantage of freshness to beat back assailants already vanquished with the sharpness of the cold and a killing march, within three or four hours, as men that thought nothing too great for them, return'd fiercely upon the same men after their refreshment, when they were enter'd into defensible houses.

If it were a romance, we should say after the success that the heroes did it out of excess of gallantry, that they might better signalize their valour upon a foe who was not vanquished to their hands by the inclemency of the season; but while we are relating wonders of Providence we must record this as such a one as is not to be conceived from a relation, in the admirable mercy that it brought forth. But to those who saw it and shar'd in it, it was a great instruction that even the best and highest courages are but the beams of the Almighty, and when he witholds his influence, the brave turn cowards, fear unnerves the most mighty, makes the most generous base, and great men to do those things they blush to think on. When God again inspires, the fearful and the feeble see no dangers, believe no difficulties, and carry on attempts whose very thoughts would at another time shiver their joints like agues. The events of this day humbled the pride of many of our stout men, and made them after more carefully seek God, as well to inspire as prosper their valour; and the Governor's handsome reproaches of their faults, with showing them the way to repair, retriev'd their straggling spirits, and animated them to very wonderful and commendable actions.

In Cheshire that same month the Parliamentarians won a notable victory at Nantwich, where Sir William Brereton – reinforced by Fairfax's Northern army – beat the Royalists under Sir John Byron. Further south, Parliament gave command of the forces of the West Midlands to Basil Fielding, the Earl of Denbigh. Later Cheshire, Derbyshire and Lancashire were placed under him as well. Denbigh's part in the civil war lacks glamour and has been largely ignored by historians, but he did a useful if unspectacular job in maintaining Parliament's cause in his province. Policing the local Royalists, together with opposing threats to the Midlands by the flying armies, kept him more than busy.

Much of Denbigh's region, especially the shires bordering Wales, were Royalist in sympathy. The inhabitants of three small villages in Shropshire, for example, provided the King with no less than twenty men, most of whom joined up in September 1642. A Myddleman called Richard Gough, who was a boy of eight in 1642 living in Myddle, could recall in later life those thirteen common soldiers who lost their lives for the King, and also some of the events of the civil war which stirred his village.

First, Thomas Formeston of Marton, a very hopeful young man, but at what place he was kill'd I cannot say.

Secondly, Nathaniel, the son of John Owen of Myddle, the father was hang'd before

GRAND
PLVTOES
Remonſtrance,
OR,
The Devill Horn-mad at *Roundheads* and *Brownifis*.

Wherein his Helliſh Maieſtie (by advice of his great
Counſell, *Eacus, Minos* & *Radamanthus*, with his beloved
Brethren, *Agdiſtis, Beliall, Incubus* & *Succubus*) is
pleaſed to declare,

1. *How far he differs from* Round-head, Rattle-head, *or* Prick-
eare. 2. *His Copulation with a* Holy Siſter. 3. *His decre
affeſtion to Romiſh Catholikes, and hate to Prote-
ſtants.* 4. *His Oration to the Rebells.*

Printed for the *Curriehhland*, in the yeere 1643.

Anti-popery feeling reached violent proportions in some of the Protestant tracts which poured
from the printing presses throughout the war.

the wars, and the son deserved it in the wars, for he was a Cataline to his own country.
His common practice was to come by night with a party of horse to some neighbour's
house and break open the doors, take what they pleased, and if the man of the house was
found, they carried him to prison, from whence he could not be released without a
ransom in money; that no man here about was safe from him in his bed; and many did
forsake their own houses. This Nat Owen was mortally wounded by some of his own
party in an alehouse quarrel near Bridgenorth, and was carried in a cart to Bridgenorth
to be healed, but in the meantime the Parliament party laid siege to Bridgenorth, and
the garrison soldiers within the town set the town on fire and fled into the Castle. In
which fire, this Owen, being unable to help himself, was burnt to death.

Thirdly, Richard Chaloner of Myddle, bastard son of Richard Chaloner, brother of
Allen Chaloner, blacksmith. This bastard was partly maintained by the parish, and
being a big lad, went to Shrewsbury, and was there listed, and went to Edgehill fight,
(which was October 23rd, 1642) and was never heard of afterwards in this country.

Fourthly, Reece Vaughan, he was brother to William Vaughan a weaver in Myddle,
and brother to Margaret the wife of Francis Cleaton. He was killed at Hopton Castle in
this county, where the garrison soldiers refusing fair quarter, when they might have had
it, were afterward cut in pieces when the Castle was taken by storm.

Fifthly, John Arthurs, a servant of my father's, who was kill'd at the same Castle.

Sixthly, Thomas Hayward, brother to Joseph Hayward the innkeeper then in Myddle was killed in the wars, but I cannot say where.

Seventhly, Thomas Taylor, son of Henry Taylor of Myddle, was killed, I think at Oswaldstry.

Eighthly and ninthly, William Preece of the cave, (who was commonly called Scogan of the Goblin hole) went for a soldier in the King's service and three of his sons (i.e.) Francis, Edward, and William, two of them viz. Francis and William were killed at High Ercall. The old man died in his bed, and Edward was hanged for stealing horses.

Tenthly and Eleventhly, Richard Jukes and Thomas Jukes, sons of Roger Jukes, sometime innkeeper in Myddle.

Twelfthly, John Benion, a taylor, who lived in Newton in the house where Andrew Paine lives.

Thirteenthly, an idle fellow, who was a tailor and went from place to place to work in this parish, but had no habitation. These four last named went for soldiers, when the King was at Shrewsbury, and were heard of no more, so that it was supposed that they all died in the wars. And if so many died out of these three towns, we may reasonably guess that many thousands died in England in that war.

There were but few that went out of this parish to serve the Parliament, and of them, there was none killed (as I know of) nor wounded except John Mould, son of Thomas Mould of Myddle wood. He was a pretty little fellow, and a stout adventurous soldier. He was shot through the leg with a musket bullet, which broke the master bone of his leg and slew his horse under him. His leg was healed but was very crooked as long as he lived.

There happened no considerable act of hostility in this parish during the time of the wars, save only one small skirmish, in Myddle, part of which I saw, while I was a schoolboy at Myddle, under Mr Richard Rodericke, who commanded us boys to come into the church, so that we could not see the whole action, but it was thus. There was one Cornet Collins, an Irishman, who was a garrison soldier for the King, at Shrawardine Castle. This Collins made his excursions very often into this parish, and took away cattle provision, and bedding, and what he pleased. On the day before this conflict, he had been at Myddle taking away bedding, and when Margaret, the wife of Allen Chaloner, the smith, had brought out and shewed him her best bed, he thinking it too coarse, cast it into the lake, before the door, and trod it under his horse feet. This Cornet, on the day that this contest happened, came to Myddle and seven soldiers with him, and his horse having cast a shoe, he alighted at Allen Chaloner's shop to have a new one put on.

There was one Richard Maning, a garrison soldier at Morton Corbett, for the Parliament. This Maning was brought up as a servant under Thomas Jukes, of Newton, with whom he lived many years, and finding that Nat Owen (of whom I spoke before) did trouble this neighborhood, he had a grudge against him, and came with seven more soldiers with him, hoping to find Owen at Myddle with his wife. This Maning and his companions came to Webscott, and so over Myddle Park, and came into Myddle at the gate by Mr Gittin's house at what time the Cornet's horse was a shoeing. The Cornet hearing the gate clap, looked by the end of the shop and saw the soldiers coming, and thereupon he and his men mounted their horses; and as the Cornet came at the end of the shop, a brisk young fellow shot him through the body with a carbine shot, and he fell down in the lake at Allen Chaloner's door. His men fled, two were taken, and as Maning was pursuing them in Myddle Wood field, which was then unenclosed, Maning having the best horse overtook them, while his partners were far behind, but one of the Cornet's men shot Maning's horse which fell down dead under him, and Maning had been taken prisoner had not some of his men came to rescue him. He took the saddle under his arm, and the bridle in his hand, and went the next way to Wem, which was then a garrison for the Parliament. The horse was killed on a bank near the further side of Myddle field, where the widow Mansell has now a piece enclosed. The Cornet was carried into Allen Chaloner's house, and laid on the floor; he desired to have a bed laid under him, but Margaret told him she had none but that which he saw yesterday; he prayed her to forgive him, and lay that under him, which she did.

Mr Rodericke was sent for to pray with him. I went with him, and saw the Cornet lying on the bed, and much blood running along the floor. In the night following, a troop of horse came from Shrawardine, and pressed a team in Myddle, and so took the Cornet to Shrawardine, where he died the next day.

Those two soldiers that were taken at Myddle were Irishmen, and when they came to Wem were both hang'd. For the Parliament had made an ordinance, that all native Irish, that were found in actual arms in England should be hang'd, upon which thirteen suffered. Which thing, when Prince Rupert heard, he vowed, that the next thirteen that he took should be so served; which happened not long after. For Prince Rupert in the summer after, viz. 1644, came with a great army this way, and made his rendezvous on Holloway Hills (as he had done once before, and his brother Prince Maurice at another time), and took his quarters all night at Cockshutt, and the next day he made his rendezvous at Ellesmeare. At which time, Mr Mitton, of Halston, was General of the Parliament forces in this county, and was a valiant and politic commander; and hearing the Prince made only his rendezvous at Ellesmeare and intended to go forward, the General hoping to find some stragglers in Ellesmeare, that stayed behind the army, came with a troop of horse through byways, but when he came to the gate that goes out of Oateley Park, he found that he was come too soon, for there was three or four troops of horse at Oateley Hall, which got between him and home; and therefore, when he and all his men were come through the gate they shot a horse dead up to the gate, to keep it from opening. But the others soon broke down two or three ranks of pales, and followed so close, that all the General's men before they came to Ellesmeare were taken, except the General, and one George Higley (a little fellow). At last, one that had a good horse overtook the General, and laid his hand on his shoulder, and said, 'You are my prisoner'. But Higley struck the other in the face with his sword, which caused him to fall, and so the General and Higley turned down the dark lane that goes towards Birch Hall and others went straight into the town. But the General and Higley escaped, and when they came to Welsh Frankton there they made a stay and one other of his men came to them. The General had lost his hat, and being furnished again, he went to Oswaldstry, a garrison for the Parliament.

The next day the Prince caused these prisoners to be brought before him, and ordered thirteen of them to be hang'd. They cast the dice on a drum head to see who should die, and amongst them there was one Phillip Litleton, who had been servant and keeper of the park to my old master, Robert Corbett of Stanwardine, Esq. This Phillip saw Sir Vincent Corbett, of Morton Corbett, ride by, and said to some that stood by, 'If Sir Vincent Corbett did know that I were here, he would save my life'. Upon this a charitable soldier rode after Sir Vincent and told him what one of the prisoners said. He came back immediately, and seeing Phillip, he alighted from his horse and fell on his knees before the Prince (who sat there on horseback to see the execution) and begg'd for the life of Phillip, which was readily granted on condition he would never bear arms against the King. Phillip promised and escaped, and afterwards no more Irish were hang'd.

II

In Cromwell Country

After the Edgehill campaign Captain Oliver Cromwell and his troop of horse quitted Essex's ranks to serve in their own country. Cromwell was a most active commander. In January 1643 he secured the town of Cambridge and arrested the Royalist Sheriff of Hertfordshire; in March he suppressed a potential Royalist plot to seize Lowestoft on the Suffolk coast; by the end of April he had raised the siege of Crowland in Lincolnshire; Royalists of Newark met defeat at Grantham at his hands in May; while in July he recaptured Stamford, took Burleigh House and relieved Gainsborough. Parliament recognised these sterling services by appointing him Governor of the Isle of Ely and second-in-command to the Earl of Manchester in the army of the Eastern Association, which was formed that summer.

By September Cromwell had raised ten troops in his regiment of horse, the famous Ironsides. Like other Puritan officers he favoured 'godly and honest men' as his officers and troopers. They were 'most of them freeholders and freeholders' sons', wrote Bulstrode Whitelocke, 'who upon a matter of conscience engaged in this quarrel'. If Cromwell could not find Puritan gentlemen as officers he was content to appoint men of the right calibre from the lower social orders for the reason he gave to the Suffolk Commissioners in a letter of 29 August: 'I beseech you be careful what captains of horse you choose, what men be mounted; a few honest men are better than numbers. Some time they must have for exercise. If you choose godly honest men to be captains of horse, honest men will follow them. . . . I had rather have a plain russet-coated captain that knows what he fights for, and loves what he knows, than that which you call a gentleman and is nothing else. I honour a gentleman that is so indeed.'

But if Cromwell rejoiced in his 'godly, precious men' there were many in the Parliamentarian army who were profoundly suspicious of such a method of selecting officers. An officer of dragoons in Manchester's army, a Presbyterian by persuasion, wrote irritably: 'When any New Englishman or some new upstart Independent did appear there must be a way made for them by cashiering others, some honest commander or other, and those silly people put in their command. If you look upon his own regiment of horse see what a swarm there is of those that call themselves the godly; some of them profess they have seen visions and had revelations.'

Cromwell probably regarded such religious experience as an advantage rather than a disqualification. Before the end of September he wrote with satisfaction: 'My troops increase. I have a lovely company. You would respect them, did you know them. They are no Anabaptists, but honest, sober Christians. They expect to be used as men.'

Cromwell's swift action at Lowestoft led to the capture of Thomas Knyvett, a Norfolk Royalist gentleman who was closely related by marriage to Sir Hugh Cholmley, the Royalist Governor of Scarborough. Knyvett happened to be in Lowestoft when the Royalists gathered there to seize the place, but he strenuously denied any involvement in the plot. A week later he wrote to his wife from his place of confinement in Cambridge:

Dear Heart,

'Tis no small comfort to me in the midst of my afflictions to hear of your welfare and to receive such divine cordials from a sincere heart. I humbly thank God I have my health very well yet. It has been our good fortune hitherto to light into the hands of gentlemen that have treated us very fair and with much courtesy. Monday night brought us hither, where there was great expectation of our coming and spectators stood to bid us welcome. That night there was a great alarm begun about eight o'clock, which lasted almost all night. The fear was of forces approaching from Oxford, but since we hear no further of it. God Almighty frame and temper the hearts of both sides to a peaceable way and send us a happy accommodation, before destruction and ruin rages too far in this Kingdom.

We are billeted in the 'Rose', the chiefest inn in the town, sixteen of us, where we have very good lodging and a very good ordinary at eighteen pence a meal. I know not how long we shall continue here. We hope well, because we heard the last night the Commissioners have some design to remove us to Jesus College. If we shall fall into this happiness, in so much misery we must acknowledge God's providence in disposing of us so well, where we shall, I hope, have better means to serve God, both in private and the public chapel.

If you write anything to Mrs Hampden [John Hampden's mother and Cromwell's aunt], I pray let it be only to use her interest to Colonel Cromwell that I may be fairly treated here 'til we shall be released. If we go to the College, there's some of us will study like pig-hogs. We are now in the midst of the school of Mars, nothing but drums and trumpets all the day long. We read our Lowestoft business in the diurnal with much joy, because all false concerning dangerous plots for anything I ever was acquainted with. God of heaven forgive the devices of these horrible lies to wrong innocent men. Good sweet heart, with the help of Will Harrison, manage our poor affairs as well as these distracted times will admit. I dare not yet write such directions as I would in my own business. I hope the malice of our neighbours will not stretch to the utter ruin of us. God has the disposing of all things, and will deliver those that trust in him. Dear heart, be patient and cheerly, for God be praised, so am I, and I glory as much in suffering for my conscience and a good cause as any can do in imprisoning. God Almighty bless you and yours and my stock. The same God, I hope, will bring us together again. Farewell.

Your faithful loving husband,

T.K.

March 23, 1642

I would I had my cloth cloak to my suit. When I know where we shall settle, I will write again concerning Jack's coming.

On 6 April, when Knyvett wrote again, he had still not exchanged words with Colonel Cromwell, 'although I wrote some compliments to him yesterday morning. I cannot perceive that Mrs Hampden has wrote anything to him yet concerning me'. The comforts of the 'Rose' had worn thin, but not his sense of humour: 'I was never so weary of a tavern in my life. I think I shall get such a surfeit of it I shall never abide to come near one again. A fine song that! Well, prithee be merry, and so will I as long as I can. . . .' His next letter came from Windsor Castle:

Dear Heart,

I know my sudden remove from Cambridge has been a greater affliction to you than to me; for, cheer up yourself, I humbly thank God I was not in better health since I saw you than now I am. And though the malice of our own countrymen thought us in too good a condition at Cambridge, yet, maugre their spites, God has given us more favour in the eyes of strangers here than we could reap from those that owe it us. God I doubt not but will reward them according to their deserts. We are now agitating our remove to London. As soon as you can put your house and goods into some reasonable way of defence or protection, I would have you make haste to Harry Ellsing's. All my fellow wives are there, soliciting their husbands' enlargement, and why stayest you so long? Yet I chide you not, for I had rather endure here a while longer than have you rashly leave our affairs at sixes and sevens. . . . You may now write Lady, for we are all poor Knights of Windsor. They have lodged us in their houses. Poor men, they have turned them out and put us in, and 'ere long we shall be as poor as they. We had but two rooms for seven of us the first night, and but one bed for us all. I hope you will say we now lay like pighogs indeed. We are since better accommodated, thanks be to the good women here, who are full of courtesy, yet still seven to our two rooms and shiting house.

We are now become housekeepers and got good things about us, but, to put us in mind of mortality, we trade all in earth. For our bodies we shall do reasonably well and for our souls God has so provided for us, as we never wanted a divine amongst us since our restraint. Doctor Young, a prebend of Norwich, is our chaplain, our fellow prisoner: a patient, quiet sober man. We had the liberty to go to church forenoon and afternoon here in the Castle where we heard wonderful sermons. The great news here is all from Reading; the town is fiercely besieged and they as strongly defend. What will be the issue God knows. Much blood has been spilt there already and abundance of maim'd men carried to London in carts. 'Tis said his Excellency will give no quarter and, so far as we hear, they desire none from him. 'Twill be a bloody business before that town be plundered. God in mercy turn people's hearts in charity one to another. The Lord Gray and Colonel Hampden are the chief in the army. Sir Arthur Aston and Colonel Fielding and many other old soldiers defend the town. Some reports it impregnable; our doorkeepers will not allow it to hold out above three days. Variety of humours makes various reports, so God's holy will be done. I was forced to leave all my clothes at Cambridge, so as I fear I shall be lousy before I shall get any change, but 'tis all our cases. Good dear mother, be hearty and merry, and pray to God. For the rest, God Almighty bless and keep you all there and us here and send us a happy meeting. Commend me kindly to all you thinkest love me. Farewell.

Your faithfullest friend living,
T.K.

from our
Palace at Windsor Castle. April 22, 1643
My fellow prisoners presents their service to you, by name. . . .
And your dear bully boy.
A knot of male contents!

After about two months imprisonment in the Castle, Knyvett was discharged by order of the Governor, the Earl of Essex, though there still seem to have been some restrictions placed on his personal liberty. His adventure at Lowestoft now placed him at the mercy of the two most notorious Committees which Parliament set up at the beginning of the Civil War. The so-called Committee of Examinations, established to investigate possible enemies of Parliament, seized some indiscreet letters from Knyvett to his wife and soon threatened him with more imprisonment again. Meanwhile the Committee for Sequestrations also had him in their clutches.

A fortnight before the troubles at Lowestoft, Parliament had decreed that its opponents should be made to contribute towards the cost of the war by having their personal estates, lands and rents confiscated. Branches of the Committee for Sequestrations were appointed in every county to carry out the provisions of the ordinance, and their agents had authority to break open locks, bolts, bars or doors where any concealment was suspected. Informers were offered a shilling in the pound on a delinquent's estate for 'discovering' an offender. The Norfolk committee issued a warrant in respect of Knyvett's possessions but he successfully asked the Earl of Manchester to intervene on his behalf. That won him a postponement but the threat of further proceedings hung over him for another year. 'Sweetheart, this business has almost broke my heart,' he wrote to his Katherine, 'I am glad to read some comfort in your letters, yet when I look back upon my condition I am struck blank again, seeing myself environ'd with eyes and ears that seeks my ruin.'

The bitterness which sequestration engendered between former friends and neighbours was perhaps the most enduring and unhappy social consequence of the war. A Royalist could compound for his estates by paying a fine. As this could be as low as one tenth of their value – not much more than a favourite daughter's dowry in some cases – many Royalists recovered relatively easily from sequestration. Others sold most of their estates to pay the fine, and these could not be recovered at the Restoration. But the miserable anxiety and the hard feelings caused as lands changed hands in this forced way cannot be measured. The threat of sequestration filled Knyvett's letters for a year or more, and it is salutary to record that his case occupies but two lines in the 4,000 pages of the five printed volumes recording the decisions of the Committee for Compounding. These volumes convey the magnitude of the social upheaval and personal suffering incurred by those who backed the wrong side.

At the opposite end of the political spectrum to Knyvett in East Anglia stood Ralph Josselin, a Puritan vicar in the large Essex village of Earls Colne. In 1642, the year of his daughter's birth, Josselin actively supported the cause of Parliament, as he records in a diary which throws much light on the Puritan ministry of the day.

My wife now growing big and ill my mother came from Olney to us upon a Tuesday lecture day April 12. After sermon having waited upon God in his house, my wife called her women and God was merciful to me in my house giving her a safe deliverance, and a daughter which on Thursday April [21st] was baptized by the name of Mary: Mr Rich. Harlkenden, Mr John Little, Mrs Mary Mildmay and my wife's mother being witnesses. I entertained my neighbours all about. It cost £6 and 13s 4d at least. They showed much love to me from all parts. God blessed my wife to be a nurse, and our child thrived and was even then a pleasant comfort to us. God wash it from its corruption and sanctify it and make it his own. But it pleased God my wife's breasts were sore which was a grievance and sad cut to her but with use of means in some distance of time they healed up.

This Spring times grew fearful. In the rising of the year about Midsummer we began to raise private arms. I found a musket for my part and the King was beginning to raise an army. The Parliament did the like. Aug. 1: we met at Colchester to underwrite, where for my part for my affection to God and his gospel having endeavoured public promoting it beyond my estate I underwrit and paid in to Mr Crane £10, but my rings wanted something so it fell short nigh 3s. Being at London I provided for myself sword, halbert, powder and match. The drums now also began to beat up, for my part I endeavoured to encourage others to go forth. Our poor people in tumults arose and plundered divers houses, Papists and others, and threatened to go further which I endeavoured to suppress by public and private means.

Edgehill battle being fought, Wednesday following being the fast day, I was told the news as I was going down the churchyard to sermon. The time and place hinted the answer of our prayers on the Lord's day, being the day and the time of battle, when I was earnest with God for mercy upon us against our enemies. Upon this the country was raised and I for my part sent a man out with a month's pay, but he returned presently but spent the most of my money.

In spring now my wife weaned her daughter and began to breed again. God gave us both our health in a greater measure than I had had before or my wife of late days. I should have mentioned our associating [in the Eastern Association] in which service I underwrit a whole [set of] arms. They went out to our great charge, and did little or no good. I began now to find my means grow scant, that notwithstanding all our industry and good husbandry and many gifts that I could have but little upon which I gave notice to the town to prevent it that I might not be forced to leave them. June 10, 1643: my wife's father died. The Lord prepare us for our latter ends and give us mercy with him through Jesus Christ.

Essex was far from the cockpits of war, but Josselin like most educated Englishmen followed military events closely. Besides contributing his taxes to the Eastern Association he also acted in a voluntary capacity in the local regiment. His diary records these services in the context of his daily life as a minister:

May 12: At Pebmarch, God good in the love and society of friends. Mr Sheppard [vicar] of Maplestead accused by his maid for endeavouring to abuse her, his patience was so moved that he stroke her on the mouth whereupon she bled much, it made much against him. The Lord discover truth, shame us in ourselves and preserve us from reproach. It might have been my condition if mercy had not prevented it.

18: The Lord was good to us this week in outward mercies and favours, peace and plenty, my little daughter only somewhat ill with cold. The Lord good to me in the work of his day. Dispose my heart more and more to his service, pardon my failings and accept me in Jesus Christ.

19: Paid 2 years tenth to the Parliament's messenger, £1 14s 2d. The messenger received from me for his pains, 3s. His power was harsh; his carriage was yet indifferent courteous. 'Tis a trial to be thus dealt withal. I bless God my spirit was under, and I hope ever shall.

25: This week the Lord was good to us in our health and outward mercies. My little daughter Mary had a great cold, strained and spit much blood. I hope the Lord will preserve her. My wife through God's goodness held out very well (though weakly in the want of a maid servant. God in his good time will supply us).

28: This day was a day of public humiliation wherein God was good to me. Oh when shall I learn more and more to love him. My daughter Mary very ill with a cold, exceedingly straining by fits and fetching up blood. We went to my Lady Honywood's who gave us divers things for her. My wife used oil and found it wrought presently upon her upwards and downwards.

June 1: This day the Lord was good to me in his ordinances. Oh make me a son of gracious and holy peace, and let his word and ordinances be advantage to us. Mary continued ill; we used means. The Lord bless them. God stedded [supplied] us with a young servant, the Lord fit her for us and bless her under us. She came May 29 1645.

The news was sad tousward that the King was coming down to Newark, had faced Leicester. God knows how soon we may be alarm'd indeed.

2: A comfortable meeting of ministers at Stanway. At home an alarm. Leicester lost. [Prince Rupert stormed Leicester on 30 May 1645.]

7: An alarm to raise our regiment of horse. The field officers [being] from home, I was resolved to have sent orders to have raised them, but the Colonel coming home at night I only assisted him in his work that night.

8: Preached at Coggleshall. God was good to me in the day and work, and in the week my wife and daughter somewhat weakly.

10: I was out with our regiment. We marched to Saffron Walden, mustered. I

11: sang psalms, prayed and spoke to our soldiers on the common at Walden and

12: also at Halstead. God was good to us in accommodating us and preserving us. Mr Josselin of Chelmsford broke his leg at Walden; his horse threw him. Our soldiers resolute, some somewhat dissolute. The Colonel was pleased to honour me to be his comrade. I shall never forget his great love and respect. I found my family well, I praise God at my return; abundance of love made my wife grieve for which I must the more respect and love her. I rode to my sister at Wenden. I had not seen her in divers years. The Lord has made a difference in our outward conditions. I gave her and her children 6s. Lord thou canst do more than return it again to me.

14: At my Lady Honywood's we agreed to meet on Tuesday to seek God for our armies and I went to prayer. Even while we were in prayer our armies were conquering [at Naseby], the Lord's name be praised and receive the glory of all.

The victory at Naseby did not seem as final to contemporaries as it does to us. It certainly did not relieve Josselin's anxieties about a Royalist invasion into the Eastern Association. On 18 June the Essex Committee appointed him officially as chaplain to his friend Colonel Harlkenden's regiment. On 10 July he received with much satisfaction fifty shillings – five days pay – from his colonel: 'this is the first money that I received of the States,' he wrote. 'God can this way pay in my layings out in his cause and service.' Soon he was called upon to earn his money in the field. On 24 August he exchanged pulpits with his cousin and preached at Upper Yeldham. 'In the night I heard the drums beat at Nether Yeldham. It proved an alarm upon the King's coming down to Huntingdon.'

August 27: Fast day. I preach'd once after that I rode to my Colonel's quarters to Great Chesterford, where we had an alarm of the enemy's advance to Cambridge, and presently of his intentions to fall upon our own quarters.

31: I preach'd at Royston one sermon where our quarters were for present. God good to us in our march, in our accommodations his name for ever be praised.

September 4: Returned home safe with our troops. No damage to any man. One horse shot in the leg through a mistake. My horse's eye hurt. God good to me in enabling me for my journey. I found my wife indifferently cheerful. Only in my absence, she was wondrous sad and discontented.

7: This week God good to us in our return of peace. The enemy fled before us and gone down to other parts of the kingdom. Good in our health and plenty in seasonable harvest weather, in his sabbath, in some measure enabling me for the work and service of the same.

9: Some failing that had promised to go along with me, I went alone towards Major Haynes. Come safe to Cambridge. Heard he was at Grantham or Lincoln, upon which I resolved home and so went to bed in Sydney College.

10: Having the opportunity of a convoy I resolved to find him out. We came safe to Huntingdon. There I refresh'd myself with Mrs Taylor. Hearing that divers of their Cavaliers rode upon the road we made ready for our defence and march'd on. Before we came at Stangate hole, Captain Warner and divers in his company overtook us. At Stilton I met the welcome news that Major Haynes at 9 of clock was at Stamford. Much ado I persuaded them to march that night to Wainsford bridge, 7 miles in the night. Our supper was a hard egg, and tough cheese, and pretty coarse lodging. Blessed be God we had anything.

11: I and three more in the morning rode to Stamford, 5 miles. Found the Major who was riding unto Grantham, very glad of my company. We quartered at Mr Wolphs, a grand malignant here. We had good lodging and diet.

12: A day of public humiliation for Scotland. Preached once at Saint Mary's, Stamford.

13: Continued at Stamford. Heard the good news of Bristol [surrendered by Prince Rupert on 10 September]. Saw the sad face of Burleigh House. A little surfeited with eating grapes.

14: Lord's day. Continued at Stamford. Preach'd two sermons. Very ill with my cold. One hurt with his own pistol upon the guard.

15: An alarm that the enemy with horse was entering our quarters. The guard said they descried a great body of them. The Major had a fall. God preserved him. It proved false and was soon quieted.

16: We march'd through Rutlandshire, a pleasant little county, to Bilsden in Leicestershire. Colonel Rossiter with four troops of horse came up to us. We quarter'd that night at Houghton at a poor house. Beef to our supper; pitiful black bread; I got a white loaf crust. Our lodging was upon straw and a quilt in our clothes. I slept well, I bless my God. Heard that Montrose was entered England.

17: March'd out with a short breakfast. Rendezvous'd at Leicester, where Colonel Rossiter's troops march'd from us. Beheld the ruins of a brave house, sometimes the Earl of Devonshire's. Nothing standing but the stone work. From hence we march'd towards Ashby. Refresh'd ourselves upon the way. But our meat smelt. I pocketed two white loaves against the worst.

Quartered at Ibstocke, Laud's living. Now Dr Lovedyn, a great Cavalier. Our diet very good and lodging indifferent.

18: March'd in the head of two troops to Rounston in Derbyshire, thence to Ashby much infected with the plague. We faced the house. I pray'd with the Council of War. We summon'd the house. We drew off about night. Lost two men. One shot in the breeches and yet had no hurt. Killed one of the Cavaliers. Heard the news of routing Montrose. Here I eat some of my bread. We had no beer all day long. March'd back to Ibstocke. Rode in a pretty while before our troops. Six men in town, they said, of Lichfield. It scar'd our men and made them ready to run. I was in the house and heard nothing. I have cause for ever to praise God for the mercies of this day. One of the men was slain on the ground where I had stood closely a little before, not knowing of the pardue [outpost] in the ditch who shot this man presently after. . . .

19: March'd through Leicester. Saw the ruins of some part of the town.

21: Preach'd two sermons at Stamford. God good to me in the same, I hope not without good to the people. We spoil one of their church feasts this day. People are still for their old ways. . . .

22: Returned safe to Colne to my dear wife and friends. My place supplied in my absence, I praise God.

The impression from Josselin's diary is that life continued much as normal in the eastern counties, except for the occasional alarm. Other sources support that view. While the Ironsides were marching to their triumph at Naseby, and Essex was bringing up its reserves, the Essex magistrates were trying for witchcraft eighteen women – 'poor, melancholic, envious, mischievous, ill-disposed, ill-dieted' – who were condemned and sentenced to be hanged at Chelmsford Midsummer Quarter Sessions.

It was chaplains in the mould of Ralph Josselin who did so much to form the character of the Eastern Association's army. As the reputation of this army grew so did the fame of Oliver Cromwell, its Lieutenant-General of Horse. But his rise was steady rather than spectacular. In 1642 Cromwell was unknown outside his own county. In the Long Parliament he did not cut much of a figure. Sir Philip Warwick saw him there one day: 'I came one morning into the House well clad, and perceived a gentleman speaking . . . very ordinarily apparelled; for it was a plain cloth suit, which seemed to have been made by an ill country tailor; his linen was plain, and not very clean; and I remember a speck or two of blood upon his little band which was not much larger than his collar. His hat was without a hatband. His stature was of a good size, his sword stuck close to his side, his countenance swollen and reddish, his voice sharp and untunable and his eloquence full of fervour. . . .'

Courtiers such as Warwick valued exquisite clothes, polished manners and silver oratory: the Huntingdonshire squire jarred upon both their eyes and their ears. The most elegant member in the House, Lord George Digby, laughed derisively at 'that sloven', as he called Cromwell, with his untidy suit and harsh voice. 'Pray, Mr Hampden, who is that man? For I see that he is on your side by his speaking so warmly today.' Hampden answered: 'That sloven whom you see before you has no ornament in his speech; but that sloven, I say, if we should ever come to breach with the King (which God forbid!), in such a case, I say, that sloven will be the greatest man in England.' It was extraordinary prescience; but Hampden always had the highest regard for his cousin Oliver Cromwell.

During the first five years of civil war Cromwell served his long apprenticeship in the military arts at the side of Manchester and Fairfax. In April 1645, while the New Model Army was being formed, he soldiered briefly in the West Country under Sir William Waller's command. Parliament had given Waller the 'hopeless employment' of trying to relieve Taunton. In this twilight of his military career Waller observed the rising star with some interest:

And here I cannot but mention the wonder which I have oft times had to see this eagle in his eyrie. He at this time had never shown extraordinary parts, nor do I think that he did himself believe that he had them. For although he was blunt, he did not bear himself with pride or disdain. As an officer he was obedient and did never dispute my orders nor argue upon them. He did, indeed, seem to have great cunning, and whilst he was cautious of his own words, not putting forth too many lest they should betray his thoughts, he made others talk, until he had as it were sifted them, and known their inmost designs. A notable instance was his discovering in one short conversation with one Captain Giles (a great favourite with the Lord General, and whom he most confided in) that although his words were full of zeal and his actions seemingly brave, that his heart was not with the cause. And in fine, this man did shortly after join the enemy at Oxford, with three and twenty stout fellows. One other instance I will here set down, being of the same sort, as to his cunning.

When I took the Lord Percy at Andover, having at that time an inconvenient distemper, I desired Colonel Cromwell to entertain him with some civility; who did afterwards tell me, that amongst those whom we took with him (being about thirty), there was a youth of so fair a countenance that he doubted of his condition; and to confirm himself willed him to sing; which he did with such a daintiness that Cromwell scrupled not to say to Lord Percy that 'being a warrior he did wisely to be accompanied by Amazons'. On which that Lord, in some confusion, did acknowledge that she was a damsel. This afterwards gave cause for scoff at the King's party, as that they were loose and wanton, and minded their pleasure more than either their country's service or their master's good.

On 22 March 1657, Oliver Cromwell, now Lord Protector of England, summoned Waller before him at Whitehall Palace and questioned him about some allegations that he was involved in a widespread Royalist plot. 'He did examine me as a stranger,' wrote Sir William, 'not as one whom he had aforetime known and obeyed, yet he was not discourteous.' A strange man, Cromwell.

12

The Impact of War

'That country is in a most pitiful condition; no corner of it free from the evils of a cruel war. . . . Every shire, every city, many families, divided in this quarrel; much blood and universal spoil made by both where they prevail.' So wrote Robert Baillie, one of the Scottish commissioners who arrived in London in 1643, in a letter home describing the state of England as he found it after more than a year of civil war. 'Oh the sad and heart-piercing spectacles that mine eyes have seen in four years space!' exclaimed Richard Baxter. 'Scarce a month, scarce a week without the sight or noise of blood.'

But it is difficult to generalize about the impact of the civil war on the lives of ordinary people. Everything depended upon who you were and where you happened to be living. Some experienced 'the devouring sword' at first hand, while others merely read about the fighting in their newspapers and contributed their money to one side or the other. 'I lived well because I lay low,' wrote one country parson in his parish register. Occasionally a troop of horse might ride through the village, but that was as near as the actual war came to them. But the psychological implications of civil war – the shock to the body politic – were universally felt. It produced in some of the finer spirits a profound depression or melancholy. A deep sense of corporate unhappiness settled upon the nation, as the daily news of fights and garrisons won or lost continued without seeming end. 'So that hearing such sad news on one side or the other was our daily work,' wrote Baxter, 'insomuch that as duly as I was awakened in the morning I expected to hear one come and tell me such a garrison is won or lost, or such a defeat received or given. And "do you hear the news?" was commonly the first word I heard. So miserable were those bloody days, in which he was the most honourable that could kill most of his enemies.'

For those who lived in the country near garrisons or in the path of marching armies, the war brought a more tangible impact. Richard Baxter, who served as a chaplain in the New Model and had some dear friends in it, could conclude that 'it must be a very extraordinary army that is not constituted of wolves and tigers, and is not unto common honesty and piety the same that a stews or whorehouse is to chastity'. The experience of being plundered by such pre-dators, as those who have been burgled might well agree, was profoundly disturbing. Bulstrode Whitelocke's description of the plunder of Fawley Court near Henley-on-Thames in the autumn of 1642 conveys this sense of outrage.

William Cook, Whitelocke's steward, had heard that Prince Rupert was

Bulstrode Whitelocke, the eminent lawyer, whose house was looted in his absence by Cavalier troops under Sir John Byron's command in 1642, and then by Parliamentarians later in the war.

descending upon Henley. He removed Whitelocke's children to his farm on Fawley Hill and told his wife to pass them off as his grandchildren. Other faithful tenants carried away many of their master's treasured books and papers from the library, hiding them in their homes, at the rectory and in the beechwood hangars above the house. Metal objects which could be melted down by the enemy were thrown into the moat. The servants had begun to carry out the furniture when the Byron brothers rode up at the head of a column of Cavaliers and quartered their men in the house. During their occupation the troopers wrought havoc.

Sir John Byron and his brothers commanded those horse and gave order that they should commit no insolence at my house, nor plunder my goods. But soldiers are not easily governed against their plunder or persuaded to restrain it. For there being about a thousand of the King's horse quartered in and about the house and none but servants there, there was no insolence or outrage usually committed by common soldiers on a reputed enemy which was not committed by these brutish fellows at my house. Then they had their whores with them, they spent and consumed a hundred load of corn and hay, littered their horses with sheaves of good wheat, and gave them all sorts of corn in the straw. Divers writings of consequence and books which were left in my study, some of them they tore to pieces, others they burnt to light their tobacco, and some they carried away with them, to my extreme great loss and prejudice in wanting the writings of my estate and losing very many excellent manuscripts of my father's and others' and some of my own labours.

They broke down my park pales, killed most of my deer, though rascal and carrion, and let out all the rest, only a tame young stag, they carried away and presented to Prince Rupert and my hounds which were extraordinary good. They ate and drank up all that the house could afford, broke up all the trunks, chests and places. And where they found linen or any household stuff they took it away with them, and cutting the beds, let out the feathers, and took away the ticks. They likewise carried away my coach and four good horses and all my saddle horses, and did put all the mischief and spoil that malice and enmity could provoke barbarous mercenaries to commit, and so they parted.

William Cook stood by and watched the damage done by the troopers and their women with mounting rage. When he saw them mindlessly throwing wooden ploughs on their fires in the close he could contain himself no longer. He shouted at them to use the bundles of faggots stored in the wood-yard. The soldiers retorted by threatening to cast him onto a fire himself for daring to reprove them. Cook made his way home, frightened and angry, to find Sir Thomas Byron there closely studying the faces of the Whitelocke children. Cook confessed their true identity, but implored the Cavaliers not to mistreat them on their father's account. Much to his relief Sir Thomas merely petted and kissed them, saying that it would be barbarous to harm such pretty children.

Later, when the Royalists garrisoned nearby Greenlands House, Fawley Court was torn by cannon fire and looted once again, this time by the Parliamentarian besieging force under Major General Richard Browne.

The psychological effects of such acts of war upon civilians, especially women and children, must have been considerable. Richard Baxter's wife, for example, who possessed a nervous disposition, was clearly scarred by being the unwilling eyewitness of destruction and carnage. 'She had a diseased, irrestible fearfulness; her quick and too sensible [sensitive] nature was over-timorous; and to increase it . . . her mother's house being a garrison, it was stormed when she was in it and part of the housing about it burnt and men lay killed before her face and all of them threatened and stripped of their clothing so that they were fain to borrow clothes.'

At least Mrs Baxter escaped the fate which sometimes awaited women when a town was sacked after a storm. John Corbet said of Colonel Edward Massey that he would not 'at any time suffer his soldiers to ransack any place they took by storm, giving this reason, that he could not judge any part of England to be an enemy's country, nor an English town capable of devastation by English soldiers'. But in practice even Parliamentarian generals found it difficult to restrain their men. Towns could often buy their way out of trouble with a large 'donation'. In many other instances, especially where Prince Rupert and the Cavaliers were the victors, the town and its inhabitants were given over to the predators. Even allowing for propaganda, the pamphlet *Prince Rupert's Burning Love to England, discovered in Birmingham's flames* gives a vivid and accurate picture of what the inhabitants must then endure:

Having thus possessed themselves of the town, they ran into every house cursing and damning, threatening and terrifying the poor women most terribly, setting naked swords and pistols to their breasts, they fell to plundering the town before them, as well Malignants as others, picking purses and pockets, searching in holes and corners, tiles of houses, wells, pools, vaults, gardens and every other place they could suspect for money or goods, forcing people to deliver all the money they had. . . . They beastly assaulted many women's chastity, and impudently made their brags of it afterwards, how many they had ravished; glorying in their shame. Especially the French among them were outrageously lascivious and lecherous. . . . That night few or none went to bed, but sat up revelling, robbing and tyrannising over the poor affrighted women and prisoners, drinking drunk, healthing upon their knees, yea, drinking drunk healths to Prince Rupert's dog.

Nor did their rage here cease, but when on the next day they were to march forth of the town, they used all possible diligence in every street to kindle fire in the town with gunpowder, match, wisps of straw, and besomes, burning coals of fire, etc., flung into straw, hay, kid piles, coffers, any other places where it was likely to catch hold. . . .

Freequarter, plunder and highway robbery were daily occurrences for those who were anywhere near the rival armies. One Shropshire farmer reported that: 'I had eleven horses taken away by the King's soldiers and four of the eleven were worth £40 . . . the soldiers took the other nine away and I could never have them more. Since again . . . going to market with a load of corn, the Earl of Manchester's soldiers met with my men and took away my whole team of horses. . . . The King's soldiers call me "Roundhead" . . . and the Parliament's soldiers tell me I pay rent to Worcester.'

When plunderers did descend upon a house they seldom contented themselves with taking horses and money. The soldiers who visited another farmer in the Midlands were exceptionally thorough. 'They took away a good store of bacon from his roof, beef out of the powdering-tub, the pots, pans, kettles, pewter to great value, all the provisions for hospitality and housekeeping and then broke the spits as unnecessary utensils. They sold his bedding, carried away in carts, which they compelled to work with them, all chairs, stools, couches and trunks . . . and pillaged to the bare walls.'

Nor were townsmen immune from such visitations. In December 1642 the Marquess of Grandison occupied Basingstoke and demanded from the inhabitants 2,000 cloths and 500 yards of linen for the King. When the clothiers delayed, Grandison's troopers ransacked their shops. 'If you see Master Lamy,' wrote the town's apothecary to a friend in London, 'tell him he saved his purse

Though Englands Ark haue furies ſtormes jndurd
By Plotts of foes and power of the ſword
Yet to this day by Gods almighty hand
The Arks preſerud and almoſt ſafe at land

Earle of Eſſex · *Earle of Warwick* · *Earle of Mancheſter* · *Gen⁰rall Laſley* · *Sⁱʳ Tho: Fairfax* · *Leiu⁰ Gen: Cromwell*

House of Lords · House of Comõs · Aſſembly

In 1646 the ship of state could be shown still bravely afloat, while Royalists and Papists drown in tempestuous seas in a vain attempt to sink it. But Cromwell waits in the lower right-hand corner.

in going away, but they made bold with his house; he may come down safely now and see what is done. Pray God send peace, or else I see what will come to this land quickly.'

The gentry could sometimes use their family influence to good effect. Mr Wolstenholme, the eldest son of Sir John Wolstenholme of Nostel, Yorkshire, was married to Dorothy, the youngest daughter of Lord Horace de Vere and sister-in-law to Sir Thomas Fairfax. He wrote in the following vein to Ferdinando Lord Fairfax:

My Lord,

I was resolved not to have been more troublesome to your lordship for anything concerning myself; but now I see myself lie open not only to be undone by plunder, but myself, wife, children, and servants subjected to the violence and rapine of disordered soldiers, before and in the presence of your captains and officers who commanded them, and plunder in part justified to be allowed the soldier by the captain, when he had no commission to enter my house; two of my servants sore wounded who did nothing to them, in my wife's presence, and she forced to flee to her chamber for rescue, and there a naked sword tendered her by a young ruffian, who called for her and told her he came for money, and with fearful oaths that money he would have; and calling all Romish whores, wherein I thank God none with me are guilty. He had his desire in part, for he snatched a purse with a gold ring and a seal in it, from a servant that was giving some to quiet him.

By the way I beseech your lordship to take into consideration, that the sequestrator gave this commission to one Captain Swaine, to sequester and appraise all my cattle, but not to bring them away; yet he not only drove them away, but gave divers of my coach-horses to one Captain Wood, who set him on work first to do this, and who the last week plundered the same horses and two others notwithstanding. I showed him your lordship's proclamation against it. I made my address to his colonel, a very civil man, and he caused three coach-horses and a mare to be restored; but the other coach-horse and a pacing nag for my own saddle, the Captain keeps still; and now by Captain Swaine's means he may set up a coach, for he has all four, and your lordship is well acquainted with our dirty country, that I need not acquaint your lordship that my wife cannot serve God at church with the congregation but in frosty weather. Cornet Lambert yet was very civil to her, though he took the best, and your lordship was pleased to say I should likewise have him again, you were so far from taking the rest. Some other colts never backed he detains likewise for his own use; he drove away my milch kine, my draught oxen, and five fat oxen, which were for my own expense, and are valued very high; and either I must purchase them or lose them. Yet I procured so much favour with Mr Lodge, by means of a friend, as to have my cattle again, all but what Captain Swaine hath disposed of; upon promise to pay the rate within a few days, if I procured not your lordship's order to stay the payment. Truly, my lord, money is very precious with me, and where to borrow so much I yet know not.

My sufferings are infinite every way; my family great, and consequently my charge, and for my own security I dare not now lessen. I beseech your lordship's order to quit it, or to abate it in some reasonable measure, that I may live; and for the abuses of the two captains and their officers and soldiers, that you would cause them to be examined by Mr Lodge, and whom else you please, and upon certificate of their demeanour, contrary to their commission and your lordship's proclamation, your lordship would make them examples for the safety of your poor servants and the rest of the county, and God will bless you in doing justice, and I shall remain,

Your lordship's humble servant,
John Wolstenholme

Nostel, December 22nd, 1644

About three weeks since I had four fatting cattle taken from me for the heath garrison, and eight fat sheep. Those your commanders there yet gave me a bill for, but when to be paid God knoweth; but they set a value of them less than I am rated to pay for my goods now taken. I beseech your lordship give me leave to defend my house according to law, against any but such as show your lordship's commission, because I live in fear of my life with all my family; and except I have your lordship's warrant herein, I dare not do it; as I both would and could barely do in defence thereof.

The burdens of war – plunder, tax and the decline of trade – hit the poor especially hard. This account by an Oxfordshire labourer who was unlucky enough to live near the south Warwickshire Parliamentary garrison of Compton House, with an unscrupulous commander, Major George Purefoy, speaks for itself:

The Petition of Thomas Tasker of Epwell, Oxfordshire, labourer, to the Right Worshipful the Committee of Accounts for the County of Warwick.

Your petitioner, being a poor man and aged, in December 1644, in the middle of the night, a party of Major Purefoy's soldiers . . . came into his house and violently took away the most part of his household goods, to the value of £10 or upwards and also took away your petitioner to Compton where he was unjustly imprisoned by the space of five or six days, and nothing being alleged against him, the Major came to him and used many harsh speeches and so gave order to the Marshal for to release him, but never examined him of anything at all, neither would he give him leave to speak for himself to desire any of his goods again.

His humble request unto your worships is that you will be pleased for to take into your considerations that he may be satisfied for his goods in regard he and his wife are aged, and the sudden fight hath made them both so sickly and weak that they are altogether unable to get their living. . . .

They [the soldiers] had in money 10s, 7 pairs of sheets, 3 brass kettles, 2 brass pots, 5 pewter dishes and other small pewter, 4 shirts, 4 smocks, other small linens, 2 coats, 1 cloak, 1 waistcoat, 7 dozen of candles, 1 frying pan, 1 spit, 2 pairs of pot hooks, 1 peck of wheat, 4 bags, some oatmeal, some salt . . . a basket full of eggs . . . pins, bowls, dishes, spoons, ladles, drinking pots and whatsoever else they could lay their hands on. . . .

Generals on both sides attempted with varying degrees of urgency and success to restrict the impact of war upon civilians by punishing their culprits. The papers of the twenty-two courts martial held in Sir William Waller's army in 1644, the only such records to survive, give us some indication of what all the armies tried to do. Waller's army behaved better than the notorious followers of General Goring, but he was far from effective when it came to stamping out illegal plundering. In April 1644, at Farnham, a major was ordered to arrest two of his troopers, one called Henry Wilcocke, for robbing a miller called Thomas Collier. But Collier apparently did not obey a summons to come and give testimony against them. Later courts martial tried similar cases. Thomas Williams, a marshal, being found guilty 'as a countenancer of plunderers, a drunkard and an abuser of prisoners', was sentenced to be drawn up on tiptoe by the wrists with a pair of handcuffs for a quarter of an hour and afterwards to be cashiered from the army never to return again. For robbing Judith Whiteing a soldier named Garrett Harbert was sent to the gallows. At the same court in Abingdon on 23 July David Rogers and Robert Baven, having confessed to plundering a doublet and a pattern for a pair of breeches from a tailor at Woodstock, were ordered to 'lie neck and heels together one whole day and be fed with no other food than bread and water'. Henry Stone, who had plundered a shirt, an apron and some other trivial things, received the 'gatlop', a severe whipping as he ran between two rows of soldiers. John Whitaker was hanged for robbing a man on the highway.

These punishments, the sum total for offences involving civilians, did not seem to have much effect, for in December, when the remnant of the army was back in Hampshire with its headquarters in the market town of Petersfield, the following order was read at the head of every regiment: 'Whereas many abuses and violences are daily offered and practised upon countrymen, both in their dwelling and travelling on the road by soldiers in plundering their horses, cattle, sheep and other provisions from them, some of which intended for the market: it is this day ordered by the Council of War that no soldiers upon any pretence whatsoever shall from henceforth plunder, seize or take away any of the goods, sheep, cattle, horse or horses, whether by exchanging or otherwise, from any countryman or other traveller on the road, nor molest in their person or goods any man or woman coming to or from the market without express order from the General or other superior officer having power thereunto, upon pain of death without mercy.'

Two weeks later William Quincy, a quartermaster in Waller's own regiment of horse, paid with his life for disobeying this order by commanding a party which robbed a gentleman on the road near Alresford of six pounds, his horse and sword. His chief accomplice, Corporal Nicholas Read, 'shall be forthwith in the head of the regiment disgracefully cashiered in the army, his sword broken over his head, never to bear arms again in the army'.

Reading these accounts of pillage and robbery it becomes understandable why the Clubmen appeared towards the end of the war. During 1645, Clubmen Associations were formed in Shropshire, Worcestershire and Herefordshire, Wiltshire, Dorset and Somerset, Berkshire, Sussex and Hampshire, and South Wales. These were bands of militant neutrals – sometimes small armies – who sought rather ineffectively to protect their homelands from the ravages of both sides. Sometimes they were led by the local gentry. Both Royalists and Parliamentarians fought against them, disbelieving in their claims to be neutral. The New Model Army scattered them in the West as a prelude to dealing with the Royalists.

In addition to the plundering common to both sides, the Roundheads indulged in a form of destruction that was generally anathema to the Royalists. They broke into churches and removed such 'popish relics' as organ pipes, white surplices and coloured vestments. Captain Harry Birch, a Royalist, told the Marquess of Ormonde in a letter that he had been inside the Hawarden

Church shortly after such a visitation and found the pages of the Book of Common Prayer scattered up and down the chancel. In the stained glass windows the Roundheads had 'left whole bodies of painted bishops, though in their rochets', contenting themselves with knocking out the faces to do as little damage as possible. But they destroyed any words in 'the language of the Beast', such as *hoc fecit* or *orate.* The altar rails had been destroyed and the communion table removed from the east end of the chancel to the body of the church. Captain Birch confessed himself 'weary of these truths'.

The element of restraint which Birch mentioned is worth emphasising, for the Puritans are so often credited with the wanton destruction of art in churches. Granted their detestation of idolatry and the symbols of Rome, the Puritans were generally very selective in the damage they did and often showed some aesthetic awareness. For instance, the superb medieval stained glass in King's College Chapel at Cambridge was spared, although Roundhead foot soldiers used the nave as a drill hall. The great west window in St George's Chapel, Windsor, stands today as full of pre-Reformation figures of saints and popes as when Cromwell and his officers gazed upon it. In the same glorious building more than three hundred stone angels survived the war intact. Despite their need for metal, the Roundheads even respected the heraldic array of Garter stall-plates and the iron tabernacle work of Edward iv's tomb. Like most cathedrals and churches, St George's Chapel emerged from the civil war without major harm.

Monuments to the departed were not safe, because zealous but illiterate soldiers sometimes could not distinguish them from other statues. Before the war Sir William Waller had built himself a fine tomb in Bath Abbey for himself and his first wife: soldiers hacked and scratched away the features on the faces of their two reclining effigies. There is a bust of a little boy placed in a church just outside Peterborough during the war which bears these touching words:

> To the courteous Souldier:
> Noe crucifixe you see, noe Frightfull Brand
> Of superstitions here, Pray let mee stand.
> *Grassante bello civili*

Perhaps the postscript in 'the language of the Beast' was a mistake, for some soldier in the Eastern Association's forces has defaced the bust with his sword.

The economic effects of the civil war were uneven and often temporary. Damaged buildings could be replaced, bringing employment to the building crafts. Almost everyone shared in some way or other the economic burden of the war: heavy taxes, fines, sequestrations and goods stolen or requisitioned in exchange for worthless warrants. Those in the way of armies suffered most. Mr Daniel, who rented a farm at Euborne near Newbury, saw his fences utterly destroyed, his crops wasted and his buildings battered by shot – damage worth one hundred pounds. As for life and limb, Thomas Hobbes estimated that about one hundred thousand people were killed during the war. That figure may not be so far off the mark as modern historians often claim it to be, if the ravages of disease among soldiers and civilians are taken into account.

Trade came almost to a halt for long stretches of time in the West, North and Midlands during the civil war. In the West, for example, the agriculture and industries of the Severn valley suffered severely as tenants fell behind in their rents and trade almost disappeared. The drovers of North Wales petitioned the King in 1643 because the stop put to the cattle trade threatened thousands of Welsh families with ruin. The clothiers of Gloucestershire, cut off from their London market, could no longer employ men and also petitioned the King to allow them to take their cloths to London. Unemployment and economic depression characterized all the West Country's industrial towns and villages, bringing riots in their train at the end of the war. In 1645 the markets of Bristol were deserted and its trade was as derelict as its buildings; a quarter of the city's population had perished, mostly from the plague the year before. Of course there were always merchants, tradesmen and shop-keepers who did well from the war, quite apart from the profiteers in corn and other basic commodities. Some cloth-makers, sword-makers, armourers, spurriers, saddlers, hat-makers, boot-makers and the like must have thrived on fat orders from the armies.

The merchants who probably lost most of their profits lived in towns or cities in the King's hands, such as Worcester and Newcastle. When the King revoked a former proclamation and forbade the cloth trade with London without special licence, Worcester's merchants promptly petitioned to be exempted. Although the King relaxed the ban his marauding soldiers on the highways still seized Worcester cloth. Cities such as Worcester, which endured long sieges, suffered considerable war damage. The poorer inhabitants tended to become homeless for they lived in the suburbs which were either cleared to improve fields of fire or burnt by the enemy. People in smaller market towns fared slightly better as they were seldom bombarded. Yet Beaminster, after French and Cornish Royalist soldiers had clashed there in 1644, was 'the pitifullest spectacle that man can behold, hardly an house left not consumed by fire'. The risk of destruction by flames was greatly increased during the war.

Many townsfolk, of course, also lost their lives as well as their possessions when obstinate defenders exposed them to the hazard of a storming. As early as February 1643 Rupert sacked Cirencester, a Puritan town in Royalists' eyes. 'The value of the pillage was very great, to the utter ruin of many hundred families.'

Henry Townshend in beleaguered Worcester has left us a vivid account of the damage wrought by the Royalist garrison on the town and surrounding countryside:

Our soldiers in the night, through the carelessness and connivance of their officers,

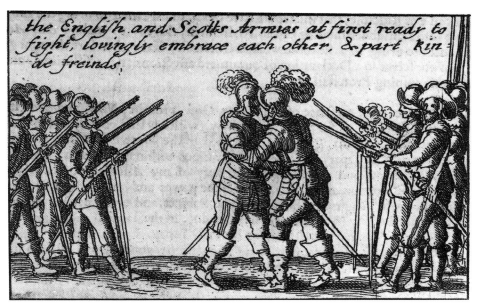

the English and Scotts Armies at first ready to
fight, lovingly embrace each other, & part kin-
de freinds,

At the end of the war the King gave himself up to the Scots army near Newark in 1646. The Scots entered the war on Parliament's side, but the King hoped to exploit their differences with their English allies.

steal into the country about Kempsey and Pirton, and take all sorts of cattle from off the grounds, fat or lean, and as soon as they have them knock them down and kill some, sell others, though they be not fit man's meat nor they necessitated. And when the country men come to demand them this answer returned, 'It is better they had them than the enemy', and so a poor honest man ruined in one night what he hath laboured for all his days. Other soldiers take the insolency to pull down men's back houses upon pretence of fuel, and to sell it for liquor that most part of the suburbs of St Peter's in Sidbury is defaced. And begin likewise in the City to tear in pieces the coaches of gentlemen which are in Backsides, and also the outhousing in the College. So wicked are the Irish soldiery chiefly and given to spoil and ruin, and the chief officers so remiss and careless in doing justice and punishing some severely for a terror to others, that shortly it is feared some great inconvenience within the close, yet wherein the soldier himself is concerned, you shall behold most exact justice *per sequentium* with that industry, appearance of officers to sit in judgement and a small – at most then only pretending or concerned – delinquency against the person or reputation of a soldier or a difference between him and a citizen or countryman punished with all extremity of power.

That all good Christians may insert in their Litany:

From the plundering of soldiers, their Insolency, Cruelty, Atheism, Blasphemy and Rule over us,

Libera nos Domine.

And

That it may please thee to resettle the good old Protestant religion and peace from civil wars in these three kingdoms of England, Scotland and Ireland.

O Christe audi nos.

173

The sea blockade of Newcastle's coal trade with London and the continent was disastrous for that Royalist city. It was a two-edged weapon, however, for London housewives used coal for cooking and they soon felt the want. In July 1643 Alderman Adams of London went to the House of Commons and said that 'he was commanded to recommend to this House the great and pressing necessities of coals, which will so pinch the poor that the consequences thereof will be full of horror and danger'. After the severe winter of 1643-4 the inventor of a substitute for coal commented:

'Some fine nosed city dames used to tell their husbands: "O husband! We shall never be well, we nor our children, whilst we live in the smell of this city's seacoal smoke. Pray, a country house for our health, that we may get out of this stinking seacoal smell." But – how many of these fine nosed dames now cry, "Would to God we had seacoal! O the want of fire undoes us! O the sweet seacoal fire we used to have . . ." thus now they see the want of what they slighted in times past.'

Parliament passed an ordinance to control coal prices, but it was not very effective. In May 1643 coal fetched 50 shillings the chalder, 20 shillings above the legal price. Hostile critics suggested that profiteers would soon push it up to three pounds. There was talk of a rebellion in the City if it reached that height. Meanwhile, Newcastle petitioned the King successfully against the imposition of a double duty on coal, on the grounds that it would completely destroy the trade of the port. Already it was in a parlous state. Before the war some ten thousand men worked the colliery at Newcastle, either underground or on boats and lighters ferrying coal to the four hundred or so vessels which were moored in the Tyne at any one time. But in April 1644 only four ships cleared the customs at Newcastle, one carrying coal to Hamburg. The labourers in the colliery, like the leading coal merchants in the city itself, were Puritan or radical Protestant in religion. In July 1642 they had joined an unsuccessful attempt to force the Earl of Newcastle's soldiers from the newly-erected bulwarks around the town. Only an overwhelming show of force kept such towns loyal to the King.

At least the civil war brought an opportunity for employment to those who were out of work. The alacrity with which many common soldiers changed sides when taken prisoner suggests that they valued their wages (roughly the same as those of a farm labourer) more than their cause. The trade of soldiering, however, held little appeal to the majority of sensible Englishmen. They had no desire, in Whitelock's words, to 'leave a soft bed, close curtains and a warm chamber to lodge upon the hard and cold earth; to leave the choicest and most delicate fare of meats and wines for a little coarse bread and dirty water, with a foul pipe of tobacco; to leave the pleasing discourse and conversation of friends, wives and children for the dreadful whistling of bullets, and bodies dropping dead at one's feet'.

On the other hand, beggars could not be choosers. Adam Martindale, who was just nineteen when war broke out, shortly afterwards lost his job as tutor to the children of a Manchester merchant when his master first fortified his house for the King and then went to soldier at Wigan, a Royalist garrisoned town, having paid off his servants. Martindale was now redundant, and could entertain no hope of going to Oxford University where he had a place promised him so that he could read for holy orders. He returned to his father's house at Prescot. His account graphically illustrates the impact of the civil war upon the life of a Puritan yeoman's family in Lancashire.

Going home to my father, he received me kindly; but things were now woefully altered for the worse from what I had formerly known them. My sister was married to a noted Royalist, and, going to live about two miles from Lathom, which the Parliament's forces accounted their enemy's headquarters, they were sadly plundered by those forces passing the road wherein they dwelt. The great trade that my father and two of my brethren had long driven, was quite dead; for who would either build or repair an house when he could not sleep a night in it with quiet and safety?

My brother Henry, who was then about twenty-four years of age, knew not where to hide his head, for my Lord of Derby's officers had taken up a custom of summoning such as he and many older persons, upon pain of death, to appear at general musters, and thence to force them away with such weapons as they had, if they were but pitchforks, to Bolton; the rear being brought up with troopers, that had commission to shoot such as lagged behind, so as the poor country-men seemed to be in a dilemma of death, either by the troopers if they went not on, or by the great and small shot out of the town if they did.

This hard usage of the country to no purpose (for what could poor cudgeliers do against a fortified place?) much weakened the interest of the Royalists (called the Cavaliers) and many yeoman's sons, whereof my brother Henry was one, went to shelter themselves in Bolton, and took up arms there. . . .

Now I was in a great strait how to dispose of myself. I abhorred to live idly and burden my father, and besides I could no more be safe there than my brother Henry, for being above eighteen years old (whereas sixteen would have brought me in) I was as liable to the danger of dancing attendance at the general musters, and thence to Bolton, as he. To avoid both these inconveniences if possible, (though I was still rather too young,) I enquired after a school. . . .

Rainford being still open for me, I removed thither, having the promise of some substantial inhabitants, that they would send me their children upon the usual rates that my predecessors had, and also find me my diet by turns, as was customary also there. The first they performed well, and I had a pretty full school; the second they never offered to do, but suffered me to depend upon my father for it, whose house had been so ransacked and stripped by rude soldiers, that he had scarce necessary goods left him for the plainest sort of housekeeping. Besides, I had great disturbance given me by several papists about me, and by a pragmatical constable, animated (as I thought) by them, who notwithstanding that the Parliament forces had so prevailed as to take Wigan and

Warrington, Preston, and divers less considerable places, still warned me to musters; and though I excused myself as a piece of a clergyman, and kept away, I could not tell how it would go with me, if I should be surprised and carried to Lathom, counted then an impregnable place, where they did what they pleased within themselves.

But among all these troubles, I met with two cordials helping to support my spirit: (1) The marriage of my brother Henry to an holy young woman of pious parentage, with whom he lived comfortably at a new brick house, which he built near Warrington thriving fast in goodness and his outward estate to his very death. (2) A sermon that I heard at St Helen's, preached by Mr Smith the minister there. He was under no great account for his abilities, but pious and serious, and in that sermon he did so lay forth the desperateness and damnableness of a natural estate, without conversion, (which before that time I had little minded) that I was roused to purpose, and this proved like a sharp needle, drawing after a silken thread of comfort in due season, so as if I may, without presumption, lay claim to a work of grace, (as I humbly hope) he was the chief instrument under God, and accordingly I honoured him as my spiritual father to his death. . . .

I accepted the motion, and he carried towards me pretty civilly, and in regard he was the only justice of peace in that part of the county besides his military employment, I got money under him so as might well have satisfied me. But his family was such an hell upon earth, as was utterly intolerable. There was such a pack of arrant thieves, and they so artificial at their trade, that it was scarce possible to save anything out of their hands, except what I could carry about with me, or lodge in some other house. Those that were not thieves (if there were any such) were generally (if not universally) desperately profane and bitter scoffers at piety, and these headed by one that had a mighty influence over the colonel, and was (I never knew why) become mine implacable enemy.

I was therefore well content to come down a peg lower, accepting of the chief clerk's place in the foot regiment, which place (though below the other for profit and credit) gave me better content; for now I lived in peace, and enjoyed sweet communion with the religious officers of the company, which used to meet every night at one anothers' quarters, by turns, to read scriptures, to confer of good things, and to pray together. My work also was easy enough, and such as gave me time for my studies, being only to keep a list of the officers' and soldiers' names, and to call them upon occasion. Nor was I to carry either musket, pike, halberd, or any other weapon, only for fashion sake I wore a sword, as even ministers in those days ordinarily did.

But in this condition I remained not long, for the quarter-master of the troop being no scholar, would needs have me into it, to assist him in making tickets, though under the name and notion of clerk of the troop, to whose office, in strictness, it belonged not. But that work was not great; and the rest of my employment was much-what the same with that in the company. I was not by my office either to wear armour, or buff-coat; to stand upon guard, or to ride out as a scout. And accordingly I was not furnished with a charging-horse, war-saddle, pistols, holsters, or carbine, but only with a little hackney, and an ordinary saddle and bridle to ride along with the rest; and here also I had the comfort and benefit of some devout persons' company. After some time, Mr Thompson, the chaplain of the regiment, was sent to us to tender to us the Covenant and to satisfy any that should make scruple, which he did so effectually, that I think not one refused it.

In this easy employment of clerk of the troop and deputy quarter-master, I continued till the taking of Liverpool by Prince Rupert; in which space of time, the garrison at Lathom making some sallies out in the night, did such exploits as the colonels for the parliament took for unsufferable affronts, and laid siege to it. This was instrumental to bring an old house upon our heads: for the prince going to raise the siege at York, (where he received a great overthrow) the Earl of Derby brought him through Lancashire, where his army, after two smart repulses, took Bolton by storm (the works having been sleighted, and in very bad order) putting about one thousand eight hundred to the sword. Then spreading themselves up and down the country, made woeful work wherever they came. My brother Henry was so lately married, that he easily secured those few goods he had, together with himself and his wife, in the garrison at Warrington. My brother Thomas secured himself and some choice goods there also, but the rest, together with his poor wife and children, were at the mercy of his enemies, who were so severe that they scarcely left his family anything in the world to subsist on. But his great stock of cattle were seized upon by a great papist in the neighbourhood, intentionally for his own use, but eventually for my brother. But my poor father fared much worse, for they took the old man prisoner, and used him most barbarously, forcing him to march in his stockings, without shoes, and snapping his ears with their firelock-pistols. His house they plundered of everything they thought worth carrying away, in carts which they brought to his door to that purpose, and were sore troubled (good men!) that the walls being stone, and the roof well shot over within, they could fasten no fire upon the house, though they several times essayed so to do. His stock of cattle they wholly drove away, and he never had an hoof again, amongst which was an excellent colt, almost ready for service, which, in regard of its high mettle and curious shapes, resembling its dam, which was a gallant mare, he valued an high rate. This, being exceeding hard to be taken, they were resolved to shoot, (out of perfect malice to him,) but at last, with difficulty, they caught her, and away she went with the rest. ... .

When Liverpool was surrendered upon terms of free-quarter, though Rupert's men, upon their first entrance, did (notwithstanding these terms) slay almost all they met with, to the number of three hundred and sixty and, among other, divers of their own friends, and some artificers that never bore arms in their lives, yea, one poor blind man; yet the first that I met with offered me quarter before I asked.

Though I lost there, in a manner, all I had, viz: my mare, books, money, and clothes, and my relations were in such distress as even now I declared, I was sufficiently provided for, and my spirit cheerfully supported throughout a tedious imprisonment of about nine weeks, though I neither knew where I should be supplied for a week beforehand, nor by what means I could expect deliverance.

When I was at last set at liberty, a free-school was vacant, and (as it were) waiting for me, in Over Whitley, in Cheshire, with which I closed when I lacked a few weeks of twenty-one years old; and this was a perfect manumission from the hated life I had lived about two years among soldiers; though mine office was all along to employ my pen, not my sword, and to spend ink, not spill blood.

Not all Englishmen hated the soldier's profession as did Adam Martindale. Like the King himself, many English gentlemen found that the active life of a soldier in the field gave them good health. Some of them, such as Colonel John Hutchinson, discovered rather late in the day that they would like to continue as soldiers. It was civil war they abhorred, not war as such. Even Sir William Waller, who so much detested 'this war without an enemy' and feigned indifference when his military employment came to an end, sought secretly to enlist as a mercenary in the service of Venice at the earliest opportunity.

Service in the armies of Parliament certainly provided opportunities for social advancement. At first the rival armies were officered by men of much the same social status, but gradually new men from the middle, lower middle and artisan classes moved into positions of responsibility, both on the committees which ran the war in each county and in the forces themselves. John Hampden's shepherd, Thomas Shelbourne, rose to be colonel of Cromwell's double regiment of Ironsides, and there were other similar stories. The more conservative Puritan gentry objected to these newcomers as much on social grounds as on account of their often unorthodox or radical religious views. As Lucy Hutchinson writes with disdain, 'almost all the Parliament garrisons were infested and disturb'd with like factious little people, insomuch that many worthy gentlemen were wearied out of their command, some oppressed by a certain sort of people in the House whom, to distinguish from the most honourable gentlemen, they called *worsted stocking men*'.

These words illustrate how the Civil War allowed ordinary people to participate in local and national politics. In some of their minds it prompted ideas of popular sovereignty which herald the dawn of modern democracy.

The war produced a religious ferment as well as stimulating social change. The Reformation had become the popular possession of the middle and lower ranks of society, especially in the towns. With the bible as their authority half-educated Puritan preachers challenged the monopoly of religion enjoyed by the university-trained clerics. In the armies, officers and soldiers would sometimes preach to each other. The Royalists accused their enemies of encouraging women to preach as well, clearly contrary to the word of scripture and the natural order which required them to be subordinate to their husbands. Stung by such charges, Anne Lady Waller even wrote a letter to the Royalist editor of *Mercurius Aulicus*, 'wherein she tells us that we have hitherto spoken unrighteously of her, for as yet (she protests) she never preached, but says she knows not what we may drive her to; assuring us on her honour that she only interpreted some difficulties in the Word, which her Ladyship calls "undoing hard chapters". According to which phrase her husband's army is almost quite expounded'.

Cromwell stands in a slippery place, directing a fickle mob in felling the Royal Oak of Britain, along with Magna Carta, the law and holy writ. Royalist cartoons were quite as vivid as their Parliamentarian equivalents.

Like such other Puritan ladies as Lady Fairfax and Lucy Hutchinson, Lady Waller participated fully in the civil war at the side of her husband. Marriage for the Puritans meant a complete partnership in the service of God, and wives expected to share in their husbands' political and even military decisions. The editor of *Mercurius Aulicus* ridiculed Lady Waller throughout 1644 as a stereotype of such Puritan ladies, so that 'no week can pass without an unmannerly flirt or fling at her'. At Abingdon church Lady Waller had said 'Stand off, good people, that the soldiers can see me'. A fortnight later she was pressing for Henry Marten, a radical republican member of Parliament, to be Governor of Reading. She was said to dominate her husband throughout the war, as she 'used to do at Winchester church, where if he offered to speak about doctrines or uses her ladyship would rebuke him, saying "Peace, Master Waller, you know your weakness in these things", since which time Sir William has ever gone for the weaker vessels. Upon another occasion she thrice greeted her husband: "O thou man of God, come kiss me!"' Again, she pushed Sir William into going up to London to protest against Major-General Browne's usurpation of his authority in the south Oxfordshire area.

In this war of rival newspapers the Parliamentarian editors sprang to Lady

Waller's defence: 'She is not like your Court madams, Aulicus; uses no oil of talc, no false teeth, no wanton frisking gate, no catterwauling [i.e. going after the opposite sex] in Spring Garden. She bestows not all her time upon her body and leaves none for the soul. She cannot measure out a whole morning with curling irons and spend the afternoon in courting and vanity and toying. But every morning her soul is made ready before her body. She looks not so much what clothes, as what virtues are convenient to wear . . .'

In fact this stereotype of the Royalist lady is partly misleading. From Queen Henrietta Maria downwards, Royalist wives often felt as fully involved in the struggle as their Puritan counterparts. Wardour Castle and Lathom House, to give but two examples, were held for the King by the wives of their owners. Many more Royalist ladies shared the hardships of their husbands. Sir Hugh Cholmley paid a handsome tribute to his wife:

My wife was at London, when at Scarborough I declared for the King; and they, being nettled that they had lost a person so useful to them as I had been, did not only pass some sharp votes in the House of Commons against my person, but plundered my wife of her coach-horses, and used her coarsely. Yet she procured a pass to come to me, and, with her two girls, the elder then not above eight years of age, came to Whitby in a ship, having so prosperous and quick a passage, as she said she would never go up and down again to London but by ship. I had now been a year from her; and she being within London, and not understanding the causes why I quitted the Parliament, or the true state of the difference between the King and Parliament, was very earnest and firm for their party; but, after I had unmasked to her the Parliament's intent, and clearly presented to her their proceedings and the state of affairs, she then was as much against them, and as earnest for the King, and continued so to her death. After she had been two or three days at Whitby, I brought her to Scarborough, where I was then governor for his Majesty by a commission from the Marquis of Newcastle, general for the King in the North parts, and was governor both of the town and castle. . . .

At the beginning of February following began the siege of Scarborough town, when my wife, who would not forsake me for any danger, desired me to send into Holland my two girls, whom I parted with not without great trouble, for I was fond of them; with them I sent to wait on them a French gentlewoman, a chamber-maid, a man-servant; and a grave minister, one Mr Remmington, and his wife, to be superintendants over all. We were in the town and castle besieged above twelve months, during which time my dear wife endured much hardship, and yet with little shew of trouble; and though by nature, according to her sex, timorous, yet in greatest danger would not be daunted, but shewed a courage even above her sex.

At the King's Court it was fashionable for women to take an interest in politics. When Lady Fanshawe rejoined her husband, who was on the Prince of Wales' Council at Bristol in 1645, she soon fell an easy victim to that fashion:

My husband had provided very good lodgings for us, and as soon as he could come home from the Council, where he was at my arrival, he with all expressions of joy received me in his arms and gave me an hundred pieces of gold, saying, 'I know that you that keeps my heart so well will keep my fortune, which from this time I will ever put into your hands as God shall bless me with increase'. And now I thought myself a queen, and my husband so glorious a crown that I more valued myself to be call'd by his name than born a princess, for I knew him very wise and very good, and his soul doted on me, upon which confidence I'll tell you what happened.

My Lady Rivers, a brave woman and one that had suffered very many thousands pounds loss for the King, and that I had a great reverence for and she a kindness for me as a kinswoman, in discourse she tacitly commended the knowledge of state affairs and that some women were very happy in a good understanding thereof, as my lady [Aubigny], Lady [Isabella] Thynne, and divers others, and yet none was at first more capable than I; that in the night she knew there came a post from Paris from the Queen, and that she would be extreme glad to hear what the Queen commanded the King in order to his affairs, saying if I would ask my husband privately, he would tell me what he found in the packet, and I might tell her. I that was young, innocent, and to that day had never in my mouth, 'What news', began to think there was more in inquiring into business of public affairs than I thought of, and that it being a fashionable thing would make me more beloved of my husband (if that had been possible) than I was.

When my husband returned from Council, after welcoming him home, as his custom ever was, he went with his handful of papers into his study for an hour or more. I followed him. He turning hastily said, 'What would you have, my life?' I told him I heard the Prince had received a packet from the Queen, and I guessed it that in his hand, and I desired to know what was in it. He smiling replied, 'My love, I will immediately come to you. Pray you go, for I am very busy.' When he came out of his closet I revived my suit. He kissed me and talked of other things. At supper I would eat nothing. He as usual sat by me and drank often to me, which was his custom, and was full of discourse to the company that was at table. Going to bed I asked again, and said I could not believe he loved me if he refused to tell me all he knew, but he answered nothing but stopped my mouth with kisses, so we went to bed. I cried and he went to sleep; next morning very early, as his custom was, he called to rise, but begun to discourse with me first, to which I made no reply. He rose, came on the other side of the bed and kissed me, and drew the curtain softly and went to court.

When he came home to dinner, he presently came to me as was usual, and when I had him by the hand I said, 'You do not care to see me troubled.' To which he, taking me in his arms, answered, 'My dearest soul, nothing upon earth can afflict me like that; and when you asked me of my business it was wholly out of my power to satisfy you. For my life and fortune shall be thine, and every thought of my heart, in which the trust I am in may not be revealed; but my honour is my own, which I can not preserve if I communicate the Prince's affairs, and pray you with this answer rest satisfied.' So great was his reason and goodness, that upon consideration it made my folly appear to me so vile that from that day until the day of his death I never thought fit to ask him any business, but that he communicated freely to me, in order to his estate or family.

Women also performed the more traditional task of acting as nurses. Not all the wounded or sick, especially those that fell into enemy hands, were as fortunate as those treated by Lucy Hutchinson after a skirmish outside Nottingham. As a girl she had been brought up in the Tower of London, where her father Sir Allen Apsley was Lieutenant. Her compassionate mother set her a good example. Apart from spending some of her annual allowance of £300 buying scientific equipment for Sir Walter Raleigh, then a prisoner, she made broths and medicines for the sick. Despite the anger of one Puritan zealot, a minister newly-commissioned as a captain named Palmer, Lucy Hutchinson continued the family tradition.

'There was a large room which was the chapel in the Castle. This they had fill'd full of prisoners besides a very bad prison which was no better than a dungeon, call'd the Lion's Den. And the new Captain Palmer and another minister, having nothing else to do, walk'd up and down the Castle yard insulting over and beating the poor prisoners as they were brought in. In the encounter one of the Derby captains was slain and only five of our men hurt, who for want of another surgeon were brought to the Governor's wife, and she having some excellent balsams and plasters in her closet, with the assistance of a gentleman that had some skill, dressed all their wounds (whereof some were dangerous, being all shots) with such good success that they were all cured in convenient time.

After our hurt men were dressed, as she stood at her chamber door, seeing three of the prisoners sorely cut and carried down bleeding into the Lion's Den, she desired the marshal to bring them into her, and bound and dressed their wounds also; which while she was doing, Captain Palmer came in and told her his soul abhorr'd to see this favour to the enemies of God. She replied, she had done nothing but what she thought was her duty in humanity to them, as creatures, not as enemies. . . .

The field armies had their complement of chirurgeons (or surgeons) and physicians to treat the sick and wounded. The methods of treatment available were primitive by our standards and left room for much disagreement. In an amusing early demarcation dispute between the two branches of the profession Richard Allen, chirurgeon to the train of artillery under Sir William Waller, was accused at a court martial of disobeying the orders of Doctor Pratt, Physician of the army, to let a gunner's blood. Thomas Peasly, Pratt's messenger, had met Allen and demanded to know the whereabouts of the chirurgeon attached to the company of firelocks (the musketeers armed with flint-locks who guarded the train). Allen snatched the paper from him, read it, and said that he had let the man's blood some time ago. Immediately falling into a passion, he tore the paper and called Doctor Pratt 'Fool! Ass! Coxcombe!' Allen confessed to using those words, and that he would not administer the doctor's physick, 'being a duty nothing belonging to him as a chirurgeon'. As his punishment he was sentenced to be cashiered and imprisoned until the next council of war.

Scarred and maimed soldiers could be seen long after the war. After the

Restoration many Royalist veterans petitioned the magistrates for war pensions, and their cases are recorded in the Quarter Sessions. They convey a note of grim reality missing from many later accounts of the Civil War. At Cropredy Bridge, for example, James Sleamaker 'received a cut from the enemy in the face and had his bowels trod out with a horse and was run through with a sword to the unparalleled hazard of his life'. Sergeant William Stoakes of Shepton Mallet served throughout the war. He was severely wounded at Marston Moor and captured at Naseby. Now a very poor man with a wife and five small children, he had 'lost the use of his limbs and is not any way able to work for their maintenance. And since it has pleased God to restore his sacred Majesty (whom God prosper) to the throne of his late father's kingdom, your petitioner hopes that some comfort and refreshment will be provided for the maintenance of himself and his poor family. . . .' He was given a pension of forty shillings a year.

'The greatest calamity of war is the perniciousness of it to men's souls,' wrote Baxter. The effect of the Civil War upon English spirits, as opposed to property or bodies, is infinitely more difficult to assess. Undoubtedly almost everyone experienced the war as a national tragedy, which depressed the finer spirits and caused not a few suicides in battle. Except for the sprinkling of professional soldiers on both sides most Englishmen in arms were soon heartily sick of the fighting, and loathed the discomforts of life in the army. Like their civilian compatriots they longed for a return of those long summer days

> When gardens only had their towers,
> And all the garrisons were flowers;
> When roses only arms might bear,
> And men did rosy garlands wear.

Andrew Marvell, who penned these words, was tutor to Sir Thomas Fairfax's daughter at Nunappleton in Yorkshire, a house famed for its lovely gardens. But in the bustle and smoke of London a greater poet, John Milton, espied a different England in the making, an England roused to new creative vigour by the impact of war. The nation could not return to the sleepy innocence of a lost paradise. Conscious of God's special calling, endowed with gifts for inventive industry and scientific discovery for the universal good, England must walk forward into an unknown future guided by the lights of faith and reason. Milton protested eloquently against Parliament's imposition of censorship on the press because he believed passionately that truth could be known through free discussion. In the travail of war he perceived a spiritual rebirth of the nation.

Lords and Commons of England, consider what nation it is whereof you are and whereof you are the governors – a nation not slow and dull, but of a quick, ingenious, and piercing spirit, acute to invent, subtle and sinewy to discourse, not beneath the

The young John Milton, who in 1644 prophesied a new birth for the nation after the travail of civil war.

reach of any point the highest that human capacity can soar to. . . .

Methinks I see in my mind a noble and puissant nation rousing herself like a strong man after sleep, and shaking her invincible locks. Methinks I see her as an eagle mewing her mighty youth, and kindling her undazzled eyes at the full midday beam; purging and unscaling her long-abused sight at the fountain itself of heavenly radiance; while the whole noise of timorous and flocking birds, with those also that love the twilight, flutter about, amazed at what she means.

Although wishful thinking coloured Milton's sublime vision, he had clearly sensed that powerful impulse for change in politics and religion, art and science. The more sober words of the historian of the Royal Society, which was founded in 1645, confirm the intellectual and spiritual stimulus which came in the wake of war. Bishop Sprat, who was a boy during the conflict, wrote: 'The late times of civil war . . . brought this advantage with them, that they stirred up men's minds from long ease . . . and made them active, industrious and inquisitive.' This led to 'an universal desire and appetite after knowledge'.

In 1644, when Milton prophesied in London, the civil war had yet to be won. That year the poet applied to become adjutant-general in Sir William Waller's new army. But Milton could find no employment for his sword (with which he practised sword-play every day) and served the cause to greater effect with his matchless pen. Meanwhile the armies of Parliament addressed themselves to the remaining military task of securing final victory in the field.

13

The Defeat of the Cavaliers

After the victory at Cheriton in March 1644 nothing less than 'a grand battle' would satisfy Parliament. To this end it was resolved to concentrate the armies of Essex, Waller and Manchester and then 'to wait upon his Majesty at Oxford'. Before the city could be stormed, however, the King slipped out of Oxford under cover of darkness with a flying army and made his way safely to Worcester. Leaving Waller to follow the King wherever he chose to go, Essex marched westwards to relieve the siege of Lyme.

When Waller closed upon Worcester the King again gave him the slip and headed back towards Oxford. By now the Committee of Both Kingdoms, which was attempting to give some overall strategic direction to the war, had counter-manded Essex's orders and told Waller to march into the West. But then, hearing that the King had left Oxford again, the Committee sent orders to Waller at Gloucester to oppose the King's march. In the Cotswolds Waller heard that the King had marched towards the Eastern Association, probably to draw away Manchester's army from Prince Rupert in the North. After long marches in extremely hot weather, he caught up with the King near the village of Cropredy. On 29 June Waller flung two strong columns of horse across the river Cherwell to take the Royalist army in the flank as it marched northwards, but both were severely repulsed. After some fierce fighting at the mouth of Cropredy Bridge, Waller withdrew to some high ground having lost eleven brass guns.

Just before sunset a trumpeter arrived with a message from the King to the effect that if Waller consented his Majesty's herald-at-arms would proclaim 'a gracious message' at the head of the Parliamentarian army. Waller replied that he had no commission to entertain any messages from the King without the permission of Parliament, and therefore the address must be made there. Waller did not include in his official report the revealing incident which followed hard upon this exchange: 'The trumpet said he had a private message for me, and prayed me to hear him. I replied there need be no privacy, not caring to give a handle to mine enemies, but some that were near me did persuade me to hear the man, and went out. He then presently pulled forth a letter, which to my great shame and surprise came from the Lady. . . . In it she besought me to betray my cause; and this she did so wittily and kind, that I had much ado to be angry. Before this lady's marriage I had been her suitor and did dearly love her, and she remembered me of this, and of some soft passages.

A contemporary picture of the King's flight from Oxford in April 1646.

Whether or not she was put on this by some greater than herself I never knew; but I returned for answer, that as I had never been traitor to my love, so I would not to my cause, which I should be, if I did as she would advise, and after this I heard no more. . . .'

On Sunday morning an unpleasant accident almost killed Sir William. 'Being with my officers at a council of war the floor of the room (where we were) sunk, and we all fell into a cellar that was underneath it. I lay overwhelmed with a great deal of lumber that fell upon me, and yet I bless God I had no hurt at all.' Waller did not mention the fact that old Major General Potley landed first on the cellar floor and broke his own fall. As the corpulent Colonel Holbourne then collapsed on top of Waller, Potley sustained the worst injuries and he appears to have retired from active service shortly afterwards.

With the King on the march again Waller made haste to follow him, but his weary and beaten army had lost heart. On 2 July Waller wrote to the Committee of Both Kingdoms: 'During these two days march I was extremely plagued by the mutinies of the City brigade . . . being come to their old song of "Home! Home!" . . . My Lords, I write these particularities to let you know that an army compounded of these men will never go through with their service, and till you have an army merely your own that you may command, it is in a manner impossible to do anything of importance.'

Waller expected the King to return to Oxford, but on Wednesday, 3 July he informed the committee at Derby House: 'I have just now received information that the enemy has given me another turn upon the toe and marched last night to Stow and Morton-in-the-Marsh, on his old road to Worcester. Tomorrow I intend to march after them with all possible speed with my horse and mus-keteers, leaving some behind to line the pikes and help guard the colours, which will follow easily. I cannot follow to overtake them in a direct line, but in coasting them by way of Leicester I hope to gain ground of them. . . . I am of the opinion, before this business be done, we shall be the longest winded army in England. I hope we shall never be weary of well doing, let the way be never so long and rugged.'

News of the defeat of Prince Rupert at Marston Moor on 2 July reached the King, however, and he turned again and marched into the West leaving Waller's shattered forces far behind him.

Richard Symonds, an Essex gentleman who served in Charles I's Lifeguard of Horse, kept a diary during that summer campaign as he marched with the army 'drums beating, colours flying and trumpets sounding'. He was an antiquarian, and he spent what time he could spare making notes in parish churches, recording the monuments of the leading families and their coats-of-arms. He also noted local customs or interesting sights: 'Every Midlent Sunday is a great day at Worcester, when all the children and godchildren meet at the head and chief of the family and have a feast. They call it the Mothering-day.' 'The parson's wife of Fladbury, a young woman often carrying a milk-pail on her head in the street – so far from pride.'

As the army made its way westwards the Royalist generals tightened disci-pline. Near Badminton in Wiltshire two foot-soldiers were hanged from a tree for pillaging the country villages. 'The whole army of horse and foot marched by the bodies.' At Bath another two were hanged for the same offence.

On 26 July the King entered Exeter, where he learned that the Earl of Essex and his whole army lay within seven or eight miles of Plymouth. The King then pursued Essex into Cornwall and hemmed him into Lostwithiel. After Essex had departed by sea on 1 September Major-General Skippon surrendered the army on terms. Leaving all forty-two cannon, their pikes and musket, and all carriages except one to a regiment, the soldiers were allowed to march away with their colours. All officers kept their swords, and those in the horse retained their pistols and hat-bands as well. Symonds noted down the green, blue and white colours of the foot regiments as they marched past him on the long road to London through hostile lines of Royalist soldiers.

The King himself rode about the field and gave strict command to his chief officers to see that none of the enemy were plundered, and that all his soldiers should repair to their colours which were in the adjoining closes. Yet, notwithstanding our officers with their swords drawn did perpetually beat off our foot, many of them lost their hats, etc.

Yet most of them escaped this danger till they came to Lostwithiel, and there the people inhabitants and the country people plundered some of their officers and all, notwithstanding a sufficient party of horse was appointed by his Majesty to be their convoy.

They all, except here and there an officer, (and seriously I saw not above three or four that looked like a gentleman,) were stricken with such a dismal fear, that as soon as their colour of the regiment was passed (for every ensign had a horse and rode on him and was so suffered) the rout of soldiers of that regiment pressed all of a heap like sheep, though not so innocent. So dirty and so dejected as was rare to see. None of them, except some few of their officers, that did look any of us in the face. Our foot would flout at them and bid them remember Reading, Greenland House (where others that did no condition with them took them away all prisoners), and many other places, and then would pull their swords, etc. away, for all our officers still slashed at them.

The rebels told us as they passed that our officers and gentlemen carried themselves honourably, but they were hard dealt withal by the common soldiers.

This was a happy day for his Majesty and his whole army, that without loss of much blood this great army of rascals that so triumphed and vaunted over the poor inhabitants of Cornwall, as if they had been invincible, and as if the King had not been able to follow them, that 'tis conceived very few will get safe to London, for the country people whom they have in all the march so much plundered and robbed that they will have their pennyworths out of them.

The Parliamentarian soldiers were permitted, once they reached Portsmouth or Southampton, to fight again. But they marched without food or shelter on the way, many of them stripped bare. Of the 6,000 men who left Lostwithiel on 2 September only some 1,000 reached their destinations. Starvation, disease, exposure and desertion accounted for the rest.

Only one regiment of horse surrendered at Lostwithiel; the remaining 2,000 troopers and dragoons broke out and linked up with Waller's horse in Dorset under Major-General John Middleton. 'We are a gallant forlorn hope,' Waller wrote from Shaftesbury on 24 September, as the Royalist army approached towards him. In October he fell back into Hampshire where the army of the Eastern Association and the remnants of Essex's regiments joined him. On the 15th of that month the whole Royalist army entered Salisbury after a wet, cold and windy day's march. On Tuesday the 22nd the King ordered a general rendezvous for his forces on Red Heath, near Newbury. Three days later the combined Parliamentarian armies, some 28,000 strong, had advanced within three miles of Newbury, the King's headquarters, on the east side. The weather continued very wet and cold; the Earl of Essex became ill as he marched on foot at the head of his regiments in the rain-lashed lanes of Berkshire and retired to a warm featherbed in Reading.

Thanks to a double turncoat, Sir John Urry, the Parliamentarian commanders had an accurate picture of the King's dispositions in the open fields between Newbury and Donnington Castle to the north of it. As darkness fell Waller and Cromwell led a force upon a long night march in order to take the enemy in the rear on the morrow while Manchester attacked from the east. Next morning, Sunday, 27 October, the great battle began as Manchester's men skirmished hard. But Waller's column did not arrive near the battlefield until about two in the afternoon, and then they had to storm an earth breastwork manned by four hundred men with five cannon before they could come to grips with the Royalist army. On the other side, Colonel Lisle and a thousand musketeers successfully held Shaw House against two major assaults by Manchester's foot. At four o'clock Waller and Cromwell led their regiments in the first charges against the Cavalier brigades of horse who responded in kind. Amid the smoke, noise and confusion, the King was once almost surrounded by enemy troopers, and his Lifeguard charged valiantly to rescue him. The Earl of Cleveland was taken prisoner, his men beaten, being overpowered by horse and foot. As the daylight faded the King went off the field to Donnington Castle, where he stayed for half an hour watching 'the infinite shooting of muskets on both sides in all places'. That 'sad night' he withdrew to Bath and then moved to Oxford.

On Friday, 8 November the King and Prince Rupert, who had joined him from Cirencester, marched back with 15,000 men to relieve the Castle and recover the train of artillery which had been left there. And so the two armies faced each other once again. The King having now secured his guns, the Cavaliers skirmished boldly with the enemy on Sunday morning as the cannon played on both sides. 'A musket bullet in volley shot the King's horse in the foot as he stood before his own regiment in his arms,' noted Richard Symonds. As night fell the whole Royalist army marched away in triumph in the face of the enemy with drums beating, colours flying and 'trumpets prattling their marches'.

While the King's army stood in battle array before their own forces Manchester, Waller, Cromwell and the other general officers had met for a council of war in a cottage nearby. Some officers urged that the King must be defeated before any foreign contingents could come to his aid. But Manchester assured them that no such forces would come out of France, and then gave his opinion against a battle, adding: 'Gentlemen, I beseech you let's consider what we do. The King need not care how oft he fights, but it concerns us to be wary, for in fighting we venture all to nothing. If we fight 100 times and beat him 99 he will be King still, but if he beats us but once, or the last time, we shall be hanged, we shall lose our estates, and our posterities be undone.' Whereupon Cromwell replied: 'My Lord, if this be so, why did we take up arms at first? This is against fighting ever hereafter. If so, let us make peace, be it never so base.'

The Parliamentary generals judged it expedient to send Sir Arthur Heselrige up to London to explain their actions. On 14 November, he strode into the House of Commons 'all in beaten buff, cross-girt with sword and pistol as if he had been killing his thousands . . . and there, like a great soldier in that habit, he gave a relation of what had passed, highly extolling the gallantry and conduct of all the commanders and the valour of the soldiers'. The House was not entirely satisfied with the explanations offered to it by Heselrige. Nine days later Waller and Cromwell, both newly arrived in London, received orders to speak in the

The Battle of Naseby

14th June 1645

Naseby

Mill Hill Farm

22

17

15

16

6

5

THE ROYALIST ARMY **1** The King; **2** Newark Horse; **3** and **4** King's Life Guard; **5** Prince Rupert's Bluecoats; **6** Newark horse; **7** (out of sight to right) Prince Maurice and Prince Rupert's Life Guards; **8** Prince Rupert's Horse; **9** The Queen's Regiment; **10** Prince Maurice's Regiment; **11** (out of sight to right) Earl of Northampton's Regiment; **12** Sir W. Vaughan's Regiment; **13** foot regiments under Lord Astley; **14** foot regiments under Sir Henry Bard; **15** foot regiments under Sir George Lisle; **16** Sir Thomas Howard's Regiment; **17** Northern Horse under Sir Marmaduke Langdale, and Newark Horse.

THE NEW MODEL ARMY **18** Dragoons; **19** the left wing under Commissary General Ireton, including the regiments of Colonels Butler, Vermuden, Riche and Fleetwood, Ireton's own regiments and the Association troops; **20** the forlorn hope; **21** the centre under Major General Skippon, including regiments of Sir H. Waller, Colonels Pickering, Hammond and Rainsborough, Montague and Pride; **22** the right wing under Cromwell, including regiments of Colonels Walley, Rossiter, Sheffield and Fiennes, Sir Robert Pye's Regiment and the Associated horse; **23** rearguard under Lt Col Pride; **24** the baggage train.

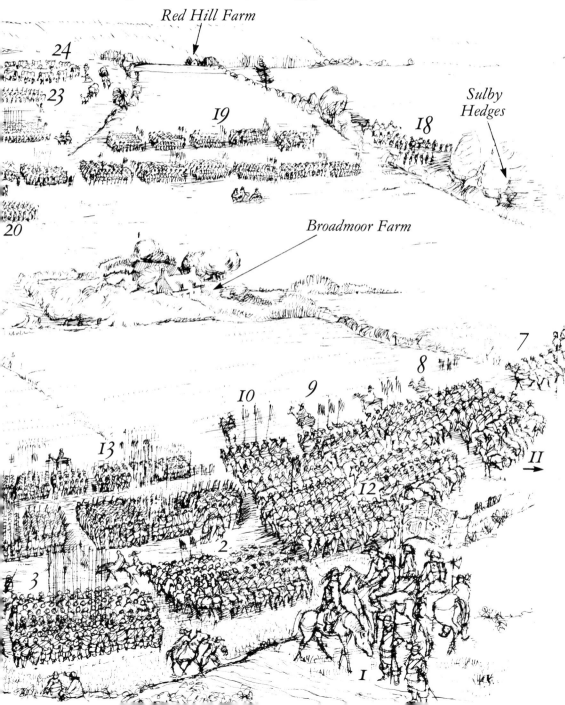

Red Hill Farm

Sulby Hedges

Broadmoor Farm

Commons. On the 25th Waller gave to the House his own version of the campaign, probably taking much the same line as Heselrige. Shortly afterwards the long-smouldering quarrel between Cromwell and Manchester exploded when the former accused his commanding officer before the House of 'continued backwardness to all action'.

The subsequent inquest into missed opportunities at Newbury and Donnington gradually developed into a searching assessment of Parliament's generals. 'God seems not to favour the great officers: certainly we are ill served by them,' noted one Puritan. On 23 November, the Commons directed the Committee of Both Kingdoms 'to consider of a frame or model of the whole militia' and to present their report to the House. In a great speech on 9 December, Cromwell persuaded the Commons to bring in the Self-Denying Ordinance, requiring members of both Houses to surrender their commissions.

The New Model Army, which took the field in April 1645 under General Sir Thomas Fairfax, consisted of 22,000 men, divided into 6,600 horse, 1,000 dragoons and 14,400 foot, the horse formed into eleven regiments, the dragoons into ten companies and the foot into twelve regiments. The army cost £44,955 a month, a sum to be raised by a national assessment. Of the 163 officers whose homes are known, 60 came from East Anglia and 51 from London. Independents were prominent among these officers, for Fairfax was empowered to dispense with the requirement that all should sign the Covenant if he was satisfied with the godliness of a man. About forty of the officers, not more than 200 in all, are known to have risen from the ranks while as many had been tradesmen or artisans. Thirty-three officers had served an apprenticeship in London, the majority of them in the cloth trades. But contemporary assertions that the officers were 'tradesmen, brewers, tailors, goldsmiths, shoemakers and the like' are exaggerated. Lieutenant-Colonels Pride and Hewson had been respectively a drayman and a cobbler but only seven of the thirty-seven generals and full colonels were not gentlemen by birth. Whatever their background, all the officers and soldiers of the New Model had proved their worth in the profession of arms.

Fairfax marched to Taunton, but he was recalled from the West to besiege Oxford. On the news of the King's capture of Leicester, he raised the siege of Oxford on 5 June and brought Charles and Prince Rupert to battle at Naseby on 14 June. Both sides drew up their forces in the traditional manner, with the foot in the middle flanked by bodies of horse. Lieutenant-General Cromwell and Commissary-General Ireton commanded the two wings of Roundhead horse. 'I can say this of Naseby,' Cromwell recalled later, 'that when I saw the enemy draw up and march in gallant order towards us, and we a company of poor ignorant men, to seek to order our battle, the General having commanded up to order all the horse, I could not, riding alone about my business, but smite out to God in praises, in assurance of victory, because God would by things that are

The most true-to-life and evocative portrait of Oliver Cromwell – Samuel Cooper's unfinished miniature, here enlarged by about a third.

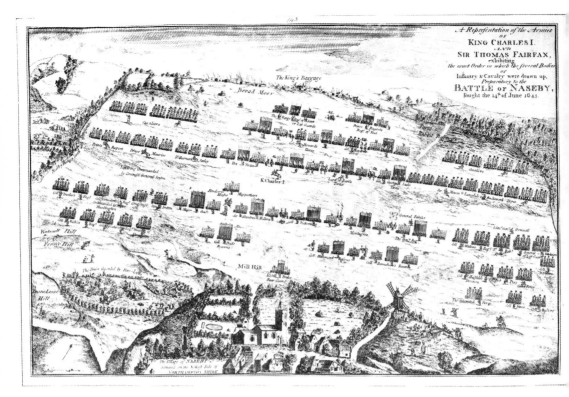

A contemporary plan of Naseby, which first appeared to illustrate Joshua Sprigge's account of the marchings of the New Model Army. It exaggerates the strength of the Royalist army.

not bring to nought things that are. Of which I had great assurance, and God did it.'

As Edward Walker makes clear, the advance of the Royalist army was caused by Prince Rupert's impatience. Lacking good intelligence of the enemy's movements he had drawn out a party of horse and musketeers to discover them. Catching sight of the van of the New Model Army he called the rest of his army forwards to join him:

This made us quit our ground of advantage, and in reasonable order to advance. Having marched about a mile and half, we could perceive their horse in the high ground about Naseby, but we could not judge of their number or intentions. To be short, the manner of our march being in full campania, gave them the means of disposing themselves to the best advantage; and the heat of Prince Rupert, and his opinion they durst not stand him, engaged us before we had either turned our cannon or chosen fit ground to fight on.

About ten of the clock the battle began, the first charge being given by Prince Rupert with his own and Prince Maurice's troops; who did so well, and were so well seconded, as that they bore all down before them, and were (as 'tis said) masters of six pieces of the rebels' cannon. Presently our forces advanced up the hill, the rebels only discharging

194

five pieces at them, but overshot them, and so did their musketeers. The foot on either side hardly saw each other until they were within carbine shot, and so only made one volley; ours falling in with sword and butt end of the muskets did notable execution; so much as I saw their colours fall and their foot in great disorder. And had our left wing but at this time done half so well as either the foot or the right wing, we had got in a few minutes a glorious victory.

The Royalist left wing consisted of five bodies of Northern and Newark horse, who were opposed by seven great bodies of horse under Cromwell, who enjoyed considerable advantage of ground. Being flanked and pressed back, the Cavaliers at last gave ground and fled. Four of the Roundhead bodies pursued them while the rest charged against the Royalist foot. Joshua Sprigge, who served as chaplain to Fairfax, gives an eyewitness account of this action:

The enemy this while marched up in good order, a swift march, with a great deal of gallantry and resolution. . . . It is hard to say whether wing of our horse charged first; but the Lieutenant-General not thinking it fit to stand and receive the enemy's charge, advanced forward with the right wing of the horse, in the same order wherein it was placed. Our word that day was, *God our strength*; their word was, *Queen Mary*.

Colonel Whalley being the left hand on the right wing, charged first two divisions of Langdale's horse, who made a very gallant resistance, and firing at a very close charge, they came to the sword: wherein Colonel Whalley's divisions routed those two divisions of Langdale's, driving them back to Prince Rupert's regiment, being the reserve of the enemy's foot, whither indeed they fled for shelter, and rallied. The reserves to Colonel Whalley were ordered to second him, which they performed with a great deal of resolution. In the mean time, the rest of the divisions of the right wing, being straitened by furzes on the right hand, advanced with great difficulty, as also by reason of the unevenness of the ground, and a cony-warren over which they were to march, which put them somewhat out of their order in their advance. Notwithstanding which difficulty, they came up to the engaging the residue of the enemy's horse on the left wing, whom they routed, and put into great confusion; not one body of the enemy's horse which they charged but they routed, and forced to fly beyond all their foot, except some that were for a time sheltered by the brigade of foot before mentioned. . . .

The horse of the enemy's left wing being thus beaten from their foot, retreated back about a quarter of a mile beyond the place where the battle was fought. The success of our main battle was not answerable; the right hand of the foot, being the General's regiment, stood, not being much pressed upon. Almost all the rest of the main battle being overpressed, gave ground, and went off in some disorder, falling behind the reserves. But the colonels and officers, doing the duty of very gallant men, in endeavouring to keep their men from disorder, and finding their attempt fruitless therein, fell into the reserves with their colours, choosing rather there to fight and die, than to quit the ground they stood on. The reserves advancing, commanded by Colonel Rainsborough, Colonel Hammond, and Lieutenant-Colonel Pride, repelled the enemy, forcing them to a disorderly retreat. Thus much being said of the right wing and

W. F. Yeames's famous Victorian painting entitled 'When did you last see your father?' It recalls Sir Thomas Byron's examination of Bulstrode Whitelocke's children at Fawley Court in 1642.

the main battle it comes next in order that an account be given of the left wing of our horse.

Upon the approach of the enemy's right wing of horse, our left wing drawing down the brow of the hill to meet them, the enemy coming on fast, suddenly made a stand, as if they had not expected us in so ready a posture: ours seeing them stand, made a little stand also, partly by reason of some disadvantage of the ground, and until the rest of the divisions of horse might recover their stations. Upon that, the enemy advanced again, whereupon our left wing sounded a charge, and fell upon them. The three right-hand divisions of our left wing made the first onset, and those divisions of the enemy opposite to them received the charge. The two left-hand divisions of the left wing did not advance equally, but being more backward, the opposite divisions of the enemy advanced upon them. Of the three right-hand divisions (before mentioned) which advanced, the middlemost charged not home; the other two coming to a close charge, routed the two opposite divisions of the enemy, (and the Commissary-General seeing one of the enemy's brigades of foot on his right hand pressing sore upon our foot, commanded the division that was with him to charge that body of foot, and, for their better encouragement, he himself with great resolution fell in amongst the musketeers, where his horse being shot under him, and himself run through the thigh with a pike, and into the face with an halbert, was taken prisoner by the enemy, until afterwards, when the battle turning, and the enemy in great distraction, he had an happy opportunity to offer his keeper his liberty, if he would carry him off, which was performed on both parts accordingly).

That division of the enemy's which was between, which the other division of ours should have charged, was carried away in the disorder of the other two; the one of those right-hand divisions of our left wing that did rout the front of the enemy charged the reserve too, and broke them; the other reserves of the enemy came on, and broke those divisions of ours that charged them; the divisions of the left hand of the right wing were likewise overborne, having much disadvantage, by reason of pits of water, and other pieces of ditches that they expected not, which hindered them in their order to charge.

The enemy having thus worsted our left wing pursued their advantage, and Prince Rupert himself having prosecuted his success upon the left wing almost to Naseby town, in his return summoned the train, offering them quarter, which being well defended with the firelocks, and a rearguard left for that purpose, who fired with admirable courage on the Prince's horse, refusing to hearken to his offer, and the Prince probably perceiving by that time the success of our right wing of horse, he retreated in great haste to the rescue of the King's army, which he found in such a general distress, that instead of attempting anything in the rescue of them, (being close followed in the rear by some of Commissary-General's, Colonel Rich's, Colonel Fleetwood's, Major Huntington's, and Colonel Butler's horse,) he made up further, until he came to the ground where the King was rallying the broken horse of his left wing and there joined with them, and made a stand.

To return again to our right wing, which, prosecuting their success, by this time had beaten all the enemy's horse quite behind their foot, which when they had accom-

Sir Thomas Fairfax, commander of the New Model Army and the victor at Naseby.

plished, the remaining business was with part to keep the enemy's horse from coming to the rescue of their foot, which were now all at mercy, except one tertia, which with the other part of the horse we endeavoured to break, but could not, they standing with incredible courage and resolution, although we attempted them in the flanks, front and rear, until such time as the General called up his own regiment of foot, (the Lieutenant-General being likewise hastening of them) which immediately fell in with them, with butt-end of muskets, (the General charging them at the same time with horse) and so broke them. The enemy had now nothing left in the field but his horse, (with whom was the King himself,) which they had put again into as good order as the shortness of their time and our near pressing upon them would permit. The General (whom God

Overleaf A graphic portrayal by the Dutch painter Jan de Wyck of the siege of Oxford by Sir Thomas Fairfax in June 1645.

preserved in many hazardous engagements of his person that day) seeing them in that order, and our whole army (saving some bodies of horse which faced the enemy) being busied in the execution upon the foot, and taking and securing prisoners, endeavoured to put the army again into as good order as they could receive, to the perfecting of the work that remained. . . .

As Edward Walker recounts, the King's departure from the field signalled a general retreat: 'At this instant the King's Horse Guards and the King at the head of them were ready to charge those who followed ours, when a person of quality, 'tis said the Earl of Cornwath, took the King's horse by the bridle, turning him about, swearing at him and saying, "Will you go to your death?" and at the same time the word being given, "March to the right hand!" (which was both from assisting ours or assailing them, and, as most concluded, was a civil command for everyone to shift for himself) we turned about and ran on the spur almost a quarter of a mile, and then the word being given to make a stand, we did so, though the [main] body could never be rallied.' Sprigge takes up the story:

Our horse had the chase of them from that place, within two miles of Leicester (being the space of fourteen miles), took many prisoners, and had the execution of them all that way. The number of the slain we had not a certain account of, by reason of the prosecution of our victory, and speedy advance to the reducing of Leicester. The prisoners taken in the field were about five thousand, whereof were six colonels, eight lieutenant-colonels, eighteen majors, seventy captains, eighty lieutenants, eighty ensigns, two hundred other inferior officers, besides the King's footmen and household servants, the rest common soldiers, four thousand five hundred. The enemy lost very gallant men, and indeed their foot, commanded by the Lord Astley, were not wanting in courage. The whole booty of the field fell to the soldier, which was very rich and considerable, there being amongst it, besides the riches of the court and officers, the rich plunder of Leicester.

Their train of artillery was taken, all their ordnance, (being brass guns,) whereof two were demi-cannon, besides two mortar-pieces, (the enemy got away not one carriage,) eight thousand arms and more, forty barrels of powder, two hundred horse, with their riders, the King's colours, the Duke of York's standard, and six of his colours, four of the Queen's white colours, with double crosses on each of them, and near one hundred other colours both of horse and foot; the King's cabinet, the King's sumpter, many coaches, with store of wealth in them. It was not the least mercy in this victory, that the cabinet letters, which discover so much to satisfy all honest men of the intention of the adverse party, fell likewise into our hands, and have been since published by the authority of the Parliament, to the view of the whole Kingdom.

Certainly *The King's Cabinet Opened* proved beyond doubt to Parliament's supporters that Charles could not be trusted. For the letters documented the favours he promised to Papists and his intention of bringing an Irish Catholic army into the war on his side. These revelations stiffened the resolve of the New

Model Army. From Leicester, Sir Thomas Fairfax marched into the West again, relieved Taunton and defeated Lord Goring at Langport (10 July). Bridgwater was taken on 23 July and Bristol successfully captured after a three weeks siege (10 September). In October a detachment under Cromwell stormed Basing House after local forces had closely besieged it for weeks; it was the twentieth Royalist garrison overcome by the New Model Army.

Two celebrated artists were taken prisoner there, the Bohemian engraver Wenceslaus Hollar, and old Inigo Jones who was carried out sick and naked in a blanket. Hugh Peter, the New Englander who served as chaplain to the train of artillery and enjoyed Cromwell's confidence, describes the scenes of devastation when he followed the soldiers into the house.

In the several rooms, and about the house, there were slain seventy-four, and only one woman, the daughter of Doctor Griffith, who by her railing provoked our soldiers (then in heat) into a further passion. There lay dead upon the ground, Major Cuffle, (a man of great account amongst them, and a notorious papist,) slain by the hands of Major Harrison (that godly and gallant gentleman) and Robinson the player, who, a little before the storm, was known to be mocking and scorning the Parliament and our army. Eight or nine gentlewomen of rank, running forth together, were entertained by the common soldiers somewhat coarsely, yet not uncivilly, considering the action in hand.

The plunder of the soldiers contined till Tuesday night. One soldier had 120 pieces in gold for his share, others plate, others jewels. Amongst the rest, one got three bags of silver, which (he being not able to keep his own counsel) grew to be common pillage amongst the rest, and the fellow had but one half crown left for himself at last. Also the soldiers sold the wheat to country people, which they held up at good rates a while, but afterwards the market fell, and there was some abatements for haste. After that they sold the household stuff, whereof there was a good store; and the country loaded away many carts, and continued a great while fetching out all manner of household stuff, till they had fetched out all the stools, chairs, and other lumber, all which they sold to the country people by piecemeal. In these great houses there was not one iron bar left in all the windows (save only what was in the fire) before night. And the last work of all was the lead, and by Thursday morning they had hardly left one gutter about the house. And what the soldiers left, the fire took hold on; which made more than ordinary haste; leaving nothing but bare walls and chimneys in less than twenty house, being occasioned by the neglect of the enemy, in quenching a fireball of ours at first.

We know not how to give a just account of the number of persons that were within; for we have not three hundred prisoners, and it may be an hundred slain, whose bodies (some being covered with rubbish) came not to our view. Only riding to the house on Tuesday night, we heard divers crying in vaults for quarter, but our men could neither come to them nor they to us. But amongst those that we saw slain, one of their officers lying on the ground, seeming so exceedingly tall, was measured, and from his great toe to his crown was nine foot in length.

The storming of Basing House by troops under Cromwell's command in October 1645, as imagined by the Victorian artist C. W. Cope. Before Cromwell's arrival the Royalist garrison had endured a siege by local forces for several weeks.

The Marquess, being pressed by Mr Peters arguing with him, broke out, and said 'that if the king had no more ground in England but Basing House, he would adventure as he did, and so maintain it to his uttermost', meaning with these papists: comforting himself in this disaster, that Basing House was called loyalty. But he was soon silenced in the question concerning the King and Parliament, only hoping that the King might have a day again.

The remnants of the King's western forces under Lord Hopton were beaten at Torrington early in 1646. Exeter capitulated on 9 April. Fairfax then marched back to summon the King's capital at Oxford, which surrendered to him on 24 June.

As the flame of his cause flickered in England, King Charles took refuge in Wales. Looking back, Walker thought that it would have been better if the King had joined Goring in the West and tried a second battle rather than allowing his

Charles Landseer's dramatic painting of the looting of Basing House. The Marquess of Winchester sits distraught, comforted by his daughter and his dog. On the floor lies Major Cuffle. Hugh Peter is himself unflatteringly depicted, gulping wine from a glass.

forces to be destroyed by pieces. Prince Rupert left him in order to preserve Bristol. 'Thence his Majesty went to Raglan Castle and there stayed three weeks; and as if the genius of that place had conspired with our fates, we were there all lulled asleep with sports and entertainments, as if no crown had been at stake or in danger of being lost, until the marching of Fairfax, after the regaining of Leicester and the defeating of General Goring at Langport awaken'd us.'

The King was really at a loss what to do. At one time he decided to join Prince Rupert in Bristol, and he even met his royal nephew at Chepstow. Then he went to Cardiff. Dissensions among the Welsh Royalists, especially those in Glamorganshire, delayed him in south Wales. Should he go into the West or head for the North? The hope of joining the victorious Marquess of Montrose drew him northwards, but the Scots army were in his way and so he marched

into the midlands. By way of Oxford and Worcester he reached Hereford in time to save it from the besieging forces. He was marching to relieve the siege of Bristol when he heard the news that Prince Rupert had capitulated without putting up much of a fight. Edward Walker refrained from commenting on the Prince's excuses except to say 'very sure I am, had it been the misfortune of any other person to have lost this place, he would have found Prince Rupert a severe judge'.

For the King's part, as soon as he came to Hereford he despatched a messenger with this letter to Prince Rupert:

Nephew,

Though the lost of Bristol be a great blow to me, yet your surrendering it as you did is of so much affliction to me, that it makes me forget not only the consideration of that place, but is likewise the greatest trial of my constancy that has yet befallen me; for what is to be done? After one that is so near me as you are, both in blood and friendship, submits himself to so mean an action (I give it the easiest term) such – I have so much to say that I will say no more of it: only, lest rashness of judgment be laid to my charge, I must remember you of your letter of the 12 August, whereby you assured me [that if no mutiny happened] you would keep Bristol for four months. Did you keep it four days? Was there anything like a mutiny? More questions might be asked, but now, I confess, to little purpose. My conclusion is, to desire you to seek your subsistence (until it shall please God to determine of my condition) somewhere beyond seas, to which end I send you herewith a pass; and I pray God to make you sensible of your present condition, and give you means to redeem what you have lost; for I shall have no greater joy in a victory, than a just occasion without blushing to assure you of my being

Your loving uncle, and most faithful friend.

Charles R

With this letter the King sent a revocation of all commissions formerly granted to Prince Rupert.

At Hereford the King resolved to march northwards by way of Chester in order to join forces with his Scottish ally the Marquess of Montrose. Colonel Sir Henry Slingsby, a resolute Royalist who was later unjustly beheaded for resisting Cromwell's usurpation, gives us an impression of the King during these twilight weeks:

In our quarters we had little accommodation. But of all the places we came to, the best at old Radnor, where the King lay in a poor low chamber, and my Lord of Lindsey and others by the kitchen fire on hay. No better were we accommodat'd for victuals which makes me remember this passage. When the King was at his supper eating a pullet and a piece of cheese, the room without was full, but the men's stomachs empty for want of meat. The good wife troubl'd with continual calling upon her for victuals, and having it seems but that one cheese, comes into the room where the King was, and very soberly asks if the King had done with the cheese, for the gentlemen without desir'd it.

But the best was, we never tarried long in any place, and therefore might the more willingly endure one night's hardship, in hopes the next night might be better. And thus we continued our march, until we came to Chester (in September) where we found my Lord Byron in command in the town, and the enemy in the suburbs and so close that it was some hazard to the King to pass the bridge. Now our horse quarter'd about three miles off, except only the King's lifeguard and my Lord Gerrard's horse, both which were drawn into the town, and preparations made next day to have a salley. But while they were busy to carry out the dung that barricaded up the gate that led to the suburbs, a messenger came that brought the King word that Poyntz had engag'd Sir Marmaduke Langdale to fight. And a little after we heard that we had taken some colours of the enemy's, but that the King must send supplies, by reason that the enemy increas'd by that assistance they had from neighbouring garrisons which flock'd to them. Whereupon the King sends forth both my Lord of Lichfield and Lord Gerrard with those that

A contemporary plan of the siege of Newark by the Scots. The siege of the Royalist strategic stronghold in the Midlands ended when the King arrived to give himself up to the Scots army in May 1646.

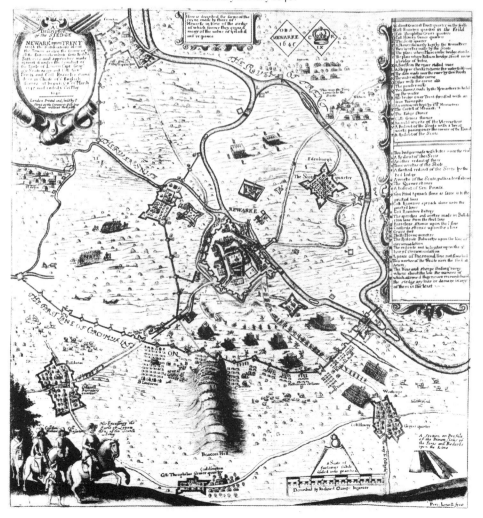

were in the town. But before they could join, our horse was beaten; and in the view of the town, and of the King. Who at the very same time was in one of the towers of the wall, looking over to see our men and their's in the suburbs exchange some bullets one with another. We took it first for the enemy till some came wounded and brought us the sad news that our horse was routed, many taken and my Lord Lichfield slain.

Here I do wonder at the admirable temper of the King, whose constancy was such that no perils never so unavoidable could move him to astonishment. But that still he set the same face and settl'd countenance upon what adverse fortune soever befell him; and neither was exalt'd in prosperity nor deject'd in adversity; which was the more admirable in him, seeing that he had no other to have recourse unto for council and assistance, but must bear the whole burden upon his shoulders, when as the general of an army, if it be destroy'd, has recourse to those that employ'd him, which will somewhat ease his heart's grief and supply the loss by new levies. And by this accident I never found him mov'd at all tho' the loss was so much the greater by my Lord of Lichfield's death, his kinsman, and whom he lov'd so dearly. But this makes him look the nearer to his own safety, and therefore gives order for his march the next day with those horse that came safe to the town; which we left without all hopes of relief, to make conditions for themselves for [the] storm, if they durst attempt no more.

Demoralized by Prince Rupert's loss of Bristol, the defeat of Montrose at Philiphaugh (13 September 1645) and his own failure to relieve Chester, the King made his way to Newark. There Prince Rupert came to take leave from him. Charles then wintered in Oxford. In late April and May 1646 he travelled in disguise through the south Midlands and gave himself up to the Scots army near Newark in order to avoid falling into Parliament's hands. The previous month had seen the defeat at Stow-in-the-Wold of his last field force, some two thousand men raised in Wales, which was on the march under Lord Astley through the Cotswolds to join him at Oxford. 'Jacob Astley being taken captive and wearied in this fight, and being ancient (for old age's silver hairs had quite covered over his head and beard), the soldiers brought him a drum to sit and rest himself upon; who being sat, he said, as was most credibly informed unto our soldiers: "Gentlemen, you may now sit down and play, for you have done your work, if you fall not out among yourselves."'

14

The Second Civil War

Having been defeated in the field King Charles deliberately sought to exploit the political divisions between his opponents. But this strategy, which relied upon obstruction and intrigue, soon ran into difficulties. The Scots prudently withdrew their army north of the border, retaining Newcastle as a security. Here the King was held in open custody, relieving the political negotiations by playing golf, chess and cards. His attempt to unite the various political elements in Scotland – the Covenanters, Montrose and other prominent Royalists – came to nothing. Parliament's commissioners also made little headway with him. Behind their backs he sent messengers with secret letters to the Queen, who was safely abroad, besides corresponding hopefully with the Irish Catholics and the Pope's agents. The truth is that Charles could not bring himself to accept the fact of his defeat, or rather Parliament's interpretation of it. Lord Hopton had spoken his thoughts in the closing days of the war; in response to Fairfax's appeal to surrender, this most able general had replied: 'God has indeed of late humbled us with many ill successes, which I acknowledge as a very certain evidence of his just judgment against us for our personal crimes. Yet give me leave to say, your present prosperity cannot be so certain an evidence of his being altogether pleased with you.'

The King's political probings from Newcastle at least revealed some inescapable conclusions. The Scots demanded too high a price – his complete acceptance of the presbyterian system – before they would commit themselves to restoring him, a step fraught with political and personal difficulties for the King. Was he desperate enough for such a concession yet? Would he ever be? Certainly his predicament could hardly be worse. Despite Henrietta Maria's infectious optimism the French would not stir themselves on his behalf. The Irish were already deep into those internecine troubles which were to be the bane of Irish history: no sane man would expect an army from that quarter to invade England. Montrose, the brilliant comet in the dark sky of Scotland, could no longer set the Highlanders on fire for him; he had taken ship for a temporary exile in Norway. The Scots could now see that they had no further use for King Charles; in January 1647 they exchanged him for a large sum of money to cover their military expenses and ordered their soldiers in Newcastle to march home.

The King was now in the hands of Parliament, a fate he had done so much to avoid during the previous year. But the political divisions of his captors, especially the tensions between Parliament and the Army, gave his devious mind some grounds for hope. The proposal to reduce the size of the New Model Army was already causing dissension. It would cost Parliament a great deal of money to be rid of this radical body, for the soldiers were owed a total of about £300,000 in all, a vast sum in those days. The problem of what to do with the Army did not become really acute until the spring of 1645, when it seemed that all Royalist resistance in England was at an end. Certainly the moderates in command of Parliament – the Presbyterians, as they were known – wished to see the dissolution of the Army, for they sensed that the ferment of radical religious and political ideas among the officers and soldiers, hatched out in those idle months spent in warm and comfortable quarters, posed a serious threat to the traditional values of English political life. For instance, at the time of the King's removal to English custody John Lilburne was attracting huge publicity for his Leveller doctrines. 'Freeborn John' preached the message that the English had lost their natural and historic freedom when the Normans imposed their aristocratic order on a democratic and egalitarian Saxon society. Mixed with a primitive apocalyptic Christian fervour, such ideas had the power to ignite the imaginations of idle soldiers.

Richard Baxter described the new temper in the Army as he experienced it towards the end of the war:

Naseby being not far from Coventry where I was, and the noise of the victory being loud in our ears, and I having two or three that of old had been my intimate friends in Cromwell's army, whom I had not seen of above two years; I was desirous to go see whether they were dead or alive; and so to Naseby field I went two days after the fight, and thence by the army's quarters before Leicester to seek my acquaintance. When I found them I stayed with them a night, and I understood the state of the army much better than ever I had done before. We that lived quietly in Coventry did keep to our old principles, and thought all others had done so too, except a very few inconsiderable persons. We were unfeignedly for King and Parliament. We believed that the war was only to save the Parliament and kingdom from papists and delinquents, and to remove the dividers, that the King might again return to his Parliament; and that no changes might be made in religion, but by the laws which had his free consent. We took the true happiness of King and people, church and state to be our end, and so we understood the Covenant, engaging both against papists and schismatics. And when the court news-book told the world of the swarms of Anabaptists in our armies, we thought it had been a mere lie, because it was not so with us, nor in any of the garrison or county-forces about us. But when I came to the army among Cromwell's soldiers, I found a new face of things which intimated their intention to subvert both church and state. Independency and Anabaptistry were most prevalent. Antinomianism and Arminianism were equally distributed; and Thomas Moor's followers (a weaver of Wisbech and Lynn, of excellent parts) had made some shifts to join these two extremes together.

Abundance of the common troopers, and many of the officers, I found to be honest, sober, orthodox men, and others tractable ready to hear the truth, and of upright intentions. But a few proud, self-conceited, hot-headed sectaries had got into the highest places, and were Cromwell's chief favourites, and by their very heat and activity bore down the rest, or carried them along with them, and were the soul of the Army, though much fewer in number than the rest (being indeed not one to twenty throughout the Army; their strength being in the generals and Whalley's and Rich's regiments of horse, and in the new-placed officers in many of the rest).

I perceived that they took the King for a tyrant and an enemy, and really intended absolutely to master him, or to ruin him; and that they thought if they might fight against him, they might kill or conquer him; and if they might conquer, they were never more to trust him further than he was in their power; and that they thought it folly to irritate him either by wars or contradictions in Parliament, if so be they must needs take him for their King, and trust him with their lives when they had thus displeased him. They said: 'What were the lords of England but William the Conqueror's colonels? or the barons but his majors? or the knights but his captains?' They plainly showed me, that they thought God's providence would cast the trust of religion and the kingdom upon them as conquerors. They made nothing of all the most wise and godly in the armies and garrisons, that were not of their way. *Per fas aut nefas*, by law or without it, they were resolved to take down, not only bishops, and liturgy and ceremonies, but all that did withstand their way. They were far from thinking of a moderate episcopacy, or of any healing way between the episcopal and the presbyterians. They most honoured the Separatists, Anabaptists, and Antinomians; but Cromwell and his council took on them to join themselves to no party, but to be for the liberty of all. . . .

When I had informed my self to my sorrow of the state of the army, Captain Evanson (one of my orthodox informers) desired me yet to come to their regiment, telling me that it was the most religious, most valiant, most successful of all the Army, but in as much danger as any one whatsoever. I was loath to leave my studies, and friends, and quietness at Coventry, to go into an army so contrary to my judgment. But I thought the public good commanded me, and so I gave him some encouragement. Whereupon he told his Colonel [Whalley] who also was orthodox in religion, but engaged by kindred and interest to Cromwell. He invited me to be chaplain to his regiment; and I told him I would take but a day's time to deliberate, and would send him an answer, or else come to him. . . .

As soon as I came to the Army, Oliver Cromwell coldly bid me welcome, and never spake one word to me more while I was there; nor once all that time vouchsafed me an opportunity to come to the headquarters where the councils and meetings of the officers were, so that most of my design was thereby frustrated. And his secretary gave out that there was a reformer come to the army to undeceive them, and to save church and state, with some such other jeers.

Baxter noted that Cromwell did not openly profess what religious opinion he held himself, uniting the Army with the common interest in liberty of con-science. Baxter, like Lucy Hutchinson, discerned in him hidden pride: 'Of a

The execution of Charles I. This painting purports to be by an eyewitness named Weesop,
although the scene differs in some respects from the account of John Rushworth quoted below.

sanguine complexion, naturally of such vivacity, hilarity and alacrity as another man has when he had drunken a cup too much; but naturally also so far from humble thoughts of himself that it was his ruin.'

With the dark spectres of popular democracy, republican agitation and religious toleration growing before their eyes, the King and the conservative majority in Parliament, those broadly of Baxter's persuasion, should have drawn together without further delay. They both wished to see England governed once more by the traditional trinity of King, Lords and Commons. That constitution, properly observed by all parties, alone promised to preserve English liberties under the law. The Lords and Commons were inclined towards that proven order, so that holders of property could once more sleep soundly in their beds at night. But there remained the unsolved problem of trust. The King made matters worse by overestimating his importance in the game. He still believed that he held the ace of trumps: the fact that he was indispensable to the constitution. Indeed he roundly told the Army's representatives when they came to treat with him: 'You cannot do without me. You will fall to ruin if I do not sustain you.' To which Commissary-General Henry Ireton replied: 'Sir, you have an intention to be the arbitrator between the Parliament and us, and we mean to be it between your Majesty and Parliament.' The King then assured the officers that 'I shall play my game as well as I can'. Again Ireton made an apt reply. 'If your Majesty have a game to play,' he said, 'you must give us leave to play ours.'

But events would not wait for the King. Without tarrying for the New Model Army's accord, Parliament voted to reduce the total armed forces in its pay from about 30,000 men to an army of 10,000 foot and 5,400 horse, which would be sent to complete the conquest of Ireland. Both Houses also resolved to bring the King back to London for further negotiations. The Army responded by strike action. Each regiment elected its own representatives known as 'Agitators' or 'Agents' – the first shop stewards in English history – to press their case. The officers connived at the mutiny. Fairfax told Parliament that he would not be held responsible if they persevered in their plan to dismiss soldiers with six weeks pay when they were owed wages for between eighteen and forty-three weeks of service. Even Sir William Waller, who headed Parliament's delegation to the Army in the summer of 1647, saw the basic injustice of these proceedings: 'For payment of arrears, I may say I was for it to the uttermost farthing . . . and, truly, herein I did but discharge my conscience. For I was ever of the opinion that a soldier's pay is the justest debt in the world.'

Mingled with this bitter dissatisfaction over their arrears of pay and their prospects for future employment, the lower ranks also resented the way that the grandees in the Army seemed to be courting the King in their fruitless quest for further concessions from him. Having fought against Charles for five long and bloody years and won victory at last, they asked, why did their senior officers still treat him with respect as if they believed his claim to be a special person? 'Why permit they so many of his deceitful clergy to continue about him? . . . Oh shame of men! Oh sin against God! What!' they exclaimed, coining a new and ominous phrase, 'to do thus to a man of blood, over head and ears in the blood of your dearest friends and fellow commoners?'

To strengthen their bargaining position the Army's leaders countenanced an attempt to seize the King that June. A junior officer called Cornet Joyce, with a body of horse, found the King at Holdenby House. John Rushworth, secretary to Fairfax, has left us an eyewitness account of the seizure which he probably obtained from Joyce himself. First Cornet Joyce set himself the task of persuading the resident Parliamentary commissioners, headed by Major-General Richard Browne, to allow him to proceed. He urged the necessity of foiling a reported Royalist plot to rescue the King and thus to precipitate the nation into a second civil war. At length Charles apparently agreed to accompany him to Newmarket, but at six o'clock in the morning of the day appointed for their departure he chose to tease Joyce. At the head of the column of troopers he called upon him to produce a commission allowing him to secure the royal person. Once more Joyce repeated all his earlier talk about a Royalist plot. 'This answer did not satisfy the King; but he asked what commission I had for doing that I did? I told his Majesty, "the soldiery of the army, or else I should not have dared to have done what I have . . ." Then said the King, "I pray, Mr Joyce, deal ingenuously with me, and tell me what commission you have?" The Cornet's answer was, "Here is my commission." "Where?" said the King. He answered, "Here." His Majesty again asked, "Where?" He answered, "Behind me," pointing to the soldiers that were mounted, and desired his Majesty that that might satisfy him. Whereupon the King smiled and said, "It is as fair a commission and as well written a commission as he had seen in his life, a company of handsome proper gentlemen as he had seen in a great while."'

Then Charles contented himself by expressing the hope that Joyce and his men would not lay violent hands on him for, he said, 'I acknowledge none to be above me but God,' a remark which reflects one of the principal causes of the English Civil War.

With the King safely in its possession the Army's more militant politicians went over to the offensive against Parliament. In a declaration on 14 June they called upon Parliament to announce a date for its own dissolution! Hard on the heels of this document came the Army's demand for the impeachment of eleven leading members of the group known as Presbyterians. The names of Waller and Browne were included on that list. Parliament decided to play for time and it invited the eleven accused members to withdraw while it negotiated. But the Army had the bit between its teeth. Hard on the heels of the declaration it sent up to London the 'Heads of Proposals', a political programme for settling the kingdom. To make matters worse the majority of the Puritan citizens of London, who supported the Presbyterian stance in politics, made it clear that they disapproved of Parliament's timid approach to the crisis. On 26 July a large

mob of apprentices demonstrated noisily in Westminster against having any more truck with the political demands of the Army. In fear of their lives, or so they said, the Speaker, eight peers and fifty-seven members of the House of Commons fled to the Army. Most of these deserters, as we must call them, were Independents by persuasion. Others sensed that the political future lay with the Army. The Earl of Manchester, who adhered more or less to the Presbyterian political position, rather surprisingly accompanied them. After this voluntary purge both Houses made ready to defend themselves. Waller, Massey, Browne and Poyntz received military commands in a new army which was to be raised in London, based upon the trained bands. Reformado officers were to be formed into regiments of horse. But it was too late. The New Model Army marched swiftly on the capital. On 6 August, after some light skirmishing in the suburbs, Cromwell rode into London at the head of the soldiers. The impeachment of the leading Presbyterians was now put in hand. The fortunate ones, such as Waller, Massey, Holles and Stapleton, made their way to the coast and took ship for the continent. The Sword now replaced Crown and Mace as symbol of real political power in England. It was a sad day for all those who had fought on both sides for the restoration of English rights and liberties.

Outwardly King Charles remained calm and cheerful, but he was now sufficiently anxious to give ground – or at least promise to do so – upon the matter of church government. Both the Scots and the Parliamentary Presbyterians still required from him the acceptance of a presbyterian order in the Church of England, but by playing off one against the other Charles intended to settle eventually for the least bad terms he could get, ones that he could perhaps repudiate 'when the King enjoys his own again' with least dishonour. Meanwhile he continued to talk with the Army's grandees who still entertained the hope of a negotiated agreement with him. The devious monarch also sought to embroil other nations in his cause. Ann Lady Fanshawe recorded for her son the story of her last sight of the King at about this time:

During his stay at Hampton Court my husband was with him, to whom he was pleased to talk much of his concerns and gave him there credentials for Spain with private instructions and letters for his service, but God for our sins disposed his Majesty's affairs otherwise. I went three times to pay my duty to him, both as I was the daughter of his servant and wife to his servant. The last time I ever saw him, when I took my leave, I could not refrain weeping. When he had saluted me, I pray'd to God to preserve his Majesty with long life and happy years. He stroked me on my cheek and said, 'Child, if God pleases, it shall be so, but both you and I must submit to God's will, and you know in what hands I am in.' Then turning to your father he said, 'Be sure, Dick, to tell my son all that I have said, and deliver those letters to my wife. Pray God bless her. I hope I shall do well.' And taking him in his arms said, 'You have ever been an honest man, and I hope God will bless you and make you a happy servant to my son, whom I have charged in my letter to continue his love and trust to you,' adding, 'And I

Opposite Charles I at his trial, by Edward Bower. The portrait was based on drawings made during the trial in Westminster Hall.

do promise you both that if ever I am restored to my dignity, I will bountifully reward you both for your service and sufferings.' Thus did we part from that glorious sun that within a few months after set, to the grief of all Christians that were not forsaken by God.

Meanwhile in the Army the officers and the soldiers' representatives engaged in the famous Putney debates upon the nature of political society. Not without some heated exchanges between radicals and the more conservative officers, they explored at tedious length such topics as the relation between property-ownership and the right to vote in elections. The Levellers advanced egalitarian views which sprang from the unfettered exercise of natural reason. Some of their ideas were centuries ahead of their time, such as Colonel Thomas Rainsborough's suggestion in Putney Church: 'I think that the poorest he that is in England has a life to live as the greatest he.'

By the end of October the radical political leaders in the Army printed their manifesto entitled *An Agreement of the People.* It called for manhood suffrage, equal electoral districts, triennial Parliaments and a purging of the House of Lords. In this Leveller programme the King received a curt mention as 'him that intended our bondage and brought cruel war upon us'. On 11 November, speaking to the Army's council, Colonel Harrison named the King again as 'that man of blood' and urged that he should be prosecuted for his crimes.

Only now did the King show some real signs of recognizing that his plight was becoming desperate. That very night he escaped from Hampton Court with Colonel William Legge, a gentleman of his bedchamber. At the riverside two other trusted gentlemen, John Ashburnham and Sir John Berkeley, met them with horses. Meanwhile Colonel Whalley, the King's custodian, had become suspicious as no sounds came from the locked royal bedchamber. Eventually he decided to make a considerable detour to try another door into the royal apartments. Whalley later described how he strode 'from chamber to chamber till we came to the next chamber to his Majesty's bedchamber, where we saw his Majesty's cloak lying on the midst of the floor, which much amazed me'.

For reasons that are still shrouded in mystery the King's companions crossed over to the Isle of Wight to enlist the help of its newly-appointed Parliamentarian governor in obtaining a ship. Colonel Robert Hammond, who was John Hampden's son-in-law and a trusted Cromwell man, would have nothing to do with the escape bid. Instead he demanded to know the whereabouts of the King. Ashburnham seems to have cracked under the strain, for he became very agitated and eventually agreed to lead Hammond to the Earl of Southampton's house in the New Forest where the King had taken refuge. 'O Jack, you have undone me!' cried Charles when he was told the identity of the man waiting in the hall below his chamber. Ashburnham desperately sought to redeem himself by offering to murder Hammond but the King, to his eternal credit, refused permission. It is possible, of course, that he may have thought that feat to be beyond the powers of his incompetent servants. Be that as it may, Hammond escorted him over the water to Carisbrooke Castle on the Isle of Wight. Thus the Army, in Edward Walker's wrestling metaphor, now had King Charles in a pinfold.

On the Isle of Wight lived a Royalist gentleman called Sir John Oglander of Nunwell, who had already suffered imprisonment in London for the King's cause.

King Charles came into our Island, Sunday the 14th of November, 1647, to my great astonishment. For, as a great while I could not be brought to believe it, so when I was certain of it, I could do nothing but sigh and weep for two nights and a day.

And the reason of my grief was that I verily believed he could not come into a worse place for himself, and where he could be more securely kept. That being the chief, yet I knew also it would be half an undoing to our poor Island in divers respects, and I pray God I be no true prophet.

Sunday morning at church I heard a rumour that the King was that night, being the 14th November, landed at Cowes. I confess I could not believe it, but at evening prayer the same day Sir Robert Dillington sent his servant to me to inform me of His Majesty's coming into the Island and that our Governor, Colonel Hammond, commanded me and my son (as he had done to all the gentlemen of the Island) to meet him at Newport the next day, being Monday, by nine in the morning.

Truly this news troubled me very much but on the Monday myself and most of the Island gentlemen went to Carisbrooke Castle to him, where he used us all most graciously and asked the names of those he knew not and, when he asked my eldest son his name, he asked me whether it was my son.

And not long after, Hammond came, when he made a short speech to us, which – as well as my old memory will give me leave – was thus, or to this purpose: 'Gentlemen, I believe it was as strange to you as to me to hear of his Majesty's coming into this Island. He informs me necessity brought him hither and there were a sort of people near Hampton Court, from whence he came, that had voted and were resolved to murder him, or words to that effect, and therefore so privately he was forced to come away and so to thrust himself on this Island, hoping to be secure here. And now, gentlemen, seeing he is come amongst us, it is all our duties to preserve his person and to prevent all comings over into our Island. I have already stopped all passages into our Island except three, Ryde, Cowes and Yarmouth, and at them have appointed guards. Now I must desire you all to preserve peace and unity in this Island as much as you can. I hear there are some such persons as his Majesty feared but I hope better, but to prevent it I would give you these cautions. If you see or hear of any people in any great number gathered together, whatsoever be their pretence, I would have you dissipate them, and timely notice given to me of it. Also, if there be any of those formerly spoken of, such as his Majesty fears, that shall offer to come into this Island, you must do your endeavours to suppress them, and all things for the preservation of his Majesty's person. And to this end I shall desire all the captains to come and renew their commissions that they may be the better authorised thereunto. And, lastly I must tell you I have sent an express to Parliament to signify his Majesty's being here and, as soon as I receive my answer, I shall acquaint you with it.'

After this speech Sir Robert Dillington moved the Colonel to know whether the gentlemen might not, after dinner, go up to his Majesty to express their duties to him. The Colonel answered, 'Yes, by all means. It would be a fit time when the King had dined. And, truly, I would invite you all to dinner, had I any entertainment, but truly I want, extremely, foul for his Majesty.' Intimating thereby that he wanted the gentlemen's assistance. Whereupon I and others promised to send into him what we had. So he thanked us and returned to the Castle to his Majesty.

Now, when we had dined, we all went up to Carisbrooke Castle, where we had not stayed half an hour before his Majesty came to us and, after he had given every man his hand to kiss, he made this speech, but not in these words but, as well as my memory will give me leave, to this effect: 'Gentlemen, I must inform you that, for the preservation of my life, I was forced from Hampton Court. For there were a people called Levellers that had both voted and resolved of my death, so that I could no longer dwell there in safety. And, desiring to be somewhat secure till some happy accommodation may be made between me and my Parliament, I have put myself in this place, for I desire not a drop more of Christian blood should be spilt neither do I desire to be chargeable to any of you. I shall not desire so much as a capon from any of you, my resolution in coming being but to be secured till there may be some happy accommodation made.'

After this he caused Mr William Legge, one of his servants, to read a kind of remonstrance, which it seemeth he left at Hampton Court when he went thence, but I shall forbear writing of that, it being in print. Mr Legge demanded of me, 'What if a greater number of these Levellers should come into our Island than we were able to resist? What course could then be taken for his Majesty's preservation?'

I answered, 'None that I knew, but to have a boat to convey him unto the mainland.'

These were all the passages on that day and, on the Thursday following, he came to Nunwell and gave a gracious visit there, and in the Parlour Chamber I had some speech with him, which I shall forbear to discover. I pray God send him happily hence and to regain his crown as his predecessor King John did here.

While his Majesty was in our Island I went (most commonly) once a week to see him, and I seldom went but his Majesty would talk with me, sometimes almost a quarter of an hour together, but all (since his close imprisonment) openly.

After February 1647, no man could see his Majesty without being informed against by these two gentlemen, Captain Robert Preston and Anthony Mildmay, that professed they would inform both Parliament and Army. The Governor himself told me he would not inform against me if I saw the King, but there were some gentlemen in the house would, which (being in the fire before), made me forbear, though much against my will.

Before the year's end both Parliament and the Scots resumed their negotiations with Charles on the Isle of Wight. In December 1647 he signed a secret treaty with the Scots: the document was sealed in a lead casket and buried in the grounds of Carisbrooke Castle. As a measure of his situation he even agreed to the establishment of the presbyterian system for a trial period. As the King did not have to take the Covenant himself, he probably felt that it would be much easier to extricate himself from this undertaking rather than from anything he concluded with Parliament. In return, the Scots agreed to establish him on his throne by force, the hidden promise which more than anything else precipitated the Second Civil War.

As part of the prelude to a resumption of fighting the King gave orders for the escape of his second son, James, Duke of York, to be engineered from St James's Palace. The design was entrusted to Colonel Joseph Bamfield, a twenty-four years old Cavalier, 'serious, handsome and of pious discourse'. Clarendon, who called Bamfield an Irishman, describes him as 'a man of wit and parts'. After the surrender of Arundel Castle to Sir William Waller in 1644 he had been employed as a spy in London, where he showed for the first time his outstanding gift for cloak-and-dagger operations. For the rescue attempt in 1648 he enlisted the help of Ann Murray, a girl who had recently fallen in love with him. Later in life Ann told the story of her part in the Duke's escape in her memoirs. In order to get girl's clothes made for James it was arranged that a gentleman attendant would smuggle out his measurements:

I had desired him to take a ribbon with him and bring me the bigness of the Duke's waist and his length to have clothes made fit for him. In the meantime C.B. [Colonel Bamfield] was to provide money for all necessary expense, which was furnished by an honest citizen. When I gave the measure to my tailor to inquire how much mohair would serve to make a petticoat and waistcoat to a young gentlewoman of that bigness and stature, he considered it a long time and said he had made many gowns and suits, but he had never made any to such a person in his life. I thought he was in the right; but his meaning was, he had never seen any women of so low a stature have so big a waist. However, he made it as exactly fit as if he had taken the measure himself. It was a mixed mohair of a light hair colour and black, and the under-petticoat was scarlet.

All things being now ready, upon the 20 of April, 1648, in the evening was the time resolved on for the Duke's escape. And in order to that, it was designed for a week before every night as soon as the Duke had supped, he and those servants that attended his Highness (till the Earl of Northumberland and the rest of the house had supped) went to a play called hide-and-seek, and sometimes he would hide himself so well that in half an hour's time they could not find him. His Highness had so used them to this that when he went really away they thought he was but at the usual sport. A little before the Duke went to supper that night, he called for the gardner (who only had a treble key, besides that which the Duke had) and bid him give him that key till his own was mended, which he did. And after his Highness had supped, he immediately called to go to the play, and went down the privy stairs into the garden and opened the gate that goes into the park, treble locking all the doors behind him. And at the garden gate C.B.

waited for his Highness, and putting on a cloak and periwig, hurried him away to the park gate where a coach waited that carried them to the water side. And taking the boat that was appointed for that service, they rowed to the stars next the bridge, where I and Miriam waited in a private house hard by that C.B. had prepared for dressing his Highness, where all things were in a readiness.

But I had many fears, for C.B. had desired me, if they came not there precisely by ten o'clock, to shift for myself, for then I might conclude they were discovered, and so my stay there could do no good, but prejudice myself. Yet this did not make me leave the house though ten o'clock did strike, and he that was entrusted, [who] often went to the landing-place and saw no boat coming, was much discouraged, and asked me what I would do. I told him I came there with a resolution to serve his Highness and I was fully determined not to leave that place till I was out of hopes of doing what I came there for, and would take my hazard. He left me to go again to the water side, and while I was fortifying myself against what might arrive to me, I heard a great noise of many as I thought coming upstairs,'"which I expected to be soldiers to take me. But it was a pleasing disappointment, for the first that came in was the Duke, who with much joy I took in my arms and gave God thanks for his safe arrival. His Highness called, 'Quickly, quickly, dress me,' and putting off his clothes I dressed him in the woman's habit that was prepared, which fitted his Highness very well and was very pretty in it. After he had eaten something I made ready while I was idle, lest his Highness should be hungry, and having sent for a Woodstreet cake (which I knew he loved) to take in the barge, with as much haste as could be his Highness went across the bridge to the stairs where the barge lay, C.B. leading him, and immediately the boatmen plied the oars so well that they were soon out of sight, having both wind and tide with them. But I afterwards heard the wind changed and was so contrary that C.B. told me he was terribly afraid they should have been blown back again. And the Duke said, 'Do any thing with me rather than let me go back again,' which put C.B. to seek help where it was only to be had, and after he had most fervently supplicated assistance from God, presently the wind blew fair and they came safely to their intended landing place. But I heard there was some difficulty before they got to the ship at Gravesend, which had like to have discovered them had not Colonel Washington's lady assisted them.

After the Duke's barge was out of sight of the bridge, I and Miriam went where I appointed the coach to stay for me and made drive as fast as the coachman could to my brother's house, where I stayed. I met none in the way that give me any apprehension that the design was discovered, nor was it noised abroad till the next day. For (as I related before) the Duke having used to play at hide-and-seek, and to conceal himself a long time when they missed him at the same play, thought he would have discovered himself as formerly when they had given over seeking him. But a much longer time being past than usually was spent in that divertisement, some began to apprehend that his Highness was gone in earnest past their finding, which made the Earl of Northumberland (to whose care he was committed), after strict search made in the house of St James's and all thereabouts to no purpose, to send and acquaint the Speaker of the

House of Commons that the Duke was gone, but how or by what means he knew not; but desired that there might be orders sent to the Cinque Ports for stopping all ships going out till the passengers were examined and search made in all suspected places where his Highness might be concealed. . . .

Alas, Ann did not receive the one reward she desired. Probably in the autumn of that year Colonel Bamfield disclosed to her that his wife was dead and proposed marriage. But she soon found out that he had deceived her and they parted company never to meet again. Her love for him, however, proved to be undying. Not until 1656 did Ann bring herself to marry Sir James Halkett, a worthy but dull man, for, as she wrote, 'nothing but the death of Colonel Bamfield could make me ever think of another'. As for Bamfield, he crowned his inglorious career in intrigue by becoming a double agent during the Commonwealth.

Had the Royalist uprisings in 1648 been better co-ordinated the outcome of the Second Civil War might well have been different. But there was no single strategic mind at work to combine the efforts of the English Cavaliers, still less to synchronise them with the Scots army which invaded under the Duke of Hamilton. The war broke out in the last week of March when the Parliamentary governor of Pembroke Castle declared for the King and most of South Wales came out in support. By the end of April the seizure of Berwick and Carlisle by Sir Marmaduke Langdale and Sir Philip Musgrave respectively opened the way south for the Scots. But political dissension in Scotland delayed the entry into England of Hamilton's army until 8 July. By that time most of Kent and much of Essex was in arms for the King. Moreover, the whole fleet now went over to the Royalist side; the sailors landed and seized the forts of Deal, Sandwich and Walmer. The Earl of Warwick, hastily reinstated as Lord High Admiral, failed to win back the allegiance of the seamen to Parliament.

The war had broken out like so many heath fires on a hot summer's day. That gave Fairfax and Cromwell the opportunity to defeat their enemy in parts. Fairfax sent Cromwell to restore order in Wales while Major-General John Lambert marched to secure Yorkshire and harry the Scots. He himself led a strong force towards Rochester in Kent, the storm centre of the most threatening uprising in the country. Fairfax decided to cross the Medway at Maidstone and approach Rochester from the east. The Cavaliers had occupied Maidstone before him. The soldiers of the New Model Army attacked them on 2 June and fought their way through the town. Old Lord Norwich, George Goring's father, now abandoned Rochester and marched towards London in the hope that the City would rise in sympathy. But Skippon still exercised firm command over the London trained bands and ordered the gates of the city to be shut.

With Skippon in front of him and Fairfax hard on his heels, Lord Norwich considered a move into Essex to join up with the Cavaliers there. He rode to Chelmsford to make the necessary arrangements, but upon returning to his camp on Blackheath he found that most of the Kentish Royalists had slipped away to their homes. About five hundred men did swim their horses across to the Isle of Dogs to continue the fight in Essex.

The Essex commanders – Sir Charles Lucas, Sir George Lisle and Lord Capel – were both capable and resourceful. On 12 June they occupied Colchester and gave a good account of themselves to Fairfax's army next day when the Ironsides attempted the town. The ensuing siege of Colchester pinned down a good part of the effective strength of the New Model Army, which could have helped to win the Second Civil War for the Royalists if others had made better use of the opportunity thus created. The navy, which had sailed to a Dutch port, welcomed as their admiral the boy Duke of York. At the prompting of his brother the Prince of Wales, who had joined the fleet, he confirmed the appointment of a prominent Presbyterian peer, Lord Willoughby of Parham, as his vice-admiral and made as his rear-admiral the experienced sailor Sir William Balten, the captain who in 1643 had fired on the Queen after she had landed in Bridlington Bay. But nobody knew what part the fleet might play in the war when it put out to sea again in June.

In England the Earl of Holland, who had now been appointed as commander-in-chief, was making ready to raise the Royal Standard once more. On 4 July he appeared at the head of a handful of Cavaliers at Kingston, but he could do nothing in Surrey and made his way northwards. Five days later he surrendered his sword in an inn yard at St Neots. On the following day Pembroke Castle surrendered, leaving Cromwell free to march north and face the Scots.

The Duke of Hamilton, a cousin of King Charles, lacked both inspiring leadership and skill in generalship. So slowly did he advance southwards that he had only reached Stainmore in Westmoreland by the end of July when Cromwell's horse were joining forces with Lambert. Cromwell himself arrived on 12 August with the infantry and train of artillery. By this time Hamilton and his English allies had marched into Lancashire. Despite being outnumbered two to one, Cromwell resolved to meet them in battle without delay.

On 17 August the invading army was strung out on the roads in long marching columns: the horse had reached Wigan while sixteen miles to their rear the foot plodded through the pouring rain into Preston. The hardest fighting at Preston took place between Sir Marmaduke Langdale's Royalists, about 3,000 strong, and Cromwell's army of nearly 9,000 around a narrow lane on the edge of Ribbleton Moor. For four or five hours Langdale's men, fighting like the Spartans at Thermopylae, withstood assault after assault. When the Roundhead army broke through to Preston they encountered the Scots attempting to form up south of the Ribble. Before this movement had been completed the Ironsides approached them. John Hodgson experienced the battle as a captain in one of Cromwell's regiments of foot:

They were drawn up very formidably. One Major Poundall and myself commanded

Left Oliver Cromwell depicted as the Anti-Christ, in a cartoon dated 1651. *Right* The Duke of Hamilton, who invaded England with a Scots army in July 1648, but whose incompetent generalship allowed Cromwell to win the Second Civil War.

the forlorn of foot; and being drawn up by the moor side (that scattering we had being not half the number we should have been), the general comes to us, and commands to march. We not having half of our men come up, desired a little patience; he gives out the word, 'March!' and so we drew over a little common, where our horse was drawn up, and came to a ditch, and the enemy let fly at us (a company of Langdale's men that was newly raised). They shot at the skies, which did so encourage our men, that they were willing to venture upon any attempt; and the major orders me to march to the next hedge, and I bid him order the men to follow me, and there drew out a small party; and we came up to the hedge end, and the enemy, many of them, threw down their arms, and run to their party, where was their stand of pikes, and a great body of colours. We drew up toward them; and on our right hand was a party of foot drawing off, that laid an ambuscade to hinder our horse, commanded by Major Smithson, from passing up the lane; and I seeing their officer, that over-run his soldiers, retreating by himself, and the soldiers a great way behind him, bid the soldiers be in readiness, and stand still; and I leaped over the ditch, and made at the champion, which was one Colonel Carleton that afterwards I knew, but he over-run me on the plain-field, which caused a great shout in our army; in which time Major Smithson was advanced as forward as we were; and the enemy coming against us with a great body of colours, we had no way to shelter ourselves, but drew over a lane where Major Smithson was, and there we kept them in play so long as our ammunition lasted, and still kept our ground.

At last comes a party of Scots lancers, and charged Major Smithson in the lane, passing by us, and put him to retreat; but they were routed immediately, and one of their commanders was running away, and I being aware of him, stepped into the lane, and dismounted him, and clapped into the saddle, and our horse came up in pursuit. My captain sees me mounted, and orders me to ride up to my colonel, that was deeply engaged both in front and flank. And I did so, and there was nothing but fire and smoke; and I met Major-General Lambert coming off on foot, who had been with his brother Bright; and coming to him, I told him where his danger lay, on his left wing chiefly. He ordered me to fetch up the Lancashire regiment; and God brought me off, both horse and myself. The bullets flew freely; then was the heat of the battle that day. I came down to the moor, where I met with Major Jackson, that belonged to Ashton's regiment, and about three hundred men were come up; and I ordered him to march, but he said he would not, till his men were come up. A sergeant, belonging to them, asked me where they should march? I showed him the party he was to fight; and he, like a true bred Englishman, marched, and I caused the soldiers to follow him; which presently fell upon the enemy and, losing that wing, the whole army gave ground and fled. Such valiant acts were done by contemptible instruments! The major had been called to a council of war, but that he cried *peccavi*. The Lancashire foot were as stout men as were in the world, and as brave firemen. I have often told them, they were as good fighters, and as great plunderers, as ever went to a field. . . . It was to admiration to see what a spirit of courage and resolution there was amongst us, and how God hid from us the fears and dangers we were exposed to. . . . Such things did God for a handful of men!

On the following day, 18 August, the Scots were in flight towards the border. Cromwell pursued them, taking thousands of prisoners. Hamilton himself was captured at Uttoxeter a week later. He surrendered himself to Colonel Thomas Waite, a Leicester officer, 'delivering to him his scarf, his George and his sword, which last he desired him to keep carefully, because it had belonged to his ancestors'. The Duke was escorted to Windsor Castle. The standards of the defeated Scots were sent up to London for display in Westminster Hall.

The collapse of morale in the defeated army is well portrayed by an eyewitness, Sir James Turner. The Scots intended to make a stand at Wigan, but their dearth of ammunition and the enclosed fields around the town made them change their minds. As they continued their retreat General Middleton's horse protecting their rear were constantly harassed by the Ironsides. As Turner marched with the last of his brigade through Wigan, word came that Middleton's horse had been beaten and the Roundheads were bearing down on them. Turner gave orders for his brigade to make a stand in the market place and present a phalanx of pikes to the enemy when they appeared. In the gathering dusk a body of disorderly horse galloped into sight. Before it was too late

Turner recognized them as belonging to their own cavalry and ordered his men to open ranks and let them through. His men refused to do so. Turner said that they were 'demented'. One tried to kill him, inflicting a serious wound. 'This made me forget all rules of modesty, prudence and discretion.' He rode up to the horsemen and asked them to charge a way through his mutinous soldiers. They would not avenge him, so Turner contented himself with shouting to his men that the enemy was upon them, which was enough to send them scurrying to the surrounding houses. The horsemen continued on their way, trampling underfoot anyone who stood in their path. Meanwhile the Scotsmen plundered the town. Two of them stole a kettle to make porridge in, and before either would let it go they were both killed by Cromwell's troopers.

Three days after the battle of Preston the starving Royalists in Colchester surrendered, bringing the Second Civil War to a virtual end. Fairfax resolved to make a stern example of the Cavalier leaders. Lord Norwich and Lord Capel were sent to the Tower of London, while Sir Charles Lucas and Sir George Lisle were sentenced to be shot. Lisle had fought valiantly at Cheriton and again at Second Newbury where he had thrown off his buff-coat in the gathering dusk so that his men could catch sight of him by his white coat. He asked the firing party to step closer to him. When the musketeers said that was not necessary Lisle replied, 'Friends, I have been nearer you when you have missed me.'

The execution of Lucas and Lisle at Colchester exemplifies a significant change of mood among the Parliamentarian soldiers. By instigating a second war the Royalists had tried their patience and civility beyond the limit. The defeated could no longer count upon being granted quarter, as Michael Hudson found to his cost in Lincolnshire. Hudson had fought at Edgehill, and he subsequently became one of the royal chaplains at Oxford. In April 1646 he and Sir John Ashburnham had organised the King's journey to the Scots Army. Imprisoned in the Tower, early in 1648 Hudson escaped in disguise 'with a basket of apples on his head' and, together with a 'drunken cheating parson called Stiles' he led a serious rising in his native county. Colonel Waite and a strong force of Roundheads eventually surrounded these Lincolnshire Cavaliers in a close near Woodcroft Hall, the home of Lord Fitzwilliam. Hudson and fifteen men retreated into the Hall and barricaded themselves in. Waite's soldiers forded the moat by placing faggots in it; then they breached the outer wall at the cost of two troopers killed and three wounded. Hudson and a few diehards fought their way up some stairs and out onto the leads of the roof where they surrendered. According to one account Hudson and three others were then thrown off the roof; another report says that they yielded on promise of quarter which was then denied to them. Being forced off the roof Hudson evidently caught hold of some projecting waterspout or stone to save himself from falling into the moat, but his fingers were promptly cut off. When he was fished from the moat the Roundheads cut out his tongue before killing him.

While Cromwell lingered in Scotland the Presbyterian majority in the Commons sent commissioners to treat with the King at Newport in the Isle of Wight. As Sir John Oglander records, the summer had been exceptionally wet – a sign of divine judgement.

I conceive the heavens were offended with us for our offence committed to one another for, from Mayday till the 15th of September, we had scarce three dry days together. Men made an ill shift with their wheat. When a dry day came, they would reap and carry it presently into the barns, although they mowed it wet. I believe most was mowed so wet that much of it will grow in the barn, and I am confident wheat and barley will bear such a price as was never known in England. His Majesty asked me whether that weather was usual in our Island. I told him that in this 40 years I never knew the like before. If it does not please the Almighty to send more seasonable weather, we shall save little pease and barley.

As for the earth, it is turned almost to water. The rivers in the Main have overflown all their neighbouring fields, the rich vales stand knee deep with water and, with the current, much corn is carried away and haycocks swimming up and down. In our Island the earth was drunk, and you might in August have gone with boat from Sandham two miles beyond Heasley.

And this is remarkable. On Thursday, being the 7th of September, the General Thanksgiving Day for killing the Scots and divers others in other places, it was from morning to night the horridest rainy day as ever I saw, insomuch as, instead of rejoicing, many had heavy hearts to see their corn spoilt, and wished it had been a day rather of humiliation than of joy and merriment. To conclude, there was almost no travelling on the earth by reason of the floods, and bogs in the highways that the rains and travelling made.

God mend all. First let us repent all our bloody sins, then we shall find His mercy, and the earth will be again propitious unto us – which God grant. But they tell us the treaty will begin on Thursday the 14th of September at Newport, and that then we shall have peace and the issue of blood will be stopped, fair weather and all things according to our hearts' desires. . . .

Hammond carried himself a good while fairly and respectfully unto his Majesty (but always as to his prisoner). One day, upon greater restraint, the King was much discontented with Hammond and said it would be wisdom in him to use him better, for one day he might be beholden to him or his son for his life. Hammond replied, 'You are grown very high since you came into the Island.' Whereupon the King said, 'Then it is my shoemaker's fault,' and, looking on the soles of his shoes, said he found himself no higher than before.

Meanwhile Sir William Waller and other exiled Presbyterian party leaders had returned from the continent and resumed their seats in the House of Commons. But in November the officers of the Army petitioned Parliament for an end to the negotiations. The soldiers asked for the King to be tried in public. While the Presbyterian leaders hesitated the Army acted. The King was removed across the Solent to a more secure prison in Hurst Castle. The Parliamentary commissioners, five lords and ten commoners, had secured the King's agreement to the establishment of the presbyterian system for three years, but he would not consent to the abolition of bishops. His answers on the church question and the question of the treatment of delinquents, as the Cavaliers were now called, were both voted unsatisfactory, but nevertheless the Commons voted on 5 December (by 129 to 83) to accept them as 'a ground for both Houses to proceed upon for a settlement of the peace of the Kingdom'.

Retribution from the Army came swiftly. Next day a party of musketeers under Colonel Pride at the doors of Parliament denied access to members favouring the Treaty of Newport and arrested some 45 others, including Sir William Waller. 'Seized upon by the Army as I was going to discharge my duty in the House of Commons,' he wrote, 'and contrary to privilege of Parliament made a prisoner in the Queen's Court. From thence carried ignominiously to a place under the Exchequer called Hell, and the next day to the King's Head in the Strand; after singled out, as a sheep to the slaughter, and removed to St James's.' Yet before accompanying the guards Waller presented them with a paper protesting against this 'high violation of the rights and privileges of Parliament and of the fundamental laws of the land'.

As many more members stayed away in protest the House of Commons was now reduced to about fifty members, all favouring or fearing the Army. An excluded Member of Parliament contemptuously called it 'this fag-end, this veritable Rump of a Parliament with corrupt maggots in it'. The name stuck. It was a derisory and disreputable assembly which lasted until 1653, a caretaker skeleton of a Parliament too feeble to do more than some token good works. The proclamation of their own power on the part of the Rump was followed by what they called an Act of Parliament (inaccurately, for the Lords refused it) establishing a high court of one hundred and thirty five persons in order to try the King for his life in Westminster Hall.

15

Rough Justice

Of the fifty-nine men who signed the warrant for the execution of King Charles the majority were army officers. Apart from Fairfax, Skippon and Lambert, almost all the regimental commanders of the New Model Army put their names to the document. Other former officers, such as Hutchinson and Ludlow, signed as well. Most of the prominent lawyers in the country steered clear of any involvement in this extraordinary trial. All the chief justices, even Oliver St John, the kinsman of Cromwell and defender of Hampden in the Ship Money case, refused to serve in the 'High Court of Justice', while other respected lawyers such as John Selden and Bulstrode Whitelocke prudently retired into the country. John Bradshaw, who presided over the trial, had begun life as attorney's clerk at Congleton in Cheshire and, although recently appointed Chief Justice of Chester, he had no repute in his profession. But then any knowledge of legal niceties was not required. When the judges met for the first time, and Algernon Sidney pointed out that technically the King could not be tried by a court, and no man by that court, Cromwell erupted angrily, 'I tell you we will cut off his head with the crown upon it!'

Towards the end of 1648 the King was moved from Hurst Castle to Windsor to await his trial. As he rode into the Henry VIII Gate he caught sight of his captive cousin the Duke of Hamilton, kneeling in the mud and murmuring 'My dear master'. In the Upper Ward the King enquired if the Presbyterian leaders arrested after Pride's Purge were also being held in the Castle, but was told that they were not there. According to a newspaper report, 'The King then went to his chair that was near the fire and leaned his arm on the backside of it, standing in a melancholy posture. A while after he went to supper, and after supper to his lodging chamber.' It was 23 December, the eve of the traditional Christmas festivities. 'The King, though the cook disappointed him of mince pies and plum porridge, yet he resolved to keep Christmas; and accordingly put on his best clothes, and himself is chaplain to the gentlemen that attend him, reading and expounding the scripture to them. . . . The King is pretty merry and spends much time reading of sermon books and sometimes Shakespeare and Ben Jonson's plays. . . . The King goes not out, only walks sometimes upon the terrace and on the galleries.' On the fly-leaf of his precious second folio copy of Shakespeare's plays he wrote the words *Dum spiro spero* (While I breathe, I hope).

The trial of Charles I was a strange affair by any reckoning. In part it was intended to be a show trial, exhibiting to all and sundry the guilt of Charles Stuart. But this aspect was overshadowed by the need for haste, as if the proceedings against the King was the last battle of the Civil War, an encounter which had to be won by swift and relentless action. The first concept of the trial was far too much of a political risk anyway. For it would give the King a platform to play in public the role of the innocent victim of circumstances. An extended performance by the royal actor could rally London to him. Therefore the Army resolved that the trial would not last for long whatever defence the King chose to offer on his own behalf. Legal forms must be observed, but the charade must have only one conclusion.

On 19 January 1649 the King was taken to St James's Palace, which was serving as a state prison for the Presbyterian leaders. From there he was carried in a closed sedan chair to Whitehall and then to a house next to Westminster Hall where he lodged during the trial. The King's guards did not let him out of their sight, talking and puffing their clay pipes while he endeavoured to say his prayers, despite his detestation of tobacco smoke. Bishop Juxon of London shared his imprisonment and acted as his chaplain.

The trial opened on the following day. Sixty-eight members of the Court had their places on a grandstand under the great window and answered their names when a roll-call was made. Lord Fairfax, as Sir Thomas had become, was not present. When his name was read a masked lady in the spectators' gallery shouted, 'He has more wit than to be here'. It is virtually certain that she was Lady Fairfax. The Clerk ignored the interruption and continued the roll-call. When he had finished the King was escorted into Westminster Hall, dressed in black and wearing upon his cloak the large embroidered Star of the Order of the Garter. Apart from his white lace collar and cuffs the black suit was relieved by the jewelled George, concealing a portrait of his wife, which hung from his neck on the blue Garter ribbon. Beneath his hat his hair was streaked with grey; his beard much longer and less well-trimmed than usual; his face drawn and even haggard. He took his place on a crimson chair in the dock, a large wooden enclosure crowded with attendants strange to him. Behind him the crowd, admitted by ticket only, and the soldiers stamped to keep warm in the vast stone unheated chamber.

Just before the charge was read by John Cook, the Solicitor General, the King tried to attract his attention so that he could speak himself by tapping him on the shoulder with his cane. The silver head fell off and – waiting in vain for someone to come forward – Charles stooped and picked it up.

Cook declared that Charles had been 'trusted with a limited power to govern by and according to the laws of the land but not otherwise, but he had conceived a wicked design to erect and uphold in himself an unlimited and tyrannical power to rule according to his will and to overthrow the rights and liberties of the people'. Following that design he had 'traitorously and maliciously levied war against the present Parliament and the people therein represented . . .' and

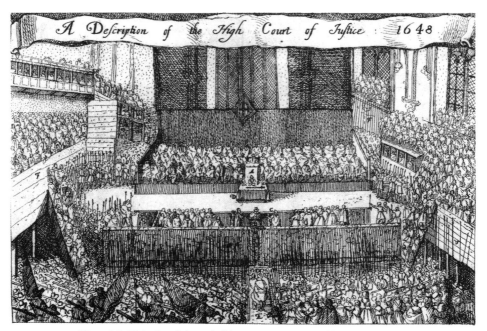

The trial. This sketch is probably contemporary, and largely accurate.

had thus been responsible for all the death, destruction and disaster which had been the result of these wars. For this cause, 'for and on behalf of the people of England', John Cook accused 'the said Charles Stuart of being tyrant, traitor and murderer and a public and implacable enemy to the commonwealth of England'.

During this accusation the King calmly surveyed the assembled judges on their benches covered with crimson cloth and turned round once or twice to look over the wooden partition at the throng behind him. At Cook's last sentence he could be seen to chuckle to himself. When President Bradshaw called upon him to reply to the charge he did so confidently and with no trace of his customary stammer. 'I would know by what power I am called hither,' he began with cool disdain. 'I would know by what authority, I mean *lawful* . . .' To emphasise the point he added that 'there are many unlawful authorities in the world, thieves and robbers by the highway . . .' Having thus by implication damned the Court by comparing it to a gang of highwaymen, he told them that he was in fact their lawful king. Bradshaw interrupted and called him to answer the charge 'in the name of the people of England'. Charles replied calmly: 'I do stand more for the liberty of my people than any that come here to be my pretended judges.' This was to be the theme of his defence: namely that he would not recognise a court which had no standing in law, and that by so doing he was protecting the liberty of his people against the tyranny of the sword. 'We are satisfied with our authority,' said Bradshaw rather lamely. The King retorted with truth, 'You have shown no lawful authority to satisfy any reasonable man.'

The second day of the trial, Monday, 22nd, saw a resumption of this debate. In frustration Colonel Hewson, one of the judges, rushed forward crying 'Justice!' and spat in the King's face. 'Well Sir,' said Charles, wiping the spittle from his face, 'God has justice in store both for you and me.' By the end of the third day the King's defence had won considerable sympathy among the spectators. Cries of 'God save the King' came from the crowd, and even some soldiers were heard to say 'God bless you, Sir'. In desperation the judges postponed the next session for three days and took evidence in private from the thirty or forty witnesses who had seen the King on the battlefield encouraging the Cavaliers to slay his subjects. The Court reassembled in Westminster Hall on Saturday, 27 January to pass sentence of death on the prisoner. But Bradshaw's opening words reiterating the charge of treason in the name of the people of England were soon interrupted by two masked women shouting 'It's a lie. . . . Not half, not a quarter of the people of England! Oliver Cromwell is a traitor!' One of them was believed to be Lady Fairfax, but she slipped out as the soldiers levelled their muskets at the public box where she sat; the muzzles so close that 'we were very hush', recalled one of the ladies who sat there.

The King now changed his tactics and eloquently asked to be heard before the Lords and Commons of Parliament. He claimed to have a new plan for a lasting peace. Before Bradshaw could formally refuse him, one of the judges, John Downes, began to suffer pangs of conscience and to mutter to his neighbours, 'Have we hearts of stone? Are we men?' Cromwell, who was sitting in the row below him, turned round and said, 'What ails you, man? Are you mad? Can you not sit still and be quiet?' Downes leapt to his feet and replied 'Sir, no, I cannot be quiet.' To prevent the discord spreading Bradshaw hastily adjourned the Court, and as they filed out Cromwell came up to Downes and called him a 'peevish troublesome fellow', refusing to agree that they should at least hear the King's proposition. (Despite his tears, Downes added his signature to the royal death warrant.) About thirty minutes later the judges returned to Westminster Hall and Bradshaw set out again the grounds for their proceedings: 'There is a contract and a bargain made between the King and his people, and certainly the bond is reciprocal, for as you are the liege lord so they are liege subjects. . . . The one tie, the one bond, is the bond of protection that is due from the sovereign; the other is the bond of subjection that is due from the subject. Sir, if this bond be once broken, farewell sovereignty. . . . Whether you have been as by your office you ought to be a Protector of England, or the Destroyer of England, let all England judge, or all the world that have looked upon it.'

That theory of a contract between King and people was the crux of the matter. From time immemorial it was the obligation of kings to defend their subjects from the assaults of enemies and maintain peace. But Charles had so misruled the country that he had embroiled it in a long and bloody civil war. Refusing the King leave to speak again Bradshaw pronounced the inevitable sentence: 'Charles Stuart as tyrant, traitor, murderer and public enemy to the good people of this nation shall be put to death by the severing his head from his body.' The King tried to speak again, stammering badly now; and as the guards made ready to remove him by force he called out: 'I am not suffered for to speak . . . hold! Expect what justice the people will have. . . .' Colonel Axtell's musketeers rushed forwards, their matches smouldering, and hurried him from the hall with rough cries of 'Justice! Execution!'

On 29 January the death warrant, duly signed by a number of the judges, was delivered to the King's gaolers. He was to die next day. That afternoon he was allowed to say goodbye to his children, Princess Elizabeth, aged thirteen, and Henry, Duke of Gloucester, who was nine. They burst into tears at the sight of their father. The rest of his children were on the Continent, but these two had been in the care of the Earl of Northumberland throughout the Civil War. He told Elizabeth why he was being put to death, begged her not to grieve and asked her to tell her mother of his undying love for her. Henry he took on his knee. 'Sweetheart,' he said, 'now they will cut off your father's head . . . and perhaps make you a king.'

Next morning the King arose at his accustomed time. There was a white hoar-frost on the ground and he donned two shirts lest he should be seen to shiver on the scaffold and be thought afraid. Like all the devout Protestants of his time he looked upon death as a 'second wedding day' with Christ, and he dressed himself carefully. After receiving the sacrament from Bishop Juxon he was ready for the scaffold. John Rushworth, who wrote the following account, was almost certainly in the crowd who saw him die:

This day his Majesty was brought from St James's, about ten in the morning, walking on foot through the Park, with a regiment of foot for his guard, with colours flying, drums beating, his private guard of partisans with some of his gentlemen before and some behind, bareheaded; Dr Juxon, late Bishop of London, next behind him and Colonel Thomlinson (who had charge of him) to the gallery in Whitehall, and so into the cabinet chamber where he used to lie, where he continued at his devotion, refusing to dine (having before taken the Sacrament), only at about twelve at noon he drank a glass of claret wine and ate a piece of bread.

From thence he was accompanied by Dr Juxon, Colonel Thomlinson, Colonel Hacker and the guards before-mentioned through the Banqueting House, adjoining to which the scaffold was erected, between Whitehall Gate and the gate leading into the Gallery from St James's. The scaffold was hung round with black, and the floor covered with black, and the axe and block laid in the middle of the scaffold. There were divers companies of foot and horse on every side of the scaffold, and the multitudes of people that came to be spectators were very great. The King, making a pass upon the scaffold, look'd very earnestly on the block and asked Colonel Hacker if there were no higher; and then spoke thus, directing his speech to the gentlemen on the scaffold. . . .

'I shall be very little heard of anybody here,' began the King, speaking from notes on a

The King saying goodbye to his children – in a rather fanciful 19th-century version of the scene which wrongly shows Cromwell as present.

small piece of paper he had taken from his pocket, 'I shall therefore speak a word unto you here. Indeed, I could hold my peace very well, if I did not submit to the guilt as well as to the punishment.' He protested his innocence of beginning the war against the two Houses of Parliament and of any intention to encroach upon their privileges. 'They began upon me. It is the militia they began upon. They confessed the militia was mine, but they thought it fit to have it from me. And to be short, if anybody will look upon the dates of the commissions, their commissions and mine, and likewise to the declarations, will see clearly that they began these unhappy troubles, not I.' But he did not lay the guilt on Parliament, 'for I believe that ill instruments between them and me has been the chief cause of all this bloodshed.' Yet he accepted God's justice in this unjust sentence as a punishment, alluding to his part in Strafford's death. He professed his forgiveness now for all men, even the chief causers of his death.

'Now, Sirs, I must show you both how you are out of your way and I will put you in that way.' Conquest in an unjust cause would avail them nothing. 'You will never do right, nor God will never prosper you, until you give God his due, the King his due (that is, my successors) and the people their due. I am as much for them as any of you. You must give God his due by regulating rightly his Church (according to his Scriptures) which is now out of order. . . . A national synod, freely called, freely debating among yourselves, must settle this, when that every opinion is freely and clearly heard. For the King indeed I will not – ' Charles suddenly stopped and turning to a gentleman who was fingering the axe he said, 'Hurt not the axe that may hurt me.' Then he continued. The laws of the land would clearly instruct them as to their duty to the King. 'For the people truly I desire their liberty and freedom as much as anybody whatsoever; but I must tell you their liberty and freedom consists in having government, those laws by which their lives and their goods may be most their own. It is not their having a share in government; that is nothing appertaining to them. A subject and a sovereign are clean different things. . . . Sirs, it was for this that I am now come here. If I would have given way to an arbitrary way, for to have all laws changed according to the power of the sword, I needed not to have come here. And therefore I tell you I am the martyr of the people. In truth, Sirs, I shall not hold you much longer. . . .'

Dr Juxon prompted him to add something about religion, and Charles at once declared: 'I die a Christian according to the profession of the Church of England as I found it left to me by my father.' Then, looking towards the Army officers, he said, 'Sirs, excuse me for this same. I have a good cause and I have a gracious God. I will say no more.'

Then, turning to Colonel Hacker, he asked, 'Take care that they do not put me to any pain . . .' But then a gentleman coming near the axe again, the King said 'Take heed of the axe! Pray take heed of the axe!' Then the King, speaking to the executioner, said, 'I shall say but very short prayers, and then thrust out my hands.' Then the King called to Dr Juxon for his nightcap; and having put it on, he said to the executioner, 'Does my hair trouble you?' who desired him to put it all under his cap, which the King did accordingly by the help of the executioner and the Bishop. Then the King, turning to Dr Juxon, said, 'I have a good cause and a gracious God on my side.'

Dr Juxon: 'There is but one stage more. This stage is turbulent and troublesome. It is a short one. But you may consider it, it will soon carry you a very great way. It will carry you from earth to heaven, and there you shall find your great joy the prize. You haste to a crown of glory.'

King: 'I go from a corruptible to an incorruptible crown, where no disturbance can be.'

Dr Juxon: 'You are exchanged from a temporal to an eternal crown, a good exchange.'

Then the King took off his cloak and his George, giving his George to Dr Juxon saying, 'Remember!' (it is thought for the Prince), and some other small ceremonies passed. After a while the King, stooping down, laid his neck upon the block; and after a little pause, stretching forth his hands, the executioner at one blow severed his head from his body.

The crowd, who could not see much because of the black cloth draping the scaffold, but saw the axe rise and heard the shuddering blow, let out a deep fearful groan, a sound, said an eyewitness 'as I never heard before and desire I may never hear again'. 'Behold the head of a traitor!' cried the masked executioner. Soldiers at once moved forwards to disperse the people. In less than a quarter of an hour the tragic affair was over.

The King's body and severed head were put into a coffin covered with black velvet and carried to the lodging-chamber in the Palace. According to tradition Cromwell came at night to look at the King's corpse. After the remains had been embalmed and the head sewn onto the body, they were taken for burial to Windsor Castle. On Saturday, 9 February the soldiers of the garrison carried the coffin to St George's Chapel, the four corners of the black velvet pall being held by four noblemen. Behind the coffin walked Bishop Juxon carrying a closed copy of the Book of Common Prayer. Snowflakes fell on the bare heads of the mourners and lay white upon the black pall of the coffin as they neared St George's Chapel. Inside the Chapel itself there was no service and no prayers were said as the coffin was lowered into the royal vault. Having replaced the stones the Governor and soldiers left the Chapel. Beneath the majestic vaulting all was silent.

Bibliography

This bibliography gives the sources of the principal eyewitness accounts, listed in order of their appearance in the text.

THE VERNEY FAMILY Frances Parthenope, Lady Verney, *Memoirs of the Verney family from the letters . . . at Claydon House*, 3rd Ed, 2 vols, 1925.

RICHARD BAXTER M. Sylvester (ed), *Reliquiae Baxterianae, or . . . Baxter's narrative of the most memorable passages of his life and times*, 1696. Later editions.

HENRY OXINDEN D. Gardiner (ed), *The Oxinden and Peyton Letters, 1642-1670*, 1937.

LUCY HUTCHINSON *Memoirs of the Life of Colonel Hutchinson*, 1973.

LORD SPENCER A. Collins (ed), *Letters and Memorials of State . . . from the originals at Penshurst*, 2 vols, 1746.

NEHEMIAH WHARTON Sir Henry Ellis (ed), 'Letters of Sergeant Nehemiah Wharton', *Archaeologia*, Vol XXV, 1853.

SIR RICHARD BULSTRODE *Memoirs and reflections upon the reign and government of King Charles I and King Charles II*, 1721.

JOHN AUBREY *Brief Lives, chiefly of contemporaries, set down by John Aubrey, between the years 1669 and 1696*, 2 vols, 1813. Later editions.

ANTHONY WOOD A. Clark (ed), *The Life and Times of Anthony Wood*, Vol I (1623-63), 1891.

RICHARD ATKYNS and JOHN GWYN P. Young and N. Tucker (eds), *Richard Atkyns and John Gwyn*, 1967.

ANNE LADY FANSHAWE and ANNE LADY HALKETT J. Loftus (ed), *The Memoirs of Anne, Lady Halkett and Anne, Lady Fanshawe*, 1978.

SIR WILLIAM WALLER J. Adair, *Roundhead General: The Life of Sir William Waller*, 1969.

WALTER SLINGSBY C. E. H. Chadwyck Healey (ed), *Bellum Civile. Hopton's Narrative of his Campaign in the West and other papers*, Somerset Record Society, 1902.

EDWARD and ROBERT HARLEY Historical Manuscripts Commission, *Portland MSS*.

JOHN CORBET J. Washbourn (ed), *Bibliotheca Gloucestrensis: A collection of scarce and curious tracts relating to the county and city of Gloucester*, 1825.

HENRY FOSTER *A True and Exact Relation of the marchings of the two regiments of the trained bands of the City of London, being the Red and Blue Regiments . . . who marched to the relief of Gloucester*, British Library: Thomason Tracts.

EARL OF CLARENDON W. D. Macray (ed), *History of the Rebellion and Civil Wars in England*, 6 vols, 1888.

SIR HUMPHREY MILDMAY P. L. Ralph, *Sir Humphrey Mildmay, Royalist Gentleman: Glimpses of the English Scene, 1633-1652*, 1947.

ELIAS ARCHER *A True Relation of the trained-bands of Westminster, the Green Auxiliaries of London and the Yellow Auxiliaries of the Tower Hamlets, under the command of Sir William Waller, from Monday 16 October to Wednesday 20 December 1643*, British Library: Thomason Tracts.

JOHN BIRCH J. Webb and T. W. Webb (eds), *Military Memoir of Colonel John Birch*, Camden Society, New Series, Vol 7, 1873.

SIR WILLIAM SPRINGATE C. Thomas-Stanford, *Sussex in the Great Civil War and the Interregnum, 1642-1660*, 1910.

SIR THOMAS FAIRFAX R. Bell (ed), *Memorials of the Civil War, comprising the correspondence of the Fairfax Family*, 2 vols, 1849.

JOHN LISTER T. Wright (ed), *Autobiography of John Lister of Bradford*, 1842.

OLIVER CROMWELL W. C. Abbott (ed), *The Writings and Speeches of Oliver Cromwell*, 4 vols, 1937-47.

SIR HUGH CHOLMLEY *The Memoirs of Sir Hugh Cholmley*, 1787, reprinted 1870.

RICHARD GOUGH D. Hey (ed), *The History of Myddle*, 1981.

THOMAS KNYVETT B. Schofield (ed), *The Knyvett Papers 1620-1644*, Norfolk Record Society, 1949.

RALPH JOSSELIN A. Macfarlane (ed), *The Diary of Ralph Josselin*, 1976.

SIR PHILIP WARWICK *Memoirs of the Reign of King Charles*, 1813.

BULSTRODE WHITELOCKE *Memorials of the English Affairs from the beginnings of the reign of Charles I to King Charles II's happy restoration*, 1722.

THOMAS TASKER Public Records Office, State Papers 28 184, printed in *Seventeenth Century England: The Revolution and its Impact*, Open University, 1981.

COURTS MARTIAL PAPERS 'The Courts Martial Papers of Sir William Waller's Army, 1644', in J. Adair, *Cheriton, 1644 The Campaign and the Battle*, 1973.

HENRY TOWNSHEND J. W. Willis-Bond, *Diary of Henry Townshend*, Worcestershire Historical Society, 1920.

ADAM MARTINDALE R. Parkinson (ed), *The Life of Adam Martindale*, Chetham Society, 1845.

RICHARD SYMONDS C. E. Long (ed), *Diary of the Marches of the Royal Army during the Great Civil War*, Camden Society, 1859.

SIR EDWARD WALKER H. Clopton (ed), *Historical Discourses upon several occasions . . .*, 1705.

JOSHUA SPRIGGE *Anglia Rediviva . . . being the history of the . . . army under . . . Sir Thomas Fairfax*, 1647, 2nd Ed, 1854.

SIR JOHN OGLANDER F. Bamford (ed), *A Royalist's Notebook. The Commonplace Book of Sir John Oglander of Nunwell (1585-1655)*, 1936.

JOHN HODGSON *Autobiography of Captain John Hodgson*, 1806.

JOHN RUSHWORTH *Historical Collections of private passages of State . . . in five Parliaments*, 7 vols, 1659-1701.

Index

Page numbers in italics refer to illustrations

Abercrombie, Captain Jecamiah 70, 73
Adwalton Moor, battle of 100
Agreement of the People, An 218
Alton, battle of 119-21
Apsley, Sir Allen 182
Archer, Lieutenant Elias 116, 117, 119-21
Arundel Castle, siege of 121-3
Ashburnham, Sir John 218, 227
Astley, Sir Jacob 35, 48, 108, 208
Aston, Sir Arthur 35, 57, 77
Atkyns, Captain Richard 77, 89, 91, 92-3, 94, 95-8
Aubrey, John 78, 79, 109, 110

Baillie, Robert 163
Balfour, Sir William 126
Balten, Sir William 224
Bamfield, Colonel Joseph 123, 221-3
Basing House, sieges of 114, 116-17, 203-4, *204, 205*
Bath Abbey 171
Barriffe, Major William 39
Baxter, Richard 15-16, 17-18, 26-8, 46, 163, 183, 210-11, 211, 214
Baynton, Sir Edward 87
Beaminster 172
Beaumont, Sir John 35
Berkeley, Sir John 218
Bishops' War 131
Blackfriars theatre 111
Blagge, Colonel Thomas 82
Blount, Sir Henry 110
Boarstall House 82, 83, 84
Bohemia, Elizabeth of *see* Elizabeth of Bohemia
Bolton 177
Book of Martyrs (Foxe) 12
Bradford, siege of 137-8
Bradshaw, John 230, 232, 233
Brereton, Sir William 144, 148
Bridgwater 203
Bristol 160, 172, 203, 206
Brooke, Lord 41, 55, 144
Browne, Major-General Richard 165, 215, 217
Bulstrode, Sir Richard 14, 48
Burleigh House 152
Burt, Nathaniel 90
Byron, Sir John 29, 30, 75, 94, *96*, 148, 164
Byron, Sir Richard 29
Byron, Sir Robert 29
Byron, Sir Thomas 29, 52, 165, 196

Cambridge 12, 110, 153, 171
Capel, Lord 224, 227
Carisbrooke Castle 219, 220, 221
Carnarvon, Earl of 48, 108
Cavendish, William, Earl of Newcastle *see* Newcastle, William Cavendish, Earl of
Chalgrove Field, battle of 100
Chard 85
Charles, Prince of Wales 12, 48, 224
Charles I 9-10, 11, 12-13, *20*, 32, 33, *34,* 48, 52, *54,* 57, 58, 76, 100-1, *173, 186,* 187-8, 192, 202, 204-5, 206-8, *212, 216,* 218-21, 228, 229, 230-3, *232,* 234-6, *235*
Cheriton, battle of 126-9, 146, 227
Chester 207-8

Cholmley, Sir Hugh 28, 143, 154, 180
Cirencester 172
Clarendon, Earl of 11, 15, 22, 35, 144
Claydon House 59, 61, 67
Clubmen Associations 170
Cockpit theatre 111
Colchester, siege of 224, 227
Commissions of Array 12, 23, 26
Committee for Sequestrations 156
Committee of Both Kingdoms 185, 192
Committee of Examinations 156
Compton, Spencer, Earl of Northampton *see* Northampton, Spencer Compton, Earl of
Compton House 169
Cook, John 231-2
Cook, William 163, 165
Cooper, Anthony 74
Corbet, John 22, 24, 102-3, 165
Covenant 19, 67, 73
Cowper's Hill (Sir John Denham) 76
Cromwell, Oliver 142, 153, 154, 155, 161-2, *179,* 188, 189, 192, *193,* 203, 204, 211, 214, 217, 223, 224, *225,* 226, 230, 233, 236
Crowland 153
Cumberland, Earl of 131
Curzon, Sir John 112

Denbigh, Basil Fielding, Earl of 148
Denham, Sir John 76, 85
Denton, Sir Alexander 44, 67-8, *68,* 70, 73
Denton, Colonel John 73
Denton, Margaret 67, 73
Denton, Susan 68, 70, 73
Devereux, Robert, Earl of Essex *see* Essex, Robert Devereux, Earl of
Digby, Lord George 11, 161-2
Donnington Castle 188-9, 192

Eastern Association 142, 161
Edgehill, battle of 35, *44,* 48, *50-1,* 52, 55, 76, 87
Elizabeth, Princess 234
Elizabeth I, Queen of England 9
Elizabeth of Bohemia 33, 35, 39, 85-6
Eliot, Sir John 9, 15
Ennis, Lieutenant-Colonel John 48
Essex, Robert Devereux, Earl of 39, *40,* 41, 44, 48, 55, 56, 103-4, *106,* 114, 185, 187, 188
Exeter 204

Fairfax, Ferdinando, Lord 130, *139,* 167
Fairfax, Sir Thomas 130-1, 133, 134, 136-7, 167, 192, *199,* 200, 203, 204, 214, 223, 230, 231
Fairfax, Lady 231, 233
Falkland, Viscount 108, 109
Fanshawe, Anne, Lady 72, 79-80, 180-1, 217-18
Fanshawe, Sir Richard 80
Farnham Castle 12
Fawley Court 163-5, 196
Fenwick, Captain John 131
Ferrar, Nicholas 12
Fielding, Lieutenant-Colonel Edward 48
Fiennes, Captain Nathaniel 45, *46*
Finch, Lady Anne 87
Forth, Patrick Ruthven, Earl of 35, 126
Foster, Sergeant Henry 105-8, 109

Gainsborough 146

Gamul, Colonel Sir Francis 52
Gardiner, Sir Thomas 63
Gardiner, Captain Thomas 63, 64
Gell, Sir John 144, 145
Globe theatre 111
Gloucester, siege of 100-4, 105, 109
Goodwin, Colonel Arthur 72, 76, 80, 81
Goring, Colonel George 28, 35, 134, 169, 203
Gough, Richard 148-52
Grand Remonstrance 86
Grantham 146
Greaves, Edward 79
Grenville, Sir Bevil 14-15, 94
Gwyn, Captain John 105, 108

Halifax Grammar School 24
Halkett, Sir James 223
Hamilton, Duke of 223, 224, *225,* 226, 230
Hammond, Colonel Robert 218, 219, 228
Hampden, Colonel John 10, 28, 39, 55, 100, 162
Hampden, Mary 62, 68
Hampton Court 11, 217, 218
Harley, Captain Edward 99
Harley, Captain Robert 126-8
Harley, Sir Robert 99
Harrison, Sir John 79
Harrison, William 80
Harvey, Dr William 55
Henrietta Maria, Queen 11, 20, 133-4, *135,* 136, 209
Henry, Duke of Gloucester 234
Hereford 47
Heselrige, Sir Arthur 11, *93,* 97-8, 99, 189
Hillesden House 44, 67, 68, 69-70
Hobbes, Thomas 171-2
Hodgson, John 16, 224-6
Holland, Earl of 57, 224
Hollar, Wenceslaus 203
Holles, Colonel Denzil 10, 11, 41, 45, 55
Hopton, Sir Ralph 85, 86, 92, 94-5, 112, *115,* 118, 121, 126-8, 136, 204
Hotham, Sir John 28
Hudson, Michael 227
Hull 28, 139, 142
Hungerford, Sir Edward 87, 88
Hurst Castle 229
Hutchinson, Colonel John 17, 29, 30-1, 32, 145, 146, 178, 230
Hutchinson, Lucy 13, 19, 23, 29, 30, 144-5, 146, 178, 182
Hutchinson, Sir Thomas 29

'Independents' 100
Ireton, Commissary-General Henry 214
'Ironsides' 153-4, 161
Isham, Elizabeth 67, 68, 73
Isle of Wight 218-21, 228

James, Duke of York 48, 221-3, 224
James I, King of England 9
Jones, Inigo 203
Josselin, Ralph 157-61
Joyce, Cornet 215
Juxon, Bishop, of London 231, 234, 236, 237

Kidderminster 26-8
Kineton 48, 52

King, Lieutenant-General James 130
Kingston, Earl of 29-30
Kingston-on-Thames 11
Knyvett, Thomas 154-6, 157

Langdale, Sir Marmaduke 223
Langport 203
Lansdown, battle of 92-4
Lathom House 180
Laud, William, Archbishop of
  Canterbury 10, 76
Lee, Sir Henry 58
Lee, Sir Henry (son of the above) 59
Leeds 137
Legge, Colonel William 218, 220
Leicester 158, 192
Levellers 210, 218, 220
Lichfield 144
Lindsey, Earl of 32, 35, 48
Lisle, Lieutenant-Colonel Sir George
  48, 224, 227
Lister, John 137
Little Dean, fight at 89
Littlecote manor 140-1
Liverpool 177
London 11, 56-7, 103-4, 105, 109, 111, 182,
  217
Long Parliament 9, 10, 86, 161
Lostwithiel 187-8
Lowestoft 152
Lucas, Sir Charles 147, 224, 227
Ludlow, Edmund 55
Luke, Sir Samuel 69, 77
Lunsford, Colonel Sir Thomas 11, 35

Maidstone 223
Malmesbury 87
Manchester, Earl of 88-9, 217
Mandeville, Lord 10, 11
Marston Moor, battle of 142
Maurice, Prince 85, 88-9
'Malignants' 19
Marten, Henry 179
Martindale, Adam 175-8
Marvell, Andrew 183
Massey, Colonel Edward 100, 101-2,
  165, 217
Meldrum, Sir John 39
Mercurius Aulicus 76, 104, 118, 178, 179
Mercurius Britannicus 144
Mildmay, Anthony 220
Mildmay, Sir Humphrey 110-12
Mildmay, Jane, Lady 112
Mildmay, Sir Walter 110
Milton, John 183-4, 184
Montrose, Marquess of 206, 208, 209
Morley, Colonel Herbert 19, 123
Murray, Ann 221-3
Musgrave, Sir Philip 223

Nantwich 148
Naseby, battle of 84, 159, 190-91, 192,
  194-5, 198-9, 202
New Model Army 162, 173, 190, 192,
  194, 203, 210-11, 214, 215, 217, 218, 229,
  230
Newark 30, 145, 146, 173, 207, 208
Newark, Lord (later Marquess of
  Dorchester) 30-2
Newbury, first battle of 73, 105-9;
  second battle of 188-9, 192, 227
Newcastle 131, 172, 174
Newcastle, William Cavendish, Earl
  of 23, 130, 132, 133, 136-8, 142, 143
Newport Pagnell 68, 69, 70
Northampton, Spencer Compton,
  Earl of 144
Norwich, Lord 223, 227
Nottingham 28, 30-2, 33, 146-8
Nanappleton 183
Nunwell House 219, 220

Oglander, Sir John 219-20, 228
Onslow, Sir Richard 11-12
Osney Abbey 76
Oxford 68, 72, 74, 75, 76-84, 192
Oxinden, Henry 24-5

Parker, Henry 19-20
Penn, William 122
Pepys, Samuel 130
Peter, Hugh 203-4
Petersfield 170
Petition of Right 39
Pierrepont, Francis 30
Pierrepont, William 30
Porter, George 35
Portsmouth 12, 28
Powick Bridge, battle of 45-7
Preston, battle of 224
Preston, Captain Robert 220
Prince Rupert's Burning Love to England,
  discovered in Birmingham's flames 166
Protestantism 9, 15
Puritans 15-18, 23, 24
Putney debates 218
Pym, John 10, 100

Rainsborough, Colonel Thomas 218
Raleigh, Sir Walter 182
Ramsey, Sir James 39, 48
Reading 108, 155
'Rebels' 19
Reformation 19, 178
Rochester 223
Rodway, Robert 118
Roman Catholics 14
'Roundheads' 19
Roundway Down, battle of 95-8, 99
Royal Society 184
Royalists 14-15, 16, 17, 23, 25
Rudyard, Sir Benjamin 24
Rump Parliament 229
Rupert, Prince 33, 35, 44, 45, 48, 55, 56,
  77, 80-1, 86, 100, 142, 143, 146, 151, 152,
  158, 163, 165, 166, 172, 177, 186, 194,
  198, 206, 208
Rushworth, John 215, 234-6
Ruthven, Patrick, Earl of Forth see
  Forth, Patrick Ruthven, Earl of

St George's Chapel, Windsor 171, 237
St James's Palace 221
St John, Lord Oliver 76, 230
Saltonstall, Sir Richard 24
Saye and Sele, Lord 76
Scotland 100, 220-1
Scots army 173, 208-9, 223, 224-6
Scroop, Sir Adrian 52
Second Civil War 221, 223-7
Second Newbury see Newbury, second
  battle of
Selden, John 230
Self-Denying Ordinance 192
Shelbourne, Thomas 178
Short Parliament 10
Shrewsbury 35
Skipton, Sergeant-Major-General
  Philip 56
Slingsby, Colonel Sir Henry 32, 131,
  133, 206-7
Slingsby, Lieutenant-Colonel Walter
  93-4
Smith, Major-General Sir John 128
Smith, Colonel William 68, 69, 73
Spencer, Lord Henry (later 1st Earl of
  Northumberland) 35-8
Sprat, Bishop 184
Sprigge, Joshua 194, 195, 198-9, 202
Springate, Sir William 123, 126
Stamford 153
Stanhope, Sir John 144, 145
Stiles, Captain John 55

Stoakes, Sergeant William 183
Stradling, Sir Edward 35
Strafford, Earl of 10, 86
Stratton, battle of 85
Strode, William 11
Stuart, Lord Bernard 129
Stuart, Lieutenant-General Lord
  John 128, 129
Sunderland, Earl of 108
Sussex, Eleanor, Lady 58-60, 65
Sydenham, Sir Edward 56, 61
Symonds, Richard 187, 189

Taunton 203
Thame grammar school 80
Thynne, Isabella, Lady 78
Towneley, Colonel Charles 142
Townshend, Henry 41, 172-3
Treaty of Newport 229
Trevelyan, Sir John 94
Turner, Sir James 226-7

Urry, Sir John 188

Vane, Sir Henry 100
Vere, Sir Horace 86
Verney, Betty 63, 67
Verney, Cary 62, 63, 64, 67
Verney, Sir Edmund 14, 15, 28, 48, 58,
  59, 60, 61, 62
Verney, Edmund ('Mun') 14, 61, 62, 73
Verney, Edmund 59, 62
Verney, Henry 62, 62-3, 66-7
Verney, Mary 62, 67, 73
Verney, Molly 63, 67
Verney, Peg 63, 67
Verney, Pen 62, 63, 67, 70
Verney, Sir Ralph 14, 19, 58, 59, 61, 62,
  64, 65, 66, 67, 70, 71, 73
Verney, Sue 63, 73
Verney, Thomas 61, 62, 64-6, 66, 70,
  71, 73

Wagstaffe, Joseph 39, 41
Wales 223
Walker, Sir Edward 129, 194, 202
Waller, Anne, Lady 178-80
Waller, Edmund 101
Waller, Edward 80
Waller, Sir William 11, 19, 85-6, 87-8,
  91, 92, 93, 94, 95, 112, 114-17, 116, 118,
  119, 121-3, 126-8, 136, 162, 169, 170,
  171, 178, 179, 185-6, 188, 189, 214, 215,
  217, 221, 228, 229
Wardour Castle 180
Warwick, Sir Philip 130, 161
Wentworth, Thomas 35
Westminster Assembly 100
Whalley, Colonel 195, 211, 218
Wharton, Jane, Lady 72, 81
Wharton, Nehemiah 41, 43, 44, 47
Whitehall 231, 234-6
Whitelocke, Bulstrode 9, 153, 163-5,
  196, 230
Wigan 205
Wilmot, Henry, Lord 35, 95
Winceby, battle of 142, 146
Winchester, Marquess of 115-16, 204,
  205
Winthrop, John 18, 24
Wolstenholme, Sir John 167-8
Wood, Anthony 74, 77, 80, 82
Wood, Thomas 74
Woodcroft Hall 227
Worcester 45, 172-3
Wortley, Sir Francis 14, 59

York 32, 33, 131, 142, 177